A ROAD CALLED HOPE

A Gentle Guide for Discipling Teens through Trauma

CHRISTOPHER MARCHAND

WESTBOW
PRESS®
A DIVISION OF THOMAS NELSON
& ZONDERVAN

WestBow Press books may be ordered through booksellers or by contacting:

WestBow Press
A Division of Thomas Nelson & Zondervan
1663 Liberty Drive
Bloomington, IN 47403
www.westbowpress.com
1 (866) 928-1240

ISBN: 978-1-9736-7747-5 (sc)
ISBN: 978-1-9736-7748-2 (hc)
ISBN: 978-1-9736-7746-8 (e)

Library of Congress Control Number: 2019916315

Print information available on the last page.

WestBow Press rev. date: 11/11/2019

To Heather:
For your courage, love, and faithfulness. Your laughter still fills
my heart with joy. Thank you for sharing your life with me.

When I said, "My foot is slipping," your unfailing love,
Lord, supported me. When anxiety was great within me,
your consolation brought me joy (Psalm 94:18–19).

Acknowledgments

Serving in youth ministry, I often felt as if I were in the deep end of a swimming pool, treading water. I'm thankful that the Lord has provided colleagues, mentors, and friends to come alongside me. They have taught me, offered support, prayed, and walked with me when ministry got too heavy to bear alone. I'm thankful for Don Prince and Garth McMillan for offering me my first full-time job in youth ministry, serving the wonderful congregation of Gentle Shepherd Community Church. I'm thankful for Les and Lori Wiseman, Dave and Kathy Wilson, Monica Green, and John and Shirley Ferris. While we travelled with teens to concerts, ran junior-high games nights, served on mission trips, planned for worship nights, and paddled rivers on our many canoe adventures, these incredible people taught me how to love and disciple teenagers. I'd also like to thank the many teens who've allowed me to walk in their sacred space. I hope that some of your stories will help others to become more effective in discipleship and caregiving.

Thanks to the students at Steinbach Bible College (SBC), who read a few chapters of this book for a course on self-care I taught. I'm pleased that their feedback has made this a better resource. I'm also thankful to Garth Friesen, Professor of Youth Ministry at SBC, and Sam and Pauline Doerksen (Focus on the Family) for reading a portion of the early manuscript and providing constructive feedback.

I'm thankful for Eric Schroeder and the good people at WestBow Press, who valued this work right from their first read and helped me to move smoothly through the publishing process. Thanks also to my editor, Carla Lowe, for her encouragement, patience, love for correct comma placement, and sense of humor.

Finally, I can't imagine taking on a project of this size without the support of my family. Thanks to my partner, Heather, and our two adult children, Justin and Brianna. You have been my strength and my inspiration when I've wanted to give up. You are incredible people, and I am truly blessed to share my life with you.

Contents

CHAPTER 1
Seized by Love:
Helping Teens in Pain to Follow Jesus

*When we accept moment-to-moment events and tribulations
as the place where we receive God's provision, we patiently
anticipate the action of his Spirit in our lives.*[1]
—Dallas Willard

The sunshine was warm on my back and refreshing to my soul as I trimmed the raspberry bushes. With a song of praise on my lips, I was working in the garden; it was my holy place, rich with solitude and having space for prayerful reflection. A wailing scream shattered the quiet, and I looked up from my work to see what calamity was at hand.

While I was attending seminary in South Dakota, my wife was running a day care out of our home to help pay the bills. I also worked full time as a youth pastor and studied full time for my master's degree. Operating a day care is good work, but it can be exhausting. Every morning at 6:30, five children under the age of three would arrive to spend the day with her. On this sunny afternoon, I was home helping my wife, and my son, Justin, and his friend, Ryan, both two years old, were with me in the backyard. I had built a small sandbox for them to enjoy, and they had been plowing with their tractors, shoveling, and digging holes while I worked in my little garden on the opposite side of the yard.

I learned as a young father that some two-year-olds have a flare for the dramatic, with small events causing rather sensational outbursts. Ryan was one of those kids. Screaming was as natural for him as walking. If the dog knocked him over, he dropped his spoon, or he wanted a toy,

1

he would immediately break down into a bawling mess. When I had last looked over at them, Justin had been digging with a small plastic shovel and Ryan had been in his glory, navigating a small toy truck over rounded mounds of sand. As I glanced at the two of them, there was no way of knowing what had led to the howling, but I noticed Justin acting strangely. Standing beside his friend, he was looking concerned. Our eyes met, and he turned again to Ryan.

I could tell he was troubled, perhaps wondering how to respond to his friend's cries for help. After a few moments, Justin left the sandbox and began walking toward me. Reaching a halfway point between his crying friend and his father, Justin did something that I will never forget. He stopped, turned for one last look at his friend, and then raised both of his arms in the form of a human cross, with one hand reaching toward his father and one hand reaching toward his friend.

In youth ministry it isn't uncommon to feel like you're standing in the middle, with one hand holding a teenager in pain while the other reaches for God. In *Care of Souls*, David Benner wrote, "Pastoral care offers the gift of Christian love and nurture from one who attempts to mediate the gracious presence of God to another who is in need."[2] I have written this book for people serving in Christian youth ministry, which exists to share the biblical truths of God's redemptive love with adolescents and help them grow into maturing disciples of Jesus Christ.[3] Youth ministers don't engage in pastoral care as chaplains, therapists, or spiritual directors but as disciple makers. This book is for people who want to help teens follow Jesus while fearlessly engaging with the pain often associated with effective teen discipleship. While it is a book about pastoral care in youth ministry, it is first and foremost a book about discipleship; providing pastoral care in youth ministry is simply one of the ways to help teens and their families follow Jesus.

As Justin stood in our backyard, arms open wide, reaching for his friend with one hand and his father with the other, the symbolism spoke to my heart: this is what God called youth ministers to do.

Hundreds of years ago, prophets were called to speak to God's covenant people about their willful disobedience. Idolatry, murder, adultery, extortion, rape, and oppression of the poor formed an abbreviated list of ungodly behaviors found in the book of Ezekiel. The prophet wrote the words of the Lord. "I looked for someone among them who would build up the wall and stand before me in the gap on behalf of the land so I would not have to destroy it, but I found no one" (Ezekiel 22:30). This is a military image of a hole in a city wall, likely created by an enemy's battering ram. Once the enemy had created the hole, soldiers would flood through the gap. The only way to keep the enemy from overtaking your city was to station soldiers in the gap until the hole in the wall was sealed. In Ezekiel, God is looking for someone to stand up for justice, to call a halt to oppression, to break the patterns of violence, and to call the people to repentance.[4] God is looking for someone to stand in the gap.

I recently spoke with a young man interested in youth ministry as a career. He explained to me that he was interested in becoming a youth pastor because he wouldn't have to go to work early, the job seemed easy, and he wouldn't have anyone bossing him around. So much for standing in the gap.

As Justin stood in our backyard with his arms outstretched, he was standing in the gap for Ryan. He did not know how to help his friend, but he trusted his father. Those who are passionate about youth ministry are willing to stand in the gap for teens, to stand against enemies—both spiritual and physical—that threaten to disrupt, destroy, and derail faith, mental wellness, and the abundant life promised by Jesus.

No Wasted Pain

Arrested for attempted armed robbery at fifteen, I have a good sense of what it means to live a godless life. My teen years were a shipwreck of substance abuse, imprisonment, and reckless living, until Jesus got my attention through several of his faithful disciples. Ron was a prison chaplain at the time, and he rode up to my house on his black motorcycle. One of my relatives was in prison and had told the chaplain he should come and speak with me. I wasn't exactly impressed, but I did think the motorcycle was cool. We sat together at our kitchen table, and Ron told me his story. He had been associated with a bike gang transporting drugs and guns from the United States into Canada. One day the gang had turned against him, beating him and leaving him to die. His story of surviving the attack was incredible. He described how God had rescued him and begun to work in his life through followers of Jesus. He told me that he had been forgiven of his sin and that God had replaced the rage in his heart with love.

I knew there was a problem in my heart, because I hated the love in his eyes. He had become a prison chaplain so that he could help other bikers and gang members experience the love of Jesus. His story made me feel uncomfortable. I had never heard anything like it.

Over the next few years, the Spirit of God would lead others across my path to share their stories of faith in Jesus. Eventually Jesus would break through my stubbornness and rescue me from my life of sin, and I would begin the long and wonderfully painful journey of becoming a disciple. I was living in a place of abuse and addiction, full of self-hatred and rage, with no idea how to live a sober life, but God began to do an incredible work in my life. You may read about it in the ministry of Jesus and in Paul's letters to the churches, but in youth ministry, you may not always be sure that God still changes lives.

I begin this book by telling you that God's Word is true. "Therefore, if anyone is in Christ, the new creation has come: The old has gone, the new is here!" (2 Corinthians 5:17). I want you to understand that God does not waste your pain; instead, God is able to use the darkest parts of your story for his glory. God still transforms lives, still heals broken hearts, and still provides opportunities for his people to tell their unfolding stories so that he can use them as a demonstration of his grace, mercy, and love.

The Ministry of Shepherding

The book you are reading is about discipleship in the hard places of life. It is a book designed to remind you that the purpose in everything you do in youth ministry—whether you're running a games night, organizing a retreat, or sitting with a kid who hates her life—is to *help teenagers follow Jesus*. In a regular week you might spend a few hours listening to stories filled with pain. You will pray for those who have created their own discomfort, for those wounded by peers, and for those overwhelmed by suffering. I would like to propose that you think of those sacred moments of listening as powerful opportunities for disciple making.

In his book written for pastors, William Willimon described pastoral care with disciple-making language when he wrote, "Think of pastoral care as our clerical attempt to help the congregation worship the true and living God in every aspect of their lives."[5] He went on to acknowledge that one of the challenges of being a pastor is providing care that is worthy of the name Christian."[6] Use of the word *pastor* here is not intended to exclude the nonprofessional youth worker. Most youth workers are giving their time because of a calling, not as an occupation. The word *pastor* is used in Ephesians 4:11. "Christ himself gave the apostles, the prophets, the evangelists, the pastors and teachers, to equip his people for works of service, so that the body of Christ may be built up." Here the word is best defined as "one who cares for his or her flock as a shepherd cares for his or her sheep. This would include ministering to troubled people, exhorting and comforting all believers, and administering the activities in the local assembly."[7] Hoehner goes on to explain that this verse of scripture refers to a gift and not to an office or profession. When I use the phrase *pastoral care* in this book, please do not think of the occupation of pastoring; think of the ministry of shepherding. If God has called you to be a shepherd to teens in pain, then your discipling ministry is called pastoral care.

Seized to Carry a Cross

In youth ministry, the goal can mistakenly become the alleviation of pain. When we're working with suffering teens, it's a natural response. Sitting behind the thick glass barrier in the visitation room of a prison, you might hear the teenager expressing remorse for his behavior. He might beg you to speak in his defense at trial, though you know you would need to lie to find just *one* positive thing to say. You might hear self-loathing and sorrow and in that moment want desperately to rescue that teen from his misery.

But the purpose of Christian care in those moments is not to alleviate pain; rather, the goal is to serve in such a way that a teenager will come to understand his deepest need, just as Willimon has described: "To worship the true and living God in every aspect of their lives."[8] When a kid is sitting in prison, this might seem like a weird description of his deepest need. Getting out of jail is clearly the most pressing need, but that isn't a feasible solution. Whether the issue is incarceration, addictions, or self-injury, the goal remains the same. Pain is often the reason lives intersect, and as much as you and I might grieve the losses brought about by suffering, pain can create an opportunity for deeper faith in Jesus as nothing else does.

The Apostle Paul invites the Philippians to make the connection between discipleship, the experience of resurrection life, and suffering when he writes, "I want to know Christ—yes, to know the power of his resurrection and participation in his sufferings, becoming like him in his death, and so, somehow, attaining to the resurrection from the dead"(Philippians 3:10–11).

Simon from Cyrene was in the wrong place at the wrong time, just minding his own business. Luke writes that he was *seized* (Luke 23:26). Grabbed by the Roman soldiers from the crowds, Simon was made to carry the cross-beam on his shoulders.[9] Some might consider it an honor to be chosen to carry the cross for Jesus, but Simon did not likely see it that way.

I imagine you're familiar with the words of Jesus from Matthew 16:24: "Whoever wants to be my disciple must deny themselves and take up their cross and follow me." Most people probably understand these words as a personal call to follow Jesus sacrificially, but I wonder if Jesus might want to pull you out of the crowd, just as Simon was *seized*. I wonder whether Jesus is calling you to carry a cross for someone in your life, just as Simon carried his—someone too tired, too beaten down by broken relationships, or disease, or mental illness, or failure.

Late one night I got a text from a young man who told me he was thinking about killing himself. It was not a surprise; I had asked him to text me if he felt he was in crisis. During our conversation, I could tell that he was clearly overwhelmed and nearing a panic attack. "Jesus, help me; give me wisdom," I prayed. I felt dragged out onto the street—*seized!* "You there! Come carry his cross." It was too heavy for my friend to carry alone, so Jesus called on me to carry it with him.

Well, I did not sleep much that night. I lay awake praying for a man who attended the church that I serve, praying that God would give him a reason to live. He was on my mind all the next day. I prepared to talk to him and to meet with him later in the week. I knew that at any time he could text me, in crisis. I prayed for him all through the day, as the Spirit brought him to my thoughts.

Gnawing at the edges of my mind was the uncomfortable image of sitting with his brokenhearted parents after his suicide, organizing and speaking at his funeral, and living with the dread of getting the kind of phone call that no pastor ever wants to receive.

But I will continue to love him. I will walk with him through the valley of the shadow of death. I will pray with him, direct him to resources, and listen carefully. I will stand up and preach the Word of God on Sundays, and he will be one of the people sitting in the congregation. There is no way of knowing how long he will experience this mental health crisis and how long my speaking about God will create confusion, anger, and frustration. Not long ago he was a strong believer, but now, under the cloud of depression, he is not sure he has ever believed in God. Even though he might not find it comforting, I will remind him that Jesus is with him. I will hold his hand when we pray, I will look him in the eye as he curses his life, and I will tell him stories of people who have made it through the darkness of depression and come to wellness.

Being "seized" by Jesus to shepherd this young man through his pain is not a burden to me, although I feel the weight of his sadness. I suppose my interaction with him is best captured by the words of Buechner, who once wrote, "The place God calls you to is the place where your deep gladness and the world's deep hunger meet."[10] As in the case of Simon of Cyrene, getting seized does not always involve deep gladness, but when God is calling, it often does. I believe that I have been seized by Jesus and asked to carry a heavy cross with this young man.

Have you ever considered that Jesus might ask you to carry a cross for a teenager who he brings into your life? What might that look like? If you are going to answer the call of God to serve in youth ministry, there *will* come a time when Jesus will do the same to you. Henri Nouwen writes, "Who can save a child from a burning house without taking the risk of being hurt by the flames? Who can listen to a story of loneliness and despair without taking the risk of experiencing similar pains in his own heart and even losing his precious peace of mind? In short: Who can take away suffering without entering into it?"[11]

In the next chapter, I'll take some time to help you think carefully about entering into suffering as a disciple maker.

Waiting on Tables

Many years ago, while working as a server in a restaurant, I noticed a beautiful young blonde come strolling in with some friends. I arranged to switch tables with another server who was happy to give it to me. These were Bible college students, and all the servers knew that students don't tip. I enjoyed serving her that night, so much so that I pursued her until we fell in love. I have now been waiting on Heather's table for twenty-nine years!

Having worked as a server to pay for college, I have always appreciated the story of Stephen in Acts chapter 6. A dispute breaks out between the Hellenistic and Hebraic Jews over the daily distribution of food. The disciples meet to problem-solve, and Luke writes that the twelve apostles conclude that it would not be right to neglect the ministries of preaching and teaching to wait on tables (Acts 6:2). It sounds as if caring for people is not as important as preaching, and if you're not careful with this text, you could conclude that prayer and the ministry of the Word are the only ministries that will make disciples. The apostles instruct the believers to choose seven men from among them who are known to be full of the Spirit and wisdom (Acts 6:3). Yet this job description for servers seems a bit over the top. Why would Stephen and the others need to be "full of the Spirit and wisdom" if their task was distribution of food?

Years later, James, the brother of Jesus, would write that "religion that God our Father accepts as pure and faultless is this: to look after orphans and widows in their distress" (James 1:27). Unfortunately, Christians often speak of discipleship when they are referring to ministries that engage in Bible study, preaching, and prayer, while the ladies who serve in the kitchen, the guy who cleans the toilets in the church, and the people who serve in the nursery are ... helpful. They support the work of discipleship. This seems like a bunch of bunk, and it is not the kind of separation the apostles had in mind in Acts, it is *not* the reason Stephen became the first martyr, and it's certainly not what Jesus had in mind when he commissioned his followers to make disciples.

Before I begin this study of youth issues, let's take a close look at Matthew 28:16–20 to better understand what it means to "make disciples." Near the end of Matthew's gospel, an angel is sitting on a stone outside the tomb where Jesus has been buried. The tough Roman guards are so afraid that they pass out, but two gutsy women stroll up to the angel and have a normal conversation. The messenger tells the women, "He has risen from the dead and is going ahead of you into Galilee. There you will see him (Matthew 28:7)." On their way to tell the other disciples, they meet Jesus. They fall at his feet to worship him, and Jesus says to them, "Do not be afraid. Go and tell my brothers to go to Galilee; there they will see me" (Matthew 28:10).

It's easy to imagine an excited and hurried crowd of men, women, and children all heading for Galilee. The women are told, "there you will see him" and Matthew uses a plural personal pronoun, meaning the women, too, will see Jesus. The women are to give the same message to the men, but by verse 11 it's easy to forget that the women were told they, too, would see Jesus. I can't imagine the women packing lunches for the guys and sending them off for a nice visit with the resurrected Jesus. Not a chance! As a matter of fact, some believe[12] that this event in Galilee is the same referred to by Paul in his first letter to the Church in Corinth, when he writes that Jesus "appeared to more than five hundred of the brothers and sisters at the same time (1 Corinthians 15:6)." It's an important point when it comes to understanding this text. If there were a large crowd, verse 17 is easier to understand, as some doubted or hesitated when Jesus suddenly appeared. Others saw Jesus and they immediately worshipped, just as the women had done in verse 9. The word used for worship here means to lie face down on the ground in adoration. It's a term used specifically for the worship of God, and using it at the end of his gospel, Matthew draws the reader's attention to the unmistakable conclusion: Jesus is God with us.[13]

A Balanced Approach to Youth Ministry

In verse 18, Jesus begins the *Great Commission* with these words: "All authority in heaven and on earth has been given to me." The Gospel of John says that "no one has ever seen God, but the one and only Son, who is himself God and is in closest relationship with the Father, has made him known (John 1:18)." Jesus comes as Immanuel, God with us, both fully human and fully God. In Paul's letter to the Church in Philippi, he tells the believers, in beautiful poetic form, that although Jesus was in very nature God, he "did not consider equality with God something to be used to his own advantage; rather, he made himself nothing by taking the very nature of a servant (Philippians 2:6–7)." As a servant to human form, Jesus limited himself to ministry in a specific place and time, but having raised him from the dead, the Father gives Jesus not only absolute power and authority over the universe but also the freedom and the right to exercise this power.[14]

Years ago, an angry youth ministry major came to my office for academic advice. Professors in colleges are often expected to assist students in course selection so that students don't come to their final year of studies and discover they don't have enough credits to graduate. This student had a rather pressing concern. "Why do I have to take so many Bible courses? I just want to work with teens."

Being a rather verbal processor, I am not often stunned into silence; however, this young man made my jaw drop. The student was interested in working with teenagers, but he was not interested in learning scripture. Senter and Dunn explain that youth ministry involves more than merely spending time with teenagers.[15] As you see in the diagram below, those who serve in youth ministry need to understand their task biblically and theologically or run the risk of building relationships and running programs that have little to do with helping teens follow Jesus. The biblical and theological purpose is rooted in God's mission and the mandate Jesus gives to make disciples.

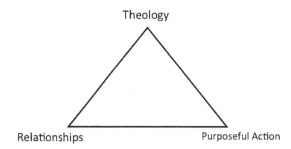

If you lean too heavily toward the biblical and theological point of the triangle, youth ministry can feel cold and impersonal. Long Bible studies and theological dialogue with no attention to relationships and personal connections can be about as exciting as watching paint dry. The intellectuals in the group will love it; the rest will be praying for the rapture.

Building healthy, safe disciple-making relationships is a critical part of effective youth ministry, but it isn't the *only* part. I was once invited to have lunch with a youth pastor from a large city church. I was teaching youth ministry at the time, and he had initiated our meeting to sharpen his ministry skills. A few moments into the conversation he said, "Youth ministry is all about relationships." He came back to that statement several times, hammering it home with greater emphasis each time.

Finally I said to him, "You are making a serious mistake: youth ministry is not *all* about relationships." He adamantly disagreed with me, and there was nothing I could do to change his mind.

The triangle serves as a reminder that there is a balance to maintain. If youth ministry gets out of balance and emphasizes relationships over theology and purposeful action, the group will never be able to make disciples. It will be a fun place to hang out and meet friends, but the ministry will lack a greater purpose. A youth ministry that leans too heavily toward relationships might have amazing small groups, a great worship band, a dynamic outreach program, and lots of kids in attendance, but without purposeful action and a theological foundation, it becomes a social club, void of spiritual formation.

I once attended a large youth conference for a major denomination in the US. During the kickoff session, it struck me as odd that the youth band was not playing worship music; the songs were all secular. Even more strange was the fact that the small group sessions were focused on self-image and strengthening relationships, with no integration of biblical or theological reflection. The entire weekend was designed with relationships and purposeful action in mind, with not a hint of Jesus.

Some youth ministries love to engage in purposeful action, such as mission trips, local service projects, and serving at food banks. Purposeful action has always played a major role in youth ministry discipleship. You might also think of purposeful action as the way to engage with teens in crisis, including short-term counselling, conflict management, addictions support, or grief care. These components of youth ministry discipleship are critical, but if the ministry begins to lean too heavily toward purposeful action, without opportunity for solid biblical and theological reflection, ministry begins to look like social work. Don't misunderstand me. Social work is necessary, and plenty of Christians are engaged in good community care, but if your calling is youth ministry, purposeful action needs to flow from the biblical mandate to *make disciples*.

Preparing for a summer mission trip, I provided an evening for parents/caregivers and teens to meet with me to discuss the details. After the meeting, a mother approached me. "My daughter doesn't really like the religious stuff, but I would like her to go anyway," she said. "Serving like this will look good on her resume." This woman was a prominent church member, and her comments provided a perfect example of purposeful action being completely removed from what it states in Matthew 25:40, that when followers of Jesus serve people in need, it's like serving Jesus himself. The point is to do all that you can to ensure that your purposeful action in ministry flows directly from a biblical and theological foundation, while nurturing healthy disciple-making relationships with teens.

Ray Anderson wisely writes, "Every act of ministry teaches something about God."[16] This statement ought to make youth workers pause for a moment of reflection. What if Anderson is right? How might you engage in acts of ministry differently? The reality is this: youth ministry is profoundly theological in nature. As you interact with teens, building safe and caring relationships, you're teaching them about God.

A junior-high boy showed up early for Bible study one night. The study was in our home, and I was playing with our young kids. He sat on the couch in silence, watching us laugh and play. The young man was still unsure about faith in Jesus; he came from a messy family situation. At the end of the night, before he left, he said, "I like coming here. It feels … peaceful." As a young father living in the chaos of what felt like a toddler invasion, I would not have used the word *peaceful* to describe our home. Days later, he shared with me over lunch that it was "weird" for him to watch me with my kids, because I never raised my voice, cursed, or hit them.

Remember Anderson's words: "Every act of ministry teaches something about God." Even watching me play with my kids was a profoundly spiritual experience for this young man, as God began to open new relational possibilities for him. Simply having me love my family in front of him became one of the primary ministry acts God used to heal him of his own father wounds and draw him closer to Jesus.

Like the student who walked into my office, you might wonder why I am "wasting time" writing about discipleship when you chose this book to learn how to help teens in crisis. I hope you'll come to understand that helping kids in crisis is not the primary purpose of youth ministry. The ultimate goal is to make disciples, and this mandate comes from Jesus's teaching, as he says to those gathered around him on the mountainside: "Therefore go and make disciples of all nations, baptizing them in the name of the Father and of the Son and of the Holy Spirit, and teaching them to obey everything I have commanded you. And surely I am with you always, to the very end of the age" (Matthew 28:19–20).

Teaching about Bible study methods, one of my college professors was fond of saying, "If you find a *therefore*, ask what it is *there for.*" It's a funny little saying, but it often comes back to me when I'm studying the Bible. You'll notice that verse 19 begins with the word "therefore." Jesus has just told the crowd that the Father has given him all authority in heaven and on earth. Now he links his authority to his commission. Don't miss the point: the universal mission commissioned by Jesus flows from his universal authority.[17]

The Christian Life in Five Words

Amber was cutting herself. One of her relatives had recently hung himself. He had developed a consistent pattern of sexually and physically assaulting her, and now that he was dead, she was filled with shame, joy, anger, remorse, and relief. She was thirteen and alone, with parents who had little interest in her. In fact, other than the teachers at her school, there was not a single caring adult in her life. She was one of the first kids the Lord brought into my life in the early days of my youth ministry.

I had only been a follower of Jesus a short time, had no ministry training, and had never been part of a youth group. As many of you have likely discovered, none of these "excellent" excuses for being passed over for ministry seem to matter much to God. Feeling incredibly inadequate for ministry, I memorized this text of scripture: "My grace is sufficient for you, for my power is made perfect in weakness" (2 Corinthians 12:9).

It didn't bother Amber that I didn't have much ministry expertise. She would call me at odd hours, sobbing into the phone, telling me she wanted to die, and often describing the cuts she had made on her arms. I had no idea what to do. I was afraid, but I listened to her, and I reminded her that Jesus cared for her and was present with her. With the combination of her life experiences and her overwhelming pain, I might as well have been describing the presence of Santa Clause in her living room on Christmas morning. Language about Christian faith was completely foreign to her. I asked Jesus repeatedly, "How do I help Amber experience your love? How do I help her experience your freedom?"

In the Great Commission, Jesus instructs his disciples to spread his teachings throughout the world. He says, "Go and make disciples of all nations." Sounds easy enough—until Amber calls you at two in the morning from her bathroom, unloading the pain of sexual assault and describing her self-injury in graphic detail. This is exactly when those in youth ministry need to get back to the word *therefore*. Jesus has conquered the grave. Jesus has defeated sin and death. Jesus has endured the cross and scorned its shame, and he now sits in active rule over the universe: "Therefore, go." Don't miss this critical point: the power and authority of Jesus Christ are connected to the work of the Church! No one is in this alone. Jesus empowers those with his own authority to make disciples.

The writer to the Hebrews will summarize the entire Christian life in five words. There's nothing magical about these words, but bringing the wisdom of Hebrews into my conversation with Amber would change everything: "Fix your eyes on Jesus" (Hebrews 12:2). She wasn't a Christian, but she was overwhelmed with pain. Fixing our eyes on Jesus is what we started to do together. Jesus slowly began to change her reality. Today, Amber is married with several children of her own, and God is using her to speak life and freedom into the lives of other young women. Alleviation of pain was not her greatest need; rather, knowing Jesus was.

Apprenticeship in Jesus

Let's take a closer look at what Jesus is intending when he commissions his followers to make disciples. The word *mathetes* is the word most commonly used for "disciple" in the New Testament, appearing in various forms over two hundred times. It comes from the Greek word *mathano*, which means "learn." To Jesus and his followers then, a *mathetes* is a learner, a student, or an apprentice, one who imitates the teacher.[18] This apprentice learns by use and practice for the purpose of acquiring a custom or habit.[19] In their groundbreaking study of adolescent spirituality in the USA, conducted from 2001 to 2005, Smith and Lundquist Denton came to the conclusion that many teens have fashioned a faith system known as Moralistic-Therapeutic Deism (MTD).[20] The basic idea is based on three premises: 1. God wants me to be good; 2. God wants me to feel good; 3. God is not personal.

This is critical to understand as you think about caring for teens in pain, who for the most part have built a theological framework around the idea that God wants them to feel good. In youth ministry, many find that their lives often intersect with the lives of teens during those moments when their theological framework is crumbling. It's also important to recognize the influence of MTD and to engage in personal and youth ministry discipleship that's firmly rooted in Christian theology and biblical wisdom.

When asked in an interview how he understood the gospel, Dallas Willard gave this answer: "Two words: *trust Jesus*."[21] He expanded, saying that a disciple trusts Jesus for everything, not just eternal life. In contrast to MTD, Willard writes, "Trusting Jesus and becoming his disciple is the same thing. I like the word *apprentice* because it means I am with Jesus, learning to do what he did. When you look at the first disciples, that is what they were doing. They watched Jesus and listened to him, and then he said, 'Now you do it.'"[22] In his book, *The Great Omission* (2006), Willard writes, "There is absolutely nothing in what Jesus himself or his early followers taught that suggests you can *decide* to enjoy forgiveness at Jesus's expense and have nothing more to do with him."[23] Writing about discipleship as apprenticeship, he continues, ". . . practicing Jesus's words, as his apprentices, enables us to understand our lives and to see how we can interact with God's redemptive resources, ever at hand."[24]

The Bible is full of verses that demonstrate this hands-on approach to spiritual formation. The Psalmist writes, "I have hidden your word in my heart, that I might not sin against you" (Psalm 119:11).

John writes, "Whoever says, 'I know him' but does not do what he commands is a liar, and the truth is not in that person" (1 John 2:4).

James writes, "Do not merely listen to the word, and so deceive yourselves. Do what it says" (James 1:27).

Finally, in his sermon on the mountainside, Jesus teaches, "Not everyone who says to me, 'Lord, Lord,' will enter the kingdom of heaven, but only the one who does the will of my Father who is in heaven" (Matthew 7:21).

One might conclude, then, that a Christian disciple is one who is learning through practice to acquire Christlike habits. I appreciate the process-oriented language used by Christopher Adsit, when he writes, "A disciple is a person-in-process who is eager to learn and apply the truths that Jesus teaches, which will result in ever-deepening commitments to a Christlike lifestyle."[25]

Participating in God's Action

God can be a bit … sneaky, sometimes. School had not been my favorite place, so attending college appeared on my bucket list somewhere down near wrestling an alligator or getting a root canal with no freezing. You get the idea. When I finally said yes to the Spirit's nudging, I thought the Lord was leading me to Bible college so that I could learn more about my faith. It came as a surprise when God *seized* me for ministry. My initial response was not faithfulness; I am more the Moses type. "You can't be serious!" was closer to the way I responded. The reality I am drawing your attention to—one I face often in ministry—is this. I, too, am a disciple in process, called to nurture faith in disciples who are in process. As I have found with the Lord, being a disciple in process is not a get-out-of-jail-free card.

Imagine the conversation in heaven. Jesus smacks his forehead in a moment of shock, as if he just remembered something. He says to the angel standing beside him, "I totally forgot! She's a disciple in process. We can't use her to make disciples. Go find someone else." That's not how this works. Ministry flows out of the person you are, and God is fully prepared to commission you, even though you'll *always* be a disciple in process. You'll likely never think you are smart enough, holy enough, pure enough, skilled enough, or even just enough to disciple someone else, but Jesus is waiting for you to say yes anyway.

To make disciples is not to coerce. It's not to force people into a direction or to threaten them with fear of punishment. Be careful not to think the nurturing of faith in a person can be reduced to a simple five-step process, like a recipe. In nurturing others in faith, it helps if we first remember the words of Jesus from Luke's gospel: "Do to others as you would have them do to you" (Luke 6:31).

Amy Jacober captures the discipling relationship beautifully. "As youth workers we are called to *intentionality*—actively seeking to join God's work in maturing adolescents, in which love, justice, and mercy unite to nurture them through the transformative power of Christ."[26]

Using similar tones of gentleness and grace, Andrew Root writes, "The purpose of youth ministry is to invite both young and old to participate in God's action. Youth ministry, like all ministry, seeks in humility to be swept up into God's own action, and therefore to participate in God's activity in our world."[27]

If these authors are correct, then I didn't bring Jesus with me when I began to disciple Amber; I joined in the work God was already doing. Some of the most effective discipleship God will call you to will take place in the most horrendous, heartbreaking, and unjust life circumstances you could imagine. In those moments, you may feel Jesus *seize* you and say, "I need you to carry this cross." The pain is not a barrier—a thing to remove before you can help—but the very life context in which you join the Spirit in the work of life transformation.

It Takes a Village

During the Napoleonic wars in Europe in the late 1700s, Dr. Dominique Jean Larrey served as a surgeon and was an important innovator in battlefield medicine. It was Larrey who first used what he called a "flying ambulance" to drive onto the battlefield and treat wounded soldiers where they lay. Larrey rejected the practice of treating the officers first and created a system of sorting that he called "triage," based on the needs of the wounded. *Triage* is a French word that means "sorting," and the practice involves the rapid evaluation and classification of casualties for treatment. "It consists of the immediate sorting of patients according to injury, the likelihood of survival, and the establishment of priority for treatment and evacuation, to assure medical care of the greatest benefit to the largest number."[28] Larrey rose to hero status among the soldiers for his ability to engage in rapid response during battle.

Triage has become common practice in mobile army surgical units, in hospital emergency rooms, and in disaster response situations. The categories are indicated by colors as follows: 1. Black = No Care. This person is dead or expected to die (lowest priority); 2. Red = First Priority. These people should be stabilized and transported to a medical facility as quickly as possible, or they will die; 3. Yellow = Delayed. Injuries are serious but not life threatening; 4. Green = Minor. The walking wounded. These people may be frightened or in pain and are still in need of medical attention. They need reassurance that their needs will be attended to in order of priority. All the wounded need to remain under observation, as their injuries may become worse.[29] When it comes to pastoral care in youth ministry, practicing the principles of triage will help in clarifying priorities and using time and energy wisely.

I got a call late one night from a teenager who was sitting in a local restaurant. She was crying and said she needed to speak with me right away; over the phone would not do. By the way she sounded, this was Code Red on the triage scale, and I knew I needed to meet with her right away to see how I could help.[30] As we sat together, she poured out her heart, telling me the story of a father who would not allow her to hang a poster of a certain rock band on her bedroom wall. She was so angry that she had slammed the door and hit the streets. *Code Red?* As a youth pastor, I learned early on that the experience of crisis and trauma are subjectively defined. To her, this was *truly* a Code Red. To me, however, this was Code Green, one of the many examples in youth ministry of encounters with the walking wounded.

Pastoral care as discipleship is a ministry of the Church. The saying "It takes a village to raise a child" comes to mind. Teens in crisis need to experience a consistently gracious worshipping community. Chap Clark captures this idea well: "The goal of youth ministry should be to make disciples of Jesus Christ who are authentically walking with God within the context of intimate Christian community."[31] Serving in my first youth ministry position in rural Ontario, I created a monthly worship night I called Power House Praise. I hoped that a night of loud worship music would draw Christian and non-Christian kids alike. One night, as I stepped onto the stage with my guitar, I noticed a group of tough-looking guys, all dressed in black and standing against the back wall. As the music began, several of them held up the flames from their cigarette lighters, slowly waving their arms as they might at a rock concert. (This is what teens did before cell phones.) The next morning when I came into the church, I noticed that the elder responsible for custodial care was in the sanctuary. Art was on his knees, scrubbing the black boot marks off the walls, right where the guys had been standing the night before. I apologized to him and picked up a sponge to help wash the walls. With tears in his eyes, that elderly man spoke words of grace to me. "Pastor Chris, don't apologize," he assured me. "This is the reason we built this church." At the next Board meeting, one of the elders in the room expressed concern over the beer bottles and cigarette butts left in the parking lot after the worship night. Again, brother Art—the oldest member at the table—spoke to the leadership and exclaimed "Praise Jesus!" with joy in his voice and tears in his eyes. Youth ministry is more effective when done in the context of a gracious faith community.

Triage for Youth Ministry

Instead of color-coded categories for youth ministry-related triage, think about your response to teens in pain using these four categories: 1. Critical Care (for those in life-and-death situations); 2. Crisis Care (for those in serious pain, who could become critical); 3. Compassion Care (for the walking wounded); and 4. Companion Care (for teen disciples caring for friends). [32] You will find a full description of the Discipleship Triage Model in Appendix A. In some of these situations, it's easy to feel completely lost, especially if discipling teens in pain is new to you. Game nights are easy. Worship nights, manageable. Bible studies, no problem. However, when there is true pain, it's easy to feel as if you have little control, inadequate answers, and few words to soothe the aching.

A family called me from a hospital waiting room one night. Two of the boys in the family were in our youth program, and the mother was one of our key youth workers. Her father had suffered a massive heart attack. I honestly had no idea what I would do when I got to the hospital, but just as I arrived, the doctors were rolling the man past the waiting room and into surgery. The woman saw her father. "Wait!" she shouted. The doctors peered over their sterile masks in anger as she blurted out, "We need to pray!" She turned to me and barked the order: "Pray!"

I will never forget the doctor's stern command: "Pray fast, preacher!" So I did. We sat for hours in the waiting room, long into the night. We prayed a little but not much. Mostly we sat in silence and shared the waiting. This, too, was helping people follow Jesus, as I will explain at the end of my chapter on grief. Take a moment now and look over the Discipleship Triage Model (Appendix A). I will refer to it as we move through the chapters together, to give you a sense of how it can be a resource for you when you're not quite sure what to do next.

The Conduit of God's Presence

Looking to Matthew's gospel (4:23), we see Jesus demonstrating his value for consistent worship, training his ministry team to preach and teach and showing them how to engage in pastoral care. The real challenge in youth ministry is understanding that sometimes the worst thing you can do is rescue a teen from suffering. In critical care, yes, it's a moral responsibility to do everything possible to help the teenager stay alive, but in ministry with the walking wounded, the goal might not be pain reduction. In his letter to the believers in Rome, the Apostle Paul writes of the value of suffering for spiritual formation. He uses words that are hard to read, especially for those sitting with kids in pain. Paul learned, through personal experience, that there is reason to glory in suffering: "because we know that suffering produces perseverance; perseverance, character; and character, hope" (Romans 5:3-4).

James, the brother of Jesus, once wrote, "Consider it pure joy, my brothers and sisters, whenever you face trials of many kinds, because you know that the testing of your faith produces perseverance. Let perseverance finish its work so that you may be mature and complete, not lacking anything" (James 1:2-4).

I sit monthly with a small group of people who are living with terminal cancer. I have on occasion found myself feeling frustrated, angry even, at their life circumstances. As I've listened to them speak about their illness, I've been surprised to hear themes of hope, resilience, and faith transformation. One woman even told me that God has become so personal to her through her suffering that she wouldn't give up her cancer, even if she had the power to do so. It was a holy moment, and as I think of her words, I am reminded again of the insights provided by Willard: "When we accept moment-to-moment events and tribulations as the place where we receive God's provision, we patiently anticipate the action of his Spirit in our lives."[33] Pain and suffering are not barriers to the movement of God's Spirit, and those things we would avoid, if given the chance, can often become the conduit of God's merciful presence.[34]

Final Words

This is a book about discipling teenagers in pain. As I write, I'm thinking about the person who might be new to youth ministry and would like to understand some of the issues he or she might encounter in work with the adolescent population. The names of people and the stories I will share will be altered to respect the confidentiality of people I have encountered in ministry. No doubt you have already noted, based on the small numbers at the ends of sentences, that I'm not writing this book on my own. This indicates that I have referred to an idea that I value, something written by someone else. It might be a word of wisdom from a youth ministry professor, a theologian, a pastor, a biblical scholar, or a specialist in a specific field. Although I haven't met any of these people, the work they've done in their own writing has helped me to provide a better resource for you.

Please refer to the reference list in the back of the book for more information about these excellent sources. I apologize if some of the websites provided are dead links by the time you read this book, but I trust that your own well-honed Google search skills will help you locate useful information, as needed. You'll also notice that I have provided reflection questions at the end of each chapter, which I hope will guide you into deeper study. You might consider reading this book with your youth ministry team and working through the questions together. I pray that you'll find this work to be a useful resource for you as you continue to help teenagers in pain to follow Jesus.

Ideas for Discussion and Reflection

1. In the opening story, Justin stands in the middle with arms outstretched. Can you think of a time when you felt you were standing in the middle, between a teen in pain and a God of compassion? Describe this encounter and the way God used you.

2. Read Ezekiel 22 and pay special attention to verse 30. What do you think God expects from those who "stand in the gap" for teens in pain?

3. Read Luke 23 and notice how Simon is seized from the crowd and made to carry the cross-beam for Jesus. Reflect on the idea of being *seized* by God for ministry. Has God ever taken hold of your heart and compelled you to pray, love, or serve someone? How does this idea fit with your thinking about discipleship?

4. Matthew 18:16–20 is often referred to as the Great Commission. Read a few biblical commentaries and see what you can discover about this text. Describe in detail the idea of apprenticeship as it relates to discipling teenagers. How could you build this into your youth ministry programming?

5. Authors Amy Jacober and Andrew Root agree that our task in youth ministry discipleship is to intentionally participate in the ongoing work of God in a teen's life. What do you think this means? What might it look like when you are sitting with a teen in pain?

1   Dallas Willard, *The Great Omission: Reclaiming Jesus's Essential Teachings on Discipleship* (New York: HarperCollins Publishing, 2006), 31.

2   David G. Benner, *Care of Souls: Revisioning Christian Nurture and Counsel* (Grand Rapids: Baker Books, 1998), 190.

3   "Statement of Purpose," *Journal of Youth Ministry*, accessed February 15, 2018, https://www.aymeducators.org/journal-youth-ministry/

4   Daniel I. Block, *The Book of Ezekiel Chapters 1–24* (Grand Rapids: Wm. B. Eerdmans Publishing, 1997), 727–728.

5   William Willimon, *Pastor: The Theology and Practice of Ordained Ministry* (Nashville: Abingdon Press, 2002), 91.

6   Ibid., 93.

7   Harold W. Hoehner, *Ephesians: An Exegetical Commentary* (Grand Rapids: Baker Academic, 2002), 544.

8   Ibid., 91.

9   Darrell L. Bock, *Baker Exegetical Commentary on the New Testament: Luke 9:51–24:53* (Grand Rapids: Baker Books, 1996), 1842.

10 Frederick Buechner, *Wishful Thinking: A Seeker's ABC* (New York: HarperSanFrancisco, 1993), 119.

11 Henri J. M. Nouwen, *The Wounded Healer: Ministry in Contemporary Society* (New York: Image Books/Doubleday, 1972), 72

12 Robert H. Mounce, *New International Biblical Commentary: Matthew* (Peabody: Hendrickson Publishers, 1991), 267.

13 Edmund D. Hiebert, "An Expository Study of Matthew 28:16–20," *Bibliotheca Sacra* 149, no. 595, (1992): 343.

14 Hiebert, 346.

15 Mark H. Senter III, "A Historical Framework for Doing Youth Ministry," in *Reaching a Generation for Christ: A Comprehensive Guide to Youth Ministry*, ed. Richard R. Dunn & Mark H. Senter III (Chicago: Moody Publishers, 1997), 109.

16 Ray Anderson, *Making the Transition: From a Theology of Ministry to a Ministry of Theology* (Grand Rapids: Wm. B. Eerdmans, 2008), 35.

17 David J. Bosch, "The Structure of Mission: An Exposition of Matt. 28:16–20," in *Exploring Church Growth* by Wilbert R. Schenk, ed. (Eugene: Wipf and Stock Publishers, 2010), 228.

18 Christopher B. Adsit, *Personal Disciple-Making: A Step-by-Step Guide for Leading a Christian from New Birth to Maturity* (San Bernardino: Here's Life Publishers, 1988), 31–32.

19 G. Abbott-Smith, *A Manual Greek Lexicon of the New Testament*, 3rd edition (New York: Charles Scribner's Sons, 1922), 277.

20 Christian Smith and Melinda Lundquist Denton, *Soul Searching: The Religious and Spiritual Lives of American Teenagers* (Oxford: Oxford University Press, 2009), 162–163.

21 "The Apprentices," *Christianity Today/CT Pastors,* accessed January 29, 2018, http://www.christianitytoday.com/pastors/2005/summer/2.20.html

22 Ibid.

23 Dallas Willard, 13.

24 Ibid., 15.

25 Adsit, 35.

26 Amy E. Jacober, *The Adolescent Journey: An Interdisciplinary Approach to Practical Youth Ministry* (Downers Grove: InterVarsity Press, 2011), 29.

27 Andrew Root, *Taking Theology to Youth Ministry* (Grand Rapids: Zondervan Publishing, 2012), 38.

28 "Mass Triage," *Disaster Medicine,* accessed February 3, 2018, https:// disaster medicine.wordpress.com/triage/

29 Ibid.

30 *This is not an endorsement for cross-gender ministry. If I were to get this same call today, I would ask a female youth worker to respond, or I would ask my spouse to respond with me. I would not go alone.*

31 Chap Clark, *Hurt: Inside the World of Today's Teenagers* (Grand Rapids: Baker Academic, 2004), 188.

32 "Discipleship Triage Model," Appendix A.

33 Willard, 31.

34 *Conduit*: a pipe used to drain water, like a downspout on the side of your house.

CHAPTER 2
The Crash of the Superhero:
Understanding Trauma in Discipleship

But Jesus said, "Someone touched me;
I know that power has gone out from me."
—Luke 8:46

I heard pieces of Sean's story in a smoke-filled room over a billiards table. When I first arrived in our small community, the senior pastor of our church suggested I visit the local high school. Introducing myself to the school administration as the new youth pastor in town seemed like a good way to start, so I made an appointment to meet with the vice principal.

Contract negotiations between the teacher's union and the education minister had not been going well, and teachers were engaged in something called "work to rule." This meant that teachers worked only as required in the terms of their contract. School administrators were scrambling to find adult volunteers to walk the halls at lunchtime, chaperone dances, drive students to events, and coach teams. It was a great time to be a youth pastor. Schools that had previously been closed to religious groups were now asking youth pastors to walk the halls at lunchtime. I volunteered to help in any way I could.

One day the vice principal called me to her office and asked me a question I'd never thought to hear in a secular school: "Would you like your own office?" I could barely breathe. I would be expected to keep a few regular office hours during the week, and teens could make appointments to see me through the school administrative assistants. It was an incredible answer to prayer, and I had amazing opportunities to care for both students and staff.

I got a call one afternoon from the school office. A youth by the name of Sean had told a friend that he wanted to kill himself. The friend was a follower of Jesus and one of the teens in our youth program. He took Sean to the office, and after speaking with him, the vice principal called me to see whether I could drive Sean to the hospital. The hospital with the psychiatric intake was an hour away, and I was sometimes called when a teen needed to be transported for a psychiatric evaluation. This occurred only if the vice principal decided that the situation wasn't an emergency. What a gift God gave me, two hours of driving with teenagers in pain! The problem with Sean was his silence; he just sat quietly, even peacefully, staring out the window. At the hospital, the physician determined that Sean was not a risk to himself. Sean had been through this process several times, and he knew that if the doctor thought he was at risk, he would have to go to the fourth floor. They would make him stay overnight, take away his cigarettes, and make him talk to someone about his feelings. So he lied.

When working with teens in crisis, I have made it my practice to find a way to be present at some point during their week. Simply sharing a lunch or taking my dog for a walk together have been valuable opportunities for discipleship. In one of our many conversations that would follow that first drive to the hospital, I discovered that Sean liked to play billiards. Often we would drive to a pool hall in a neighboring town, where we would spend time quietly shooting pool. Sometimes he would speak, but mostly we would play. As often happens in youth ministry, my heart began to break for Sean, and I prayed for months that he would come to know Jesus. He was a young teen, yet he spoke as if his life were already over. Deeply wounded by a variety of people, Sean was a time bomb of unexpressed rage, but as hard as I tried, I could not get him to open up to me.

As I was preparing for bed, my phone rang. It was Sean's mother. Sobbing into the phone, she told me that Sean had come home from school and tried to take his life. He had survived and was now in hospital. It has now been many years since my young friend tried to take his life, but even as I write these words, I *still* feel the aching in my soul.

Shortly after Sean was admitted to the hospital, it became painfully clear to me that something was seriously wrong with me. I had stopped at the only traffic light in our small town, and as I waited for the light to turn green, I felt pressure on my chest. I began to sweat and could barely breathe. As I looked up at the green light, I had no idea where I was. It's not that I didn't know which way to turn; I literally couldn't remember where I was. I turned the corner, and as I pulled my car to the side of the road, I began to sob uncontrollably. I had never cried like this before. My heart was aching. I felt like a complete failure, as if Sean's attempt to kill himself was entirely my fault.

Over the next few weeks, I would struggle constantly with feelings of insecurity, wanting desperately to quit my job and disappear. I didn't want to be around people, and I wondered whether God was trying to tell me that youth ministry was no longer my calling. I was sick, malnourished, sleep-deprived, exhausted, irritable, and unable to concentrate. As I look back, it's hard to believe that I didn't connect what was happening in my life to the trauma I had experienced.

Over my years of speaking to missionaries from war zones, youth ministry volunteers serving in the inner city, and camp ministry staff, I have found a common thread. Very few people understand that effective disciple making with people in pain can traumatize you, leading to sickness, loss of faith, and despair. Thankfully, you have a book in your hands that will help you care well. Now that you've heard about my journey into sickness, let me tell you how I have learned to stay healthy as I continue to serve in ministry.

Caring for the Wounded

Trauma comes from a Greek word that means "wound." Many of the teens you'll disciple in youth ministry will have wide, gaping wounds from things like abuse, addiction, bullying, rejection, and low self-esteem. You can expect to encounter wounded people in youth ministry, and because of the work Jesus has done in your own lives, many of you will gravitate fearlessly to those living in the aftermath of trauma.

In my work with Sean, I did everything I could to engage him, using empathy to listen, to be present in the hospital, and to sit in silence. How is it that effective youth ministry discipleship could cause me to sink into despair and even question my own faith in Jesus? How did hearing of Sean's attempted suicide translate into nightmares, loss of sleep, self-blame, and loss of meaning in my life? For years I was baffled by these questions, thinking that perhaps I had just burned out in ministry. I've since met many youth workers experiencing the same thing, and it's been a pleasure to help them understand that while there's certainly a cost to caring, there is also a way to understand what's happening to you, and there are wise choices you can make that will help you stay healthy.

After his return from Vietnam in the late 1960s, psychologist Charles Figley became interested in combat-related stress reactions. In his work with veterans, he recognized that family, friends, and even professionals could develop symptoms of traumatic stress, just from living with and caring for soldiers who had experienced war trauma. He first referred to this experience of help-related trauma as a kind of burnout, but he would come to change his terminology to *compassion fatigue*.[1] As his thinking developed, Figley described compassion fatigue as secondary traumatic stress, which he defined as, "The natural consequent behaviors and emotions resulting from knowledge about a traumatizing event experienced by a significant other. It is the stress resulting from helping or wanting to help a traumatized or suffering person."[2] Note in his definition that *knowledge about* another person's encounter with trauma is enough to cause traumatic stress.

I have found that medical staff in hospitals, people working in palliative care, and social workers tend to prefer the term *vicarious trauma*. The word *vicarious* is used to refer to an experience someone has through someone else. A father who never had the opportunity to play hockey as a boy might live vicariously through his son. He fulfills his dream to play, but he isn't physically on the ice. He experiences his joy of hockey through his son.

In Christian theology it's said that Jesus suffered vicariously for us. Jesus took the sin of humanity upon himself and died in our place; it was a vicarious suffering. Vicarious trauma happens, not through direct personal experience with trauma but through contact with someone who personally experiences trauma.[3] Pearlman writes that vicarious trauma is a "process of change resulting from empathic engagement with trauma survivors.[4] It results in the disruption of one's sense of identity, world-view, and spirituality.⁵ In *Transforming the Pain*, a helpful workbook for those healing through the effects of vicarious trauma, authors Pearlman and Saakvitne write the following:

> Vicarious traumatization is our strong reactions to grief, rage, and outrage, which grow as we repeatedly hear about and see people's pain and loss and are forced to recognize human potential for cruelty and indifference, and it is our numbing, our protective shell, and our wish not to know, which follow those reactions.⁶

After Sean's attempted suicide, I began to wonder whether I might be experiencing burnout, but I would come to understand that burnout and vicarious trauma are not the same. Burnout is the result of emotional exhaustion due to the chronic, repetitive emotional strain of dealing with people in pain. Unlike vicarious trauma, burnout stems from a pattern of emotional overload.⁷ Vicarious trauma can occur even after a single encounter with a story of trauma.⁸ Even more shocking are research findings that indicate that many volunteer emergency medical technicians have experienced vivid, involuntary, and uncontrollable thoughts, feelings, and images following a cardiopulmonary resuscitation (CPR) attempt. These findings suggest that even routine CPR has the potential to cause post-traumatic symptoms in crisis workers.⁹

I was sitting in a graduate class in 2007 the first time I read the following quote—twenty years after Sean shot himself, and my experience was finally beginning to make sense. "The vicarious experiencing of what is heard from clients can affect helpers as if the events were happening to them personally," writes Robert Hayes.¹⁰

For example, picture yourself in a car, driving to see a friend. You notice a line of cars ahead and see police flares on the side of the road. You slow down when you notice emergency vehicles ahead and you see police directing traffic. As you slowly make your way past the accident, you smell gas, you see several people on the side of the road on stretchers, and you notice one person who is still unconscious, trapped in the vehicle. Firefighters are working to free the person, but you aren't permitted to stop and watch, to see how things resolve.

As you drive away from the accident, how are you feeling? Are you afraid? Are you praying? What is happening to your body? Are your hands shaking? Is your stomach upset? Perhaps your shoulders feel tight. What about your thoughts? If you are a parent and one of your teens is currently driving, you might wonder where she is and whether she's safe. If you are a person of deep empathy and caring, it's likely your response will be different from someone who doesn't have an empathic nature. Consider for a moment what you might be experiencing if you'd recently lost a friend in a car accident. You might need to stop for a few moments to cry or to gather your thoughts. The interesting thing about your experience in the car is that although you were responding to a traumatic situation, it was not *your* trauma. You were only an observer, a witness to the accident, and yet you may have experienced physical, psychological, and spiritual similarities to the person in the accident.

When you listen to stories of pain, or you encounter tragedy in youth ministry discipleship, as I did with Sean, the things you encounter as a witness can affect you *as if the events were happening to you personally.* The survivor's horror imprints on the helper's mind, leading to behaviors and emotions that can parallel those of the primary trauma survivors."[11] Addressing therapists, Herman writes, "Trauma is contagious. In the role of witness to disaster or atrocity, the therapist at times is emotionally overwhelmed. She experiences, to a lesser degree, the same terror, rage, and despair as the patient. This phenomenon is known as traumatic countertransference or vicarious traumatization."[12]

One of the words that has become important to me in understanding how ministry can make me sick is *overwhelmed. Traumatic stress* refers to feelings, thoughts, actions, and physical and spiritual reactions when we are exposed to events that are overwhelming.[13] In addition to feeling overwhelmed in our capacity to respond, we may feel a sense of helplessness at these often-unexpected events. "Traumatic events overwhelm the ordinary systems of care that give people a sense of control, connection, and meaning ... They confront human beings with feelings of helplessness and terror and evoke the responses of catastrophe."[14]

As I look back on my time with Sean, I recognize that his attempted suicide overwhelmed my capacity to respond. I was right where I wanted to be in his life, doing what God had called me to do, engaging in discipleship with the hope that he would come to faith in Jesus. But my inability to understand what was happening to me almost destroyed my life.

Thankfully, I have learned that there is a cost to caring, and there are healthier ways to engage in discipleship with people in pain. Self-care in ministry might be a new idea to you, but I pray that as you take the journey in this book, you will learn to pay attention to your personal needs. That way God will be able to use you for the good of the teens you encounter for many years to come. Now that you know a little bit about vicarious trauma, I would like to help you understand some of the reasons youth workers make themselves sick, and I'd like to look at some better patterns for caregiving in discipleship.

Witnessing Fear

At first, Susan loved working with the kids at the drop-in. Every Thursday night, she would make beaded bracelets in the craft room, as children sat around the table and lounged on the floor. Stories from their day at school and their lives at home naturally flowed into conversation. The way she spoke with kindness and empathy made it easy for them to share, and it was rewarding for her, as relationships deepened.[15]

It wasn't long before Susan started noticing bruises and injuries on some of the children's arms. The kids were casually telling her stories of violence, stories they recounted with little emotion. After walking a nine-year-old girl home one night, Susan had just gotten her safely in the door when she heard a scream. Suddenly, the front door was thrown open and the little girl raced across the lawn and hid behind a tree near the road. Susan had heard the story of the older sister's methamphetamine use. The little girl had said she was afraid to go home because of the violence, but Susan had never experienced the fear personally.

That night, as she shared in her little friend's fear, she came to understand what it meant to live in terror. As had been my experience with Sean, Susan had no idea that this kind of caregiving could traumatize her. Susan was a classic superhero caregiver: tough as nails, fearless, able to walk dark inner-city alleys at night, and ready to fight for "her" kids if the situation called for it. She was trained in martial arts and was not the kind to back down from a challenge. You could almost hear her superhero cape flapping in the wind. It never dawned on her that her experiences of terror and trauma might take a toll. Read Susan's own words on the way trauma was affecting her life:

> I would come home after nights like that and take a shower and just bawl my eyes out, and I would just cry and cry and cry and cry. I'd cry myself to sleep because it was just so painful, but I never really made a connection between why it was hurting. I couldn't fall asleep because it just hurt so much, but I never really thought that it could all build up. Emotionally, after so long of having all of that pain and not talking to anybody about it, I started to feel as though I was being stripped of my ability to care.[16]

It's important to remember that this youth ministry "craft lady" just wanted to give a few hours a week to love some kids. She wasn't working in an emergency room at a hospital or counselling soldiers returning from battle. She was making bracelets! I hope that Susan's story will help you to understand that it's easy to experience traumatic stress in youth ministry. I want you to have this information so that you can learn to care well. Caring for people with traumatic life stories doesn't have to make you sick; you must care with wisdom. Now, before looking at a few suggestions for self-care, let's think about the nature and power of empathy.

The Double-Edged Sword

Empathy has been described as the ability to "think and feel oneself into the inner life of another person."[17] Empathic people are able to feel and even absorb other people's emotions and physical symptoms because of their high sensitivities.[18] These folks tend to gravitate to the helping professions and to youth ministry, but after a while their capacity for sharing in the inner lives of people becomes overwhelming, and trauma encounters can reduce their ability to care. Empathy is an essential tool in youth ministry discipleship, and yet it's like a double-edged sword. Empathy helps people care deeply, but it's also the primary reason they're vulnerable to vicarious trauma. Crothers explains that repeated stories of human cruelty will inevitably challenge a caregiver's basic faith and heighten his sense of personal vulnerability.[19]

As I experienced personally and witnessed in Susan's story, traumatized caregivers may become generally more fearful of other people and distrustful in close personal relationships. "When overwhelmed with the impact of stressful emotions, empaths may experience panic attacks; depression; chronic fatigue; food, sex, and drug binges; or exhibit many other physical symptoms that defy traditional diagnosis."[20] The hallmark of vicarious trauma and compassion fatigue is the reduced capacity or interest in being empathic or bearing another's suffering.[21]

Looking in the Wrong Place

Susan's world started to unravel, and she had no idea what was happening to her. After months of working at the drop-in, her emotions had begun to shut down. She felt angry most of the time, did not want to be around people—just in case someone might need her to care for them—and spent most of her time alone. She no longer answered the phone, kept the curtains drawn, and was experiencing conflict in her marriage. One sunny afternoon, Susan was waiting for a bus when she noticed a group of men walking toward her. She had heard many stories from little girls of violent experiences at the hands of men, but her home life had always been safe. As the men drew closer, she was surprised to find that her body was responding.

> (As the men walked toward me), my soul felt like a clenched fist, a clenched jaw. It was this tightness that just overwhelmed my whole body, and my palms were getting a little bit damp. I had this incredible feeling of tension just completely come over me, this anxiety. I stood there the whole time just wondering, *What is it I'm afraid of?* There was nobody else around besides these guys walking by; they stood around for a little bit and

then moved on. It's hard to describe; it wasn't fear, really, at least I don't think. I had no reason to be afraid of them; it was just this incredibly deep feeling of anxiety and tension and discomfort just with them passing. Even my palms were sweating. It just didn't make any sense.[22]

Earlier in this book, you read that the survivor's horror can imprint on the helper's mind, leading to behaviors and emotions that can *parallel* those of the primary trauma survivors. To help Susan make sense of her experience, I asked her, "If one of the young survivors of violence had been standing at that bus stop, how might her body have reacted?"

Susan's eyes lit up, and she popped out of her chair. "But that's not possible!" she exclaimed. "I've never been assaulted." If it's possible to have a full-body reaction when driving by a car accident, why would it be strange that her emotions and thoughts could parallel the behaviors and emotions of the primary trauma survivors (even though she had only been a witness to their pain)?

Imagine you're helping a friend build a house, and you've been asked to nail a few boards together. As you're lifting your hammer, you lose your grip on the nail and you strike your thumb—hard. You say something you would not want your pastor to hear and begin to dance around, as you coddle your aching thumb. The nice thing about a situation like this is the way you can make a direct and immediate connection between the pain and its source. You might toss the hammer on the ground, blaming the tool for causing your injury.

When it comes to injury due to vicarious trauma, I've found that it's common for people, like Susan, to have absolutely no clue what's happening to them or why. There is no hammer to throw, so all that's left is the pain—but there's no conscious awareness of the source. When this happened to me during my time with Sean, I honestly thought I was going crazy.

Thankfully, you can learn to recognize the signs and symptoms of vicarious trauma. If you can learn to recognize how you typically respond when you feel overwhelmed by a story of trauma, you can begin to respond in ways that are both healthy *and* restorative.

Vicarious trauma creates discomfort, and it would seem reasonable that a person experiencing discomfort would want to feel comfortable. This desire for comfort can create spiritual "dis-integration," relational tension, loss of employment, and shame. When experiencing vicarious trauma, I've found, through interviews with youth workers, that it's not uncommon for some of them to seek the solace of technology. After an encounter with a traumatic story, youth workers can turn to gaming as a narcotic that occupies the brain and numbs the mind. A youth pastor came up to speak with me after one of my workshops. He was having a hard time controlling his emotions as he blurted out, "I just can't turn it off. I keep hearing his story—even *seeing* his story—over and over in my mind." The behaviors in which you engage when you feel afraid or traumatized act like a medication, soothing, numbing the pain, and helping people manage when they feel overwhelmed.

Helping is actually not the best word to use, because the help provided by behaviors intended to medicate will eventually lead to more pain. Medicating behaviors are notorious for ending youth ministry careers, but if all you see when you look at people in pain is their behavior, you're looking in the wrong place. Behaviors meet needs. Pornography is comforting, because it meets a need—just as alcohol, gaming, exercise, food, and sex all provide a kind of comfort. The behavior often escalates, with increasingly higher doses required to numb the pain, until the youth worker discovers they're spinning out of control. Although Christians would refer to many of these medicating behaviors as sin, it's interesting and important to note that the behaviors don't actually stem from sin. They grow out of good ministry—ministry that traumatized the youth worker but didn't leave a hammer laying on the counter.

When the hammer causing the injury is called vicarious trauma, you might expect to experience symptoms such as uninvited recurring thoughts, avoidance of people, hypervigilance, disturbed sleep, demoralization, fear, a sense of alienation, isolation, withdrawal, loss of confidence, guilt, feelings of insanity, loss of control, and even suicidal thoughts.[23] Other symptoms of trauma exposure might include the inability to empathize, helplessness, chronic exhaustion, and a sense that you can never do enough.[24] When as a youth worker you encounter vicarious trauma, you may experience a toxic combination of loss that includes the loss of meaning, the loss of hope, and the loss of connection with others.[25]

As you start practicing prayerful self-awareness in ministry, listening to your body and being gentle with yourself and attentive to your desire for unhealthy medicating behaviors, you'll begin to see the hammer for what it is. And as you begin to recognize both the source and the symptoms of the pain, you can begin to engage in wise self-care, thereby experiencing the restoration of meaning, hope, and connection through Jesus and the faith community. Vicarious trauma is not a terminal illness, and even though there's a cost to caring, engaging people with empathy doesn't have to make you sick. Jesus is the master caregiver, and there is much that you can learn from his example as you look to his interactions with people in need. Let's look at one of his healing encounters and see what we might learn about the cost of caring.

Touched with Purpose

Jesus said some odd things in his life: "Go sell everything you have and give to the poor," for example (Matthew 19:21). When Peter thinks he is a spiritual rock star for suggesting he might forgive someone seven times, Jesus challenges him by saying, "Not seven times, but seventy-seven times" (Matthew 18:22). There are few words stranger than the ones Jesus speaks in Luke 8:46. Jairus, a synagogue leader, falls at his feet and begs Jesus to come and heal his little girl. She is dying, and understandably, the dad is frantic. The crowds press against him, as the disciples, acting like presidential Secret Service bodyguards, do their best to get Jesus safely to his location. Based on their circumstances, his words must have sounded crazy, and yet in Luke 8:45, Jesus says, "Who touched me?" Peter's answer captures what many people would have said: "Everybody's touching you!"

One day as I was thinking about the cost of caring, Jesus's response in 8:46 caught my attention: "Someone touched me; I know that power has gone out from me."

In his commentary on the Gospel of Luke, William Hendriksen writes, "Here, Jesus shows how he knew that someone had indeed touched him, touched him in faith and with a purpose to be healed, and this not without cost to the Healer."[26] Lenski beautifully describes the woman's actions as a *touch with a purpose*.[27] Others touched him, perhaps like a crowd mauling a celebrity outside a restaurant. She touched him out of desperation, and instantly Jesus knew her. He knew her need. He experienced her faith in her touch, and Jesus allowed his healing power to flow into her. It wasn't magic; it was the Spirit of God working through Jesus for the good of those in need.

The image of power being released from Jesus is like what you might experience when you minister to people in need. When you are touched by people in need of healing, you also release power and energy, as you care. Jesus demonstrated here one of the most important principles of healthy ministry: recognizing when power has gone out from you. It seems like a simple principle, but I have found this to be one of the most neglected practices among those serving in Christian ministry.

No Place for a Superhero

I was on a flight with my little redheaded girl, Brianna. She was around seven years old, and it was our first time flying together. As I stowed our carry-on baggage, we were laughing and enjoying the experience of sharing this adventure. As we settled into our seats, the flight attendant introduced herself and began to explain how to operate a seatbelt. Her sense of humor engaged the crowd as we prepared for takeoff. Although I had heard the presentation many times before, this time I felt anger rising up inside of me. "In the event of loss of cabin pressure, an oxygen mask will drop from the compartment above your head. Those travelling with small children, please place your own mask on first, before assisting others." This had always made good sense to me, but now that I was looking into my little girl's sparkling green eyes, I immediately thought, *I don't think so! If the cabin pressure drops, my little girl gets her mask first.* It might sound noble—even heroic—but the reality is that focusing entirely on her needs in such a situation could kill us both.

This heroic and selfless sentiment is common in the helping professions. Some people call it the Messiah complex; others refer to it as acting like a superhero. In regard to emergency workers, Beaton and Murphy write that the superhuman notion that helpers should be able to save everyone can be a burden. Many emergency workers recognize it as a God syndrome.[28] When the Messiah complex influences discipleship, you'll notice that you're constantly pushing yourself to work harder, with plenty of guilt when you stop for rest. A pastor I worked with said to me one day, "I work ninety hours a week, and I expect the same from you." His words are an excellent example of a Messiah complex. In addition to giving 110 percent, people can blame themselves for the decisions made by others—even decisions like Sean's, which were completely outside of my control.

When I was having a conversation with an inner-city youth worker traumatized by a child's sexual assault, she blurted out in anger, "If these were my kids, I'd never treat them like God does!" When you minister from this kind of theological framework, God becomes your employee, anger consumes your thoughts, and cynicism seeps through the cracks of your heart like carbon monoxide. It silently and quietly poisons faith, until you leave ministry altogether, bitter and disillusioned at God's failure to act. The sheer number and depth of the needs begin to overwhelm your capacity to respond.

When you become the Messiah, your life will begin to fall apart. Only Jesus can meet the needs. Only Jesus can carry the load. He does not call you into youth ministry only to crush you under the weight of the pain. He invites you to serve so that you might know him more deeply, trust him more faithfully, and love others in his name. When you refuse to take on the role of Messiah, learning instead to recognize when power has gone out from you and taking time to live by the biblical rhythms of Sabbath rest, you will be refreshed and begin to discover a kind of joy in discipleship that you never thought possible.

Trauma-Informed Discipleship

There's nothing like spending a week at camp, especially if you're the camp speaker! It was a hot July, and I was a few days into our week when the program director asked to speak with me. The camp speaker often functions like a chaplain, so I wasn't at all surprised when he invited me to have a conversation about a crisis. Two girls in their late teens had volunteered to spend a week as cabin counsellors. They had spent their time in typical fashion, loving on the junior-high girls in their cabin, enjoying water sports together, and worshipping at chapel every evening. Following breakfast one morning, a quiet young girl had given them a letter that she wanted them to read.

The following day, the counsellors told me they had no idea what might be in the letter. As they sat to read it together, the young cabin leaders felt sickened by the content. In the letter was a graphic description of a recent sexual assault by an older male. These two young women had wanted to serve Jesus by giving a week of their summer to disciple young girls; instead, they found themselves being traumatized by a violent story. Even though the content of the letter created strong emotions for them, they felt an obligation to read it all, to stand with this young girl as witness to her pain and to be fully present. As the teen counsellors wept through our conversation, they expressed anger and rage and disappointment. They wanted to go home, but they didn't want to desert this young woman who had made herself vulnerable. They were angry that the fun and joy of the camp environment had now been tainted by this pain. They wanted to harm the man who had caused such pain and hated the fact that they felt powerless in the face of his violence.

Youth workers have a unique passion for loving teenagers. At camp, I have watched as counsellors engage in life-changing discipleship through the most powerful means available: friendship. Richard Dunn writes, "The greatest resource spiritual caregivers offer adolescents is their own life of intimate connection with the heart of God. Like a conduit for life, the love of a spiritual caregiver links the adolescent with a real God whose real love is available amid real life."[29] This was real life. These young camp counsellors discovered the hard way that there was a personal cost to discipling teens in pain.

If you're going to engage in effective youth ministry, it'll mean intimate connection that goes far beyond planning a games night or a pool party. These kinds of events, typically associated with youth ministry, are opportunities for building safe and caring discipling relationships that provide the context for honest conversation about faith, real-life pain, and hope. A sober evaluation of youth ministry helps us to understand the critical importance of ministering from a trauma-informed perspective.

Paul Borthwick writes the following:

Youth ministry is not just discipleship groups, winter retreats, and an occasional outreach. Youth ministry in the townships of South Africa addresses issues of violence, unemployment, and a deep hopelessness in youth about their future. Youth ministry in Uganda and Thailand teaches young people a biblical response to people with HIV/AIDS. Youth Ministry in Bosnia means addressing nontraditional youth ministry topics, such as recovering from the traumas of war. Youth workers in Israel and Palestine try to exemplify forgiveness and reconciliation in the midst of a war-torn community.[30]

Borthwick challenges readers to think about youth ministry from a global perspective, and when they do, they can't avoid thinking about the impact of trauma on kids.

A youth pastor invited me to coffee a few years back, to talk about the kids in his youth group. Several of the young teens had come to the city recently from an African nation where they had been child soldiers. He was overwhelmed and sickened by the stories he was hearing. He noticed that the kids recounted with very little emotion some of the horrendous things they had experienced. He was not sure how to engage in discipleship with kids who had been soldiers. I admit, this was a new one for me as well.

But you don't have to look to South Africa or Syria to find teen victims of trauma. If you learn to look and listen carefully, you'll find these teens all around: in youth programs, schools, and camps.

Back in 2001, in his book on counselling adolescents, Wade Rowatt penned these sobering words that seem just as fitting today:

Fifty percent of today's youth may experience a major crisis before reaching the age of eighteen. They will be hospitalized, appear in court, have major parental conflicts, be crippled in an accident, attempt suicide, abuse alcohol or drugs, drop out of school, get pregnant, contract a sexually transmitted disease, be arrested, be raped, pay for or have an abortion, witness an act of violence, or experience something else of this magnitude. Many will endure multiple crises![31]

My stories of Amber and Sean correspond with Rowatt's summary of the kind of pain teens might experience, and yet it hasn't been uncommon for me to disciple teens who don't experience many, or any, of these traumatic things personally. Raised in sheltered Christian homes, some kids seem to soar through the adolescent years, excelling in their studies, participating in athletics and extracurricular interests, and serving in their church and community. If you have been a youth worker, you know that although the kids I'm describing have not personally experienced trauma, they're often overwhelmed by pain as they care for their friends. These peer helpers and teen disciple makers are at significant risk of vicarious trauma, as they hear the gory details that teens often keep secret from the adult world.

On their website, The Institute for Congregational Trauma and Growth has an excellent article by Elizabeth Power titled, "Seven Key Traits of a Trauma-informed Congregation."[32] Trauma-informed care is a key phrase these days in secular social work and care agencies. Power writes that a trauma-informed congregation will acknowledge the vast scope of adverse experiences common to persons today, to gain a better understanding of the common needs of those in the congregation and community. Much like Rowatt, she lists common traumatic events: natural disasters, violence, substance abuse, divorce, mental health concerns, and various forms of abuse.[33] In addition, congregations and staff will recognize that trauma can occur when persons perceive a threat to their well-being and their ability to cope is overwhelmed. She calls on churches to practice a perspective shift, something valuable for discipleship with people in pain.

This shift creates a "new normal," leading those in discipleship to adjust their questions from "What's wrong with you?" or "Why are you acting like that?" to *"What happened to you?"* This is a powerful paradigm shift! The article expresses the importance of bearing witness, just as the camp counsellors felt compelled to do. You need to be "compassionately curious and interested to honestly bear witness to adverse experience from the past that may be influencing fear or defense tactics in the present."[34] Trauma-informed congregations view forms of "acting out" as opportunities for building trustworthy and emotionally safe relationships. Being trauma-informed in youth ministry means that you understand that all the issues written about in this book find their source in trauma.

Practicing the Rhythms of Rest

Ninety percent of healing is awareness. It's probably not statistically accurate, but it is a helpful phrase I heard my therapist use constantly as he was helping me become a healthier person and a more effective pastor. In my early days of youth ministry, I was oblivious when it came to self-awareness. I had not given much thought to how I was treating myself, not to mention how my behavior might be affecting other people in my sphere of influence. I have discovered that developing self-awareness is something like going on vacation. Once you get to your destination, it's amazing—but before you get to that sunny beach resort, you have to find the right location, part with a bunch of cash, update your passport, finish the work on your desk, pack your clothes, and berate yourself on the way to the airport for being such a miser that you purchased the cheapest flights you could find and so had to start your day at 4:30 in the morning. The destination is amazing, but the journey can be hard.

Prayerful self-awareness is one of the most effective ways to stay healthy while you care for people in pain. One of the ways I practice this is to keep a journal detailing the way I use my time. When I have an encounter that overwhelms my capacity to respond, I put a large *X* beside the date that this occurred. Putting an *X* on the page means I noticed that a particular conversation or situation was difficult for me. The simple act of placing an *X* on the page is my way of saying, "Pay attention!" Not being all that creative, I have chosen to call these my "X days." If I have an X-day, I give myself permission to take some time off in the next five days or to treat myself to something I enjoy. This is a way of engaging in self-care that makes sense to me; it is my way of treating myself with gentleness and grace. It's one way I can remind myself that I am human.

In 2016, the church I serve gave me the opportunity to take a sabbatical. During my four months of rest and refreshment, I read several books, including *Sabbath* by Wayne Muller. At one point in the book, he recounts the stories of several professionals who work themselves almost to death. He describes these people as individuals who refuse to engage in self-awareness, who see rest as weakness, and who drive themselves to achieve—only to discover that their way of being human is actually killing them. The most memorable sentence in the book for me is this: "If we do not allow for the rhythm of rest in our overly busy lives, illness becomes our Sabbath."[35]

You will not have the sense to engage in rhythms of rest until the practice of prayerful self-awareness begins to open your mind to the reality of your human limitations and your desperate need for communion with God.

In addition to self-awareness, it's helpful to begin thinking about debriefing as a spiritual discipline. When you feel overwhelmed in your capacity to respond, when there is an X in your calendar, or when your desire for unhealthy behaviors is causing you concern, you may be experiencing vicarious trauma. As you practice self-awareness, ask yourself, "Have I heard a story that frightened me?" "Have I intervened in a crisis?" "Am I caring for someone who has been violated or has experienced loss?" "Am I afraid for someone's safety?" If the answer is yes to any of these questions, it may be wise to have a conversation. I strongly recommend that this conversation *not* be with your spouse; your spouse is not your "dumping ground." If you need to process some of your thoughts or pain, might I suggest you pay a professional therapist? If you serve in professional pastoral ministry, you need to see someone who isn't impressed by your credentials or position. I have often told pastors, "You need to go somewhere you aren't afraid to swear." I'm not advocating for regular profanity or ungodly behavior, but I'm suggesting that if you can't debrief in complete honesty, you aren't sharing with the right person. When I debrief, sometimes I'm angry. Sometimes my heart is broken. Sometimes I am disappointed with God, and I need to sit with someone who can help me honestly empty my garbage.

I'd never really given any thought to debriefing on traumatic encounters until I was part of community-care response to an adolescent fatality. It was 1996, and I was serving as youth pastor at First Baptist Church in Jackson Hole, Wyoming. A fifteen-year-old boy and two of his teenaged friends were enjoying a ride on the gravel road near our home, when his fourteen-year-old girlfriend lost control of their vehicle and drove into a ditch embankment. The young man had been sitting in the middle, with no seatbelt fastened. He went through the sunroof of the Toyota Forerunner and landed on the gravel road, which killed him instantly. His girlfriend and his best friend were taken to the local hospital but were unharmed. I was asked to visit with the girlfriend shortly after she had learned that she had killed her boyfriend. I have never experienced trauma quite like I did that day. Shortly after the accident, I sat with the boy's dad and mom in their living room. We cried, and we prayed, and we agreed to meet the next day at the funeral home to select a casket. I officiated at the funeral, and with the church full of people stunned by a senseless death, I did my best to speak words of hope. Ironically, after several days of sitting with wounded people, I had difficulty feeling any sense of hope myself. I felt spaced out and lost, and I craved solitude to process what I had experienced.

I was thankful when a social worker approached me after the funeral to ask if I would like to take part in a debriefing for those involved in the boy's death. She was inviting people in emergency, fire response, and policing services as well as the medical staff from the hospital. Although I didn't know what to expect, I thanked her for the offer and agreed to attend. When I arrived the next day, I found the room full of men, except for the therapist. State troopers with arms like tree trunks, paramedics, and fire and rescue workers sat silently, most staring at the floor, everyone trying to avoid eye contact. There was enough testosterone in the room to fill a truck, and enough macho maleness to stifle any emotional disclosure.

As unlikely as I had presumed it to be, it wasn't long before one of the officers began to talk about his feelings and of his love for his teenage daughter. With tears streaming down his cheeks, he told the group how he had gone home and wept like a baby, how he had taken his daughter in his arms and held her. It wasn't long before every single one of us was quietly crying. "Each of us was experiencing a profound sense of sadness, and yet our open and honest dialogue, our positive regard for one another, together with a skilled and sensitive therapist made this encounter one of the most profound healing experiences of my life."[36]

Debriefing trauma is a way to remind yourself that *you are not Jesus.* No one is. You and I are not divine or superhuman. Thus, when trauma threatens to make you sick, instead of tossing the weight of the world on your shoulders, you must practice letting go. When everything within you wants to isolate and move away from the trauma, you must be courageous. You must move toward the pain and seek to embrace what's most valuable, the things that trauma threatens to erode: hope, meaning, and connection with people.

Time to Lose the Cape

Edna is my favorite character in the Pixar classic *The Incredibles*. If you don't know who she is, put this book down and search for "Edna, no capes." Watch the video, and I bet you'll have a good laugh. Edna's a seamstress for superheroes. In her humorous conversation with Mr. Incredible, they talk about his new superhero uniform. He wants a cape. Edna is immediately irritated by his request and begins to recount from memory multiple stories of cape-related deaths. One superhero gets his cape snagged on a missile and is dragged to his death. Another is killed when her cape gets sucked into a jet turbine. Edna's conclusion is the youth minister's mandate: *no capes!* No Messiah complex. No superhero syndrome.

Instead, I encourage you to make a commitment that from now on, as you engage in discipleship with people in pain, you'll absolutely refuse to pose as a superhero. I suggest you fold up your cape, put it into a drawer, and then leave it there. Unfortunately, doing this may be complicated, as people in your life may not appreciate the changes in your behavior. After all, who doesn't enjoy having their own personal superhero to rescue them? Your boss might become angry. The ministry leadership team might want to turf you. Your spouse, parents, and even the teens you serve might feel like you have betrayed them. You may be told you're "not doing your job," that you're not "spiritual enough" to continue in ministry—even that you're not "following Jesus anymore." When you lose the cape, it makes people nervous, but it's truly one of the most freeing things you'll ever do. It all begins by simply learning to say no.

I have a few friends who have pinned little pieces of red cloth to their office bulletin boards as a constant reminder that they have hung up their capes. As you practice letting go of those things that fall outside of your control, you'll find yourself learning to let go even of those things that *are* within your control. As you do this, you'll discover that the world doesn't fall apart. It's a way of being faithful to the truth found in Ephesians 5:23, where Paul writes, "Keep in step with the Spirit." I become more honestly present to the presence of God when I can acknowledge—perhaps even confess—that I don't want to be the Messiah in my youth ministry. As I do this, I'm set free by the Spirit of God to be who the Spirit is creating me to be, and I'm released from the pressure to be something I'm not.

As you continue to read this book, please practice prayerful self-awareness. It's okay to put the book down for a while, go for a walk, pause, lift your pain to Jesus, or pray for a wounded friend. Please be aware that even reading stories about trauma, such as those found in this book, can lead to experiencing vicarious trauma. I have provided questions at the end of each chapter for you to use as you debrief. You might consider writing in a journal, reading the book together with a friend, or speaking to a trusted therapist about the stories and situations you've found troubling.

During my time in seminary, a professor began one class with a rather disturbing proclamation. He said: "Ministry flows out of who you are." I remember thinking to myself, *Oh, no. What if that's really true?* Ninety percent of healing is awareness, but sometimes awareness really stinks. When I was in seminary, I was after the destination, but God wanted me to pay attention to the journey.

God has you on a journey too, and for some odd reason, this book is now a part of what God is doing in and through you. Over the years I have added to my wise professor's words, as I have come to believe that ministry flows not only through *who* you are, but also through *how* you are. If you want to be used by God to bring healing to the lives of young disciples in pain, open your own wounded life to the Spirit. Be receptive to the reshaping, renewing, and resurrecting power of Jesus.

Ideas for Discussion and Reflection

1. Take a few moments to search online sources, and see if you can describe vicarious trauma in writing. What's the difference between vicarious trauma and burnout?

2. Describe empathy. Why do you think I referred to empathy as a double-edge sword? Where would you place yourself on an empathy scale—high or low (or somewhere in between)? What does this tell you about your potential for vicarious trauma?

3. Consider Luke 8:45–46. What do you think Jesus meant when he said, "I know that power has gone out from me"? On a scale of 1–10 (1 being poor, 10 being great), how good are you at recognizing when power has gone out from you? How do you recharge when you feel drained?

4. Describe a week in youth ministry from a superhero perspective. What are the long-term effects of this kind of ministry for self and others? Describe the same week from a healthy caregiving perspective.

5. What are the benefits of practicing prayerful self-awareness as you engage in discipleship with teens in pain? Can you think of any biblical support for this way of engaging in ministry?

1   Charles R. Figley, "Compassion Fatigue as Secondary Traumatic Stress Disorder: An Overview," in *Compassion Fatigue: Coping with Secondary Traumatic Stress Disorder in Those Who Treat the Traumatized*, ed. Charles R. Figley (New York: Brunner-Routledge, 1995), 2.

2   Ibid., 7.

3   Ibid., 5.

4   L. A. Pearlman, *Self-care for trauma therapists: Ameliorating vicarious traumatization* (Lutherville: Sidran Press, 1999), 52.

5   Ibid., 53.

6   L. A. Pearlman and Karen W. Saakvitne, *Transforming the Pain: A Workbook on vicarious traumatization* (New York: W. W. Norton, 1996), 41.

7   Christina Maslach, *Burnout: The Cost of Caring* (Los Altos: ISHK, 2003), 3.

8   M. A. Dutton and F.L. Rubinstein, "Working with people with PTSD: Research Implications," in *Compassion Fatigue: Coping with Secondary Traumatic Stress Disorder in Those Who Treat the Traumatized*, ed. Charles R. Figley (New York: Brunner and Mazel, 1995), 89.

9   R. D. Beaton and S. A. Murphy, "Working with People in Crisis: Research Implications," in *Compassion Fatigue: Coping with Secondary Traumatic Stress Disorder in Those Who Treat the Traumatized*, ed. Charles R. Figley (New York: Brunner and Mazel, 1995), 58.

10 Robert E. Hayes, "Healing Emergency Worker's Psychological Damage," in *USA Today*, 128, no. 2650, 1999, https://www.questia.com/magazine/1G1-55149343/healing-emergency-workers-psychological-damage

11 Judith Herman, *Trauma and Recovery: The Aftermath of Violence—From Domestic Abuse to Political Terror* (New York: Basic Books, 1992), 140.

12 Ibid., 140.

13 Mark Lerner, *It's OK Not To Be OK ... Right Now: How to Live Through a Traumatic Experience* (Melville: Mark Lerner Associates, 2006), 13.

14 Herman, 33.

15 Chris Marchand, "An investigation of the influence of compassion fatigue due to secondary traumatic stress on the Canadian youth worker" (Doctor of Ministry Thesis, Providence Theological Seminary, 2007), 120.

16 Ibid., 122.

17 Heinz Kohut, *How Does Analysis Cure?* (Chicago: The University of Chicago Press, 1984), 82.

18 Judith Orlo , "10 Traits Empathic People Share," *Psychology Today* (February 2016), https://www.psychologytoday.com/blog/emotional-freedom/201602/10-traits-empathic-people-share

19 Kathryn Betts Adams et al, "The Traumatic Stress Institute Belief Scale as a Measure of vicarious trauma in a National Sample of Clinical Social Workers," *Families in Society: The Journal of Contemporary Human Services* 82, no. 4 (2001): 364.

[20] Orloff.

[21] Joseph A. Boscarino et al, "Secondary Trauma Issues for Psychiatrists," *Psychiatric Times* 27, no. 11 (2010): 24–26, https://www.ncbi.nlm.nih.gov/ pmc/articles/ PMC3014548/

[22] Marchand, 34.

[23] Beaton and Murphy, 62.

[24] Laura van Dernoot Lipsky, *Trauma Stewardship: An Everyday Guide to Caring for Self While Caring for Others* (San Francisco: Berrett-Koehler, 2009), https://www. bkconnection.com/static/Trauma Stewardship EXCERPT.pdf

[25] L. A. Pearlman and Karen Saakvitne, *Trauma and the Therapist: Countertransference and vicarious traumatization in Psychotherapy with Incest Survivors* (New York: W. W. Norton & Company, 1995), 160.

[26] William Hendriksen, *The Gospel of Luke* (Grand Rapids: Baker Book House, 1978), 458.

[27] R. C. H. Lenski, *The interpretation of St. Luke's Gospel* (Minneapolis: Augsburg Publishing, 1946), 485.

[28] Beaton and Murphy, 69.

[29] Richard Dunn, *Shaping the Spiritual Lives of Students: A Guide for Youth Workers, Pastors, Teachers & Campus Ministers* (Grand Rapids: Zondervan Publishing, 2001), 57.

[30] Duffy Robbins, *This Way to Youth Ministry: An Introduction to the Adventure* (Grand Rapids: Zondervan Publishing, 2004), 50.

[31] Wade Rowatt, *Adolescents in Crisis: A Guide for Parents, Teachers, Ministers, and Counselors* (Louisville: John Knox Press, 2001), 3.

[32] Elizabeth Power, "Seven Key Traits of a Trauma-informed Congregation." *Institute for Congregational Trauma and Growth* (blog), posted March 1, 2018. http://www. ictg.org/

[33] Ibid.

[34] Ibid.

[35] Wayne Muller, *Sabbath: Finding Rest, Renewal, and Delight in Our Busy Lives* (New York: Bantam Books, 1999), 20.

[36] Chris Marchand, "Secondary Traumatic Stress: Recognizing the Unique Risks for Youth Ministry," *Journal of Youth Ministry*, 4, no. 1 (2005): 9.

CHAPTER 3
Unique as a Fingerprint:
Nurturing Faith Resiliency in Grief

The Lord is close to the brokenhearted
and saves those who are crushed in spirit.
—Psalm 34:18

Camp staff were getting ready for another amazing summer of ministry. Registrations were being gathered, campers being placed into cabins with eager counsellors, maintenance teams beautifying the site, and program staff working on Bible study materials, activities, and games, to ensure that this would be the best summer ever.

It's the director's job to ensure safety protocols are in place, to meet the rigorous standards for insurance, but more importantly, to make camp a safe place for kids. There's nothing like dropping off your child and feeling that sense of confidence, knowing that the people at camp will do their best to keep your child safe. But sometimes doing their best is not enough. Camp boards and directors dread it, but sometimes a death comes to camp, devastating the joy and forever forging in people's memories the summer that hearts were broken by loss.

The seventeen-year-old camp counsellor was on loan from Midway Bible Camp.[1] It was a simple assignment, not high risk or dangerous—serve Jesus by loving kids at Steeprock Bay Bible Camp. The youth had been supervising campers while swimming out to a floating dock in Lake Winnipegosis. He went under, and no one saw him surface. Within hours, search and rescue teams donned diving gear; they looked for several days for the young man's body. Social workers, counsellors, and pastors were called to provide support. Other camps in Manitoba and across Canada interrupted their season to grieve and pray as their sister camp sat in limbo, waiting for the devastating news. My daughter was serving at one of the camps that cried and prayed that week for their friends at Steeprock and Midway. The boy's family arrived at the camp shortly after his disappearance, waiting in tears and sorrow as the police methodically searched the waters for his body. News of his confirmed death finally made its way to camp ministries and churches all over Manitoba, and soon, through social media, people all over the world were grieving this tragic loss and praying for those brokenhearted by the pain.

Strapping on the Tool Belt

As a camp speaker for many years, I found myself wondering, What if I had been the speaker at Midway or Steeprock that week? What if *you* had been on the leadership team, or the board, or a cabin counsellor listening to frightened campers cry themselves to sleep? How would you help these kids grieve while at the same time managing your own pain? The Christian camp is a great place for spiritual formation—but what kinds of questions about the faithfulness of God might you hear when tragic circumstances traumatize and overwhelm those in your care?

In her article describing her season of grief, professor of Youth Ministry and youth worker Kelly Soifer describes not one but multiple encounters with fatality. These include a friend with a brain tumor, the suicide of one of the teens in her youth group, the care of some young teens who lost a twelve-year-old friend in a car accident, and the case of a fifteen-year-old who lost his own life to brain cancer. It's just a matter of time before the youth worker will be called upon to disciple teens through the pain associated with tragedy, terminal illness, and death.[2]

In youth ministry, you might picture yourself wearing a carpenter's tool belt. If you're like me, your tool for everything is the hammer—but the hammer is not very effective if you're trying to change your kitchen tap or putting together an IKEA bookshelf. Whether you are a carpenter, a plumber, or a youth worker loving kids in pain, it's a good idea to have a few specialized tools in your tool belt that you can grab in situations like that drowning at the Bible camp. Think of this book as an opportunity to select a few of those specialized tools to help you minister to teens more effectively.

Teens and Loss

Around the world, more than three thousand teenagers will die every day, totaling over one million deaths a year.[3] According to the World Health Organization, many of these deaths are preventable, with the primary causes being traffic injuries, respiratory infections, and suicide. For work in youth ministry, it's interesting to note that most teenagers killed in vehicle-related accidents are not driving, as one might expect. Most teens killed in vehicle-related accidents are pedestrians, cyclists, and motorcyclists.[4] In Canada, accidents are the leading cause of death for people ages ten to eighteen. For those ages ten to fourteen, illness and death by suicide fall into second and third place, while teens aged fourteen to eighteen are more likely to die by suicide than cancer.[5] In the United States, the leading causes of death among teenagers are unintentional injuries, homicide, suicide, cancer, and heart disease.[6] In both Canada and the USA, accidents account for nearly 50 percent of all teenage deaths! In addition, one in five people will experience the death of someone close to them by the time they reach the age of eighteen.[7]

As difficult as this is to read and process, it doesn't yet represent a full picture of the experience of loss for adolescents. Loss occurs in many situations unrelated to death. It is not uncommon for teenagers to experience loss when their family breaks apart due to separation and divorce. My son experienced loss when he tore his ACL in a soccer game and lost his opportunity to play basketball during his senior year of high school. As a chaplain for a high school football team in South Dakota, I witnessed senior students grieving as they walked off the football field for the last time. Some knew they would never play at the college level; this was the end of their football careers. To watch them weep, one would have thought they were grieving the loss of a loved one, which indeed they were. Teens experience loss when they move to a new city and begin attending an unfamiliar school. The discomfort of forming new friend groups can intensify the experience of loss, resulting in high-risk and out-of-the-ordinary behaviors in a teen's life. Then there is loss due to mental illness, loss with relational separation when an intimate friendship falls to pieces, or the loss when your friendship group goes with your ex and leaves you not only single but completely alone.

We must take care not to underestimate or diminish the loss that gets the least amount of care and attention but which can have a profound effect in the life of a teen—the loss of a beloved pet. For non-animal lovers, this loss can seem a silly thing to include alongside human death and mental illness, but loss and grief are subjective experiences. One loss often triggers other unresolved losses, resulting in deeper grief than one might have expected. I have seen animal deaths lead to an avalanche of unresolved emotions for teens who think they're no longer grieving a previous death. Their grief and loss have turned to a sense of numbness— that is, until their animal friend dies, and then they relive the old pain with the fresh pain, and life becomes unbearable once again.

The Power of Grief

Where there is loss, you will typically find people who are grieving. "Grief is a natural response to loss. It is the emotional suffering you feel when something or someone you love is taken away. The more significant the loss, the more intense your grief will be."[8] Grief is normal, grief is natural, and grief is necessary, providing a healthy way for people to cope with the loss of someone, or something, they value.[9] As I mentioned above, death is not the only cause of loss; as a matter of fact, many of the painful experiences people face in life are complicated by feelings of loss. Earlier, I referred to Willimon's quote about *helping that is Christian*. Each time you find yourself walking with teens in pain, you must discern what it is that God is asking you to do. As a Christian caregiver, I have sometimes felt that I needed to include Jesus in every conversation. I have had to learn that in some moments *not* talking about Jesus is the most Christian thing that I can do. Engaging with teens takes place through relationship, and relationships can be notoriously difficult to navigate. You can't use a one-size-fits-all mentality with people; your response must always be uniquely tailored to the individual.

Serving as a youth pastor in Sioux Falls, I would sometimes take a moment to encourage the adult Sunday school teachers. It was nothing fancy, just a quick pop-in to a classroom to say hello to the class and thank the teacher for serving. One morning after I had done this in several classrooms, one teacher approached me and said, "If you ever do that again, I will quit!"

A few moments later, a second teacher approached me with tears in her eyes and said, "I've been teaching Sunday school here for years, and no pastor has ever taken the time to visit my class or say thanks. It was so meaningful of you to drop by this morning."

What is the takeaway here? A one-size-fits-all approach is not effective in leadership nor in responding to people in pain. One leader would have appreciated a card in the mail, the other a personal contact. As I have discovered, caring for teenagers in pain requires the same kind of attentiveness and respect. Care for teens in pain may be similar, but due to the complexity of individual life history, personality, faith, and family context, your approach to discipleship may be quite different. How, then, do you help teens follow Jesus when their hearts are breaking? How do you walk with them and pray with them, when some of them will honestly and mistakenly view God as the very source of their pain?

As I want this to be a practical book about helping teens in pain, let me tell you a few stories about ministry with teens who suffered loss. Hopefully, by the time you have completed this section and the reflection questions at the end, you'll feel that you have some new tools in your tool belt to use when you're called to stand amid the pain and be the one to speak the words of hope.

Two Kinds of Death

There are only two kinds of death that one can experience, and I have engaged in plenty of conversations with people, trying to determine which would be their preference. Not many years ago, *Would You Rather* books were being used by youth workers to break the ice and get teens talking. The books were full of contrasting options, like would you rather lose your hearing or your sight? Would you rather be tall and ugly or short and attractive? It was a brilliant series of books that could even bring a room full of introverts into lively conversation and result in laughter, arguments, and sketchy moral choices.

This would be a good place for a *Would-you-rather …?* question for yourself. Would you rather suffer terribly for a year as you die with terminal cancer, but have a year to spend time with and say goodbye to family and friends, or would you rather get hit by a car tonight and die instantly, with no chance to say your goodbyes? For some, anticipated death can feel painfully, torturously slow, while for others time seems to slip away too quickly. If you have shared in this journey with a loved one, no doubt you have played this would-you-rather game in your mind. As much as you might truly hate to watch a loved one die slowly with terminal illness, by contrast, anticipated death is almost something of a gift. Although watching a loved one die slowly feels intolerable at times, anticipated death offers people time to repair relationships, to forgive, to pray, to hold a hand, to cry together, to say goodbye, and to prepare for the inevitable. Anticipated death gives people time to grieve with their loved one and to prepare their hearts for the pain of loss.

Unanticipated death causes grief pain that's unlike anything else you can experience as a human being. As with the drowning at Steeprock, teens who think they are immortal suddenly discover that even people their own age can die unexpectedly. Car accidents, heart attacks, suicide, and, in many places in the world, homicide and war, take young lives tragically and unexpectedly, leaving families and friends to grieve in shock. In both cases, anticipated and unanticipated grief, the youth worker will be a part of a multidisciplinary team, including medical professionals, social workers, a hospital chaplain or counsellor, police, and the funeral home attendants. The role of the youth worker is unique; he or she may be one of the only adults remaining in relationship with the teen who is beginning the long process of grieving the loss.

With a few well-publicized school shootings in the past few months, schools are exercising a zero-tolerance policy to threats of violence. Unanticipated violent death, and the threat of violent death, create traumatic stress and can result in feelings of terror, incapacitation, hopelessness, loss of meaning, and all the painful symptoms covered in the previous chapter. Unlike anticipated death, during which there's time to process, unanticipated death is on you in an *instant*—like a school shooter, leaving youth workers to provide an answer for the question many dread more than any other: **Why?**

I will talk more about this question in the final chapter when we look closely at questions related to suffering. Before taking a closer look at discipling teens in grief, let's think together about discipleship and the anticipated death.

Taking the Journey Together

James was one of the most effective parents I ever served with in youth ministry. A professional in his early sixties, he was the poster boy for "uncool." He always came straight from work, in a suit. It was easy to see that the kids didn't mind his lack of cool, because as soon as he walked into the room they would swarm him. His two daughters were part of our group, and they loved spending time with him, so having Dad in their space was no big deal. On occasion James would come to church in his clown suit. The kids loved it, and he enjoyed making them laugh by juggling and making balloon animals. As I said, he was the best youth ministry dad ever.

When his wife was diagnosed with terminal cancer, the entire group felt the sorrow, but some beautiful things began to happen in our junior-high ministry. Often, as we closed in prayer, kids would spontaneously gather around James and his daughters to pray. We cried together, we loved one another, and we took the painful journey of loss together as a community. James's wife lived with terminal cancer for several years before the disease finally took her life. As I witnessed in that ministry, when teens are living in the anticipation of loss, connection is one of the most powerful and healing gifts a youth ministry can provide.

When there's a Hole in Your Chest

I recently discovered on YouTube a moving video series, called *Grief Out Loud: Teens Talk about Loss*.[10] If it's still available online, I recommend you put the book down and take a few moments to listen to teens as they recall their own moving stories of grief and loss. When a person is grieving, it's common to use the word *bereaved*. The word comes from the Old English *bereafian*, meaning to deprive of or to take away by violence; to seize, or to rob.[11] In the video, fourteen-year-old Lily gives her definition of grief when she says, "Grief is sadness. It's kind of like you have this hole in your chest. Like this missing part of you."[12]

Therapist Lani Leary explains that although everybody experiences grief, the way people journey through grief is as unique as a fingerprint.[13] Some teens will want to spend time with friends; others will choose to isolate. Some will pour themselves into academics; others will turn to sports, to drugs, or to sleep. When asked for her definition of grief, Shannon replied, "Losing my dad was like losing myself."[14] Everyone feels grief differently, and yet there are similarities in the way people move through the grieving process.

One summer, a teen suicide left many in the town of Jackson Hole, Wyoming, reeling in pain. I didn't know the sixteen-year-old boy who took his life in his bedroom, but the Presbyterian pastor in town wanted to help teens process their grief, so he invited a few pastors to come and sit with any teens who might show up. We met in the evening in an empty classroom at the high school. Teens trickled in and sat on the floor, some in tears and many sitting in silence, holding one another or just staring into space. I wasn't quite sure how the pastor would proceed, but as he began to talk, I could sense a deep caring in his voice. He walked to the chalkboard at the front of the classroom and began to describe the normal process of living through grief.

For many of the young people in the room, this would be their first significant life loss, and I could easily see that the reactions were varied. As the pastor began to talk about grief with the teens, I noticed that he was using the stages of grief from Swiss-American psychiatrist Elizabeth Kübler-Ross.[15] He was careful to explain that the stages do not happen in a nice and neat, orderly fashion, and that people might very well return to the same stage several times before moving on to another.

It's important to note that because grief is as individual as a fingerprint, people may experience other stages not described in these five. I have found myself referring to these stages so frequently that I finally wrote them in the back of the Bible I use most often. Having them close at hand has been useful on many occasions.

Stages of Grief

The Psalmist writes, "The Lord is close to the brokenhearted and saves those who are crushed in spirit."[16] When grief enters a teen's life like an unwelcome guest, words like *brokenhearted* and *crushed* might resonate with their own feelings of despair. My pastor friend drew on the board for all the teens in the room to see. He explained that when people first hear news about an unanticipated death, the first reaction is usually **denial**. It might sound like this: "He can't be dead—I was just with him in class."

Another person might simply say, "This isn't happening. This can't be happening." Denial is a kind of defense mechanism that buffers the initial shock of loss, numbing people to their emotions.[17] Like electrical breakers in the home, when power exceeds the system's capacity to conduct the power, it turns off. Denial is like a breaker switch; it limits the emotional power surge. In youth ministry, it's not your job to break through denial by making teens face up to reality.

The pastor leading the conversation was gentle, helping the teens to understand the value of denial. It's a good mechanism for helping manage new and painful information; however, it's not healthy to remain in denial for a long period of time. To get the teens talking, the pastor, leading through the stages, asked the teens to gather in small groups and respond to this question: "How did you respond when you first heard the news?" Teens and adults mingled together, cried together, and began to process the pain and the shock of this new, unexpected reality.

Recently, I was sitting with two adult children planning their mother's funeral. As it was going to be my job to honor her memory, I asked them to share a few fond memories. Although I didn't know the sons, I had spent a good deal of time with their parents. Knowing that their mother had been a wonderful woman of faith, I'd thought this question to be a safe one. I was met with silence. Finally, one of the sons looked at me and said, "I have no fond memories. I am just glad she's dead." This was an anticipated death, so denial was not prominent in his grief response. I could almost feel the heat of his anger radiating from his face. **Anger** is the second stage of grief, and it is a common teen response to suicide. Feelings of anger are often mingled with guilt, as the anger is often directed toward the deceased. I have heard people at funerals say, "I am so angry that if he were here, I'd kill him." An odd thing to say, to be sure, but a statement like this illustrates the mixed emotions that cloud the mind, often creating internal chaos. Anger can be directed at the deceased, at the injustice, at the sickness, at God, at a friend whose actions or words somehow played a part in the decision to take one's life, or even at you, the caregiver.

As I sat with those two adult children planning their mother's funeral, it seemed to me that they might be directing some of their anger toward themselves. While they were glad she was dead, they were angry at the way that they had treated her.

The pastor helping the room full of teens to grieve their loss drew an arrow from denial to anger and asked if anyone felt angry at the young man for his decision. The room erupted with strong emotions as teens expressed their feelings. Some cursed, a few punched the floor, and some paced, while others simply sat and cried. It was a wonderful place to be as a youth worker, helping kids to grieve a horrible loss, but in that moment, everyone in that room desperately wanted to be somewhere else.

"The normal reaction to feelings of helplessness and vulnerability is often a need to regain control through a series of "If-only"-type statements, such as: *If only we had sought medical attention sooner … If only we got a second opinion from another doctor … If only we had tried to be a better person toward them.*"[18] If-only statements torment teens when a friend commits suicide.

I was watching football with my son and a group of rowdy college students one afternoon. It was a great day of laughter, snacking, and ribbing each other as we enjoyed the rivalry of team sports. Early the next morning, one of the young men we had spent the afternoon with walked right past my house and down the train tracks, where he made the decision to end his life. Many of the guys who had been in the room that afternoon struggled with self-blame. "If only we had noticed his sadness, maybe he would still be alive!"

Whether it's cancer, suicide, or a car accident, guilt will often accompany bargaining. You might start to believe there was something you could have done differently that might have saved a life.[19]

The pastor walking the teens through grief drew another arrow, this time from anger to **bargaining**. He directed the teens back to their small groups to talk about ways they had engaged in bargaining since they'd heard the news. As we debriefed the small group conversations, many teens described their feelings of guilt. Some had noticed their friend's sadness but had shrugged it off. Others had dismissed his violent self-talk as "typical" or "no big deal" and now they lived with guilt associated with the *if-onlys*. One of the things I liked most about the pastor's approach with the teens that evening was the way he reminded them that grief was not a moment in time; it was a *process*. It was also powerful to hear him say repeatedly that grief was a *normal* response to loss. Normalizing the feelings associated with loss is an important part of discipleship. It helps teens appreciate God's creative design, and it sensitizes them to the reality of their current needs. Normalizing also slows down you, the caregiver, and reminds you that grief can't be rushed. Grief always moves at its own pace.

"After bargaining, our attention moves squarely into the present. Empty feelings present themselves, and grief enters our lives on a deeper level, deeper than we ever imagined. This stage of **depression** feels as though it will last forever."[20] Doka wisely states that as adolescents become more independent they may also become less comfortable in seeking support from parents or other adults. This makes it more challenging for youth workers to assess whether a teen is having a difficult time coping with a loss—or to even know that a loss has occurred in a teen's life.[21]

There is no way to tell how long it will take a person to grieve, for grief operates on its own time, moving randomly, yet purposefully, through denial, anger, bargaining, depression, and finally to **acceptance**.

The Five Stages of Grief

A friend of mine lost her husband to cancer a few years ago. After several years of emotion, anger, and depression, she had a friend imply that it was time for her to "get over it." As you help kids follow Jesus through loss, it's important to remember that moving to acceptance is not the same thing as "getting over it." Life will never be the same, and although the pain will subside, there will always be a "hole in the chest." Acceptance is coming to that time when the teen has learned to live and cope with the new normal. Moving to acceptance may simply be the slow awareness that, finally, there seem to be more good days than bad ones.[22]

One of the barriers to acceptance is moving through the guilt associated with feeling good again. Laughing, eating, sleeping, and just living life can feel wrong, especially if other people in the teen's life have not yet moved to acceptance. A teenager might feel she is betraying or disrespecting her loved one's memory by moving on with her life. Normalizing feelings and helping the teen to consider what her loved one might want for her are good ways to help her move away, past the guilt and to full acceptance.

I took this journey with someone in my congregation, a gentle senior who had lost his wife to cancer. For several months, the two of us met weekly for coffee. I watched him move through shock and right over bargaining to depression, where he got stuck for a long time. It never seemed to occur to him to feel angry, just sad and lonely. After about two years, he said to me one day over coffee, "I think I'm going to be okay." We discontinued our regular meetings, and within a few months, he had met a woman his age, who has become a wonderful companion to him.

Whether it's with a teenager or a senior citizen, the discipleship journey is similar. You pray, you stay close, you grieve alongside, you sit in the pain and listen to the heartache. You say little, drink coffee, and ask the Spirit of God to fill the hole in the chest, in a way that only God can.

The First Year

In *Grief Out Loud*, the video series I referred to earlier, fifteen-year-old Tommy comments, "The hardest thing isn't losing the memories I have with my mom; the hardest thing is the memories that I won't be able to have with her in the future."[23] Tommy identifies one of the most painful realities associate with grief: the loss of future relationship. He realized that his mom would not be at his high school graduation. She would not be around to help him learn to drive. She would not be there when he brought his first girlfriend home, and there would be an empty seat in the church on the day he got married. He would miss her at Christmas, on his birthday, on her birthday, and when his basketball team won the championship. If you were to walk with Tommy on this journey of grief, it would be important to realize that these events that are supposed to bring joy to his life will only serve to remind him of his mother's absence.

During the first year, it's not uncommon to forget your loved one is no longer within reach. Tommy might pick up his phone to call his mom, only to remember that she's gone. All of life conspires to remind the teen of the loss, making it increasingly difficult to heal and sometimes leading them to process their grief in unhealthy ways. "Adolescent grief may be masked by other behaviors. Acting-out behaviors, substance abuse, and eating disorders may all be ways that the adolescent copes with loss and seeks support."[24]

In the first year, teens may experience guilt due to regret. As grief overwhelms them, some will isolate themselves, no longer finding joy in the things that once brought pleasure. Isolation leads to increased loneliness, and lack of connection can make the weight of grief seem unbearable. As others in the same family system may also be grieving, an increase in conflict and family tension are common. The effects of grief may become most obvious in difficulty sleeping, lack of energy, and decreased motivation, which can result in problems at school, work, relationships, and/or sports. Some teens will attempt to numb the pain with high-risk medicating behaviors like substance abuse, while others may consider self-harm or suicide as the only way to make the sadness stop.

During this crucial first year, there are some ways that youth workers can help teens follow Jesus, even in grief. It's common for people who experience trauma due to loss to process the question, "Who is God now?" They may never actually speak these words, but the road to processing trauma and loss often leads across this bridge. To use another metaphor, it's as though someone has removed the window you've always looked through to interact with God and replaced it with a window of a different color. As hard as you might try, you can't see God the same way, because the glass you now look through is shaded differently. You can expect teens looking through the window of grief to wonder why God doesn't look as God once did. To some, God will seem closer, while to others, more distant. Your task is to help them adjust to this new window and to help them discover that they will indeed experience God in a new way. They will now be able to relate to Jesus not only in his joy but also in his suffering. To help teens grieve through the first year, don't feel the pressure to be God's "defense attorney." If they need a place to be angry at God, give them that space. Listen to and reflect on what you're hearing, without feeling the pressure to protect God's honor.

In this first year, you're engaging in companion care—providing caregiver support, prayer, and ministry tools for friends of the grieving teen and compassion care for the teen in pain. These include a multidisciplinary approach, ongoing adult contact, spiritual nurture, and consistent youth group support.[25] Teens experiencing grief are the *walking wounded*. Although they may not be in a life-and-death crisis, if they aren't sufficiently cared for and supported, they could easily find themselves choosing unhealthy coping strategies. In providing compassion care, you might help a teen locate a counsellor or grief support group, or you might help them attend one of the Comfort Zone camps, which provide a unique setting specifically designed for teens living with loss.[26] You might also encourage teens to capture feelings and thoughts in a journal or to write their grief into a poem, a psalm, a song, or a short story. Music can provide words and feelings some teens find hard to express for themselves.

After her grandfather passed away, Christian singer and songwriter Lauren Daigle was grieving. To work through her own loss, she penned the words to one of my favorite songs, "I Will Trust in You." Daigle writes, "When You don't move the mountains I'm needing You to move / When You don't part the waters I wish I could walk through / When You don't give the answers, as I cry out to You / I will trust, I will trust, I will trust in You." Directing teens to a song like this and to Lauren's YouTube video, in which she describes the backstory for the song, is a great way to help them connect with the words that can become *their* words—*their* song—in a time when the right words can elude you.

You might also inspire a teen to paint or draw their pain and bring their art to a meeting where you can look at it together. In those moments, it's important not to look at their work as an art critic would! Quality of composition is not the point. The value of this experience is engaging the teen in conversation and reflecting back to them what you're seeing and hearing. On occasion, I've been asked to go to the grave with a teen who hopes to experience some closure. Using sand to pour out, or rose petals to drop, or flowers to lay down, or dirt to throw, or a letter to read can help a teen release feelings and find closure. Asking the deceased loved one at the gravesite for forgiveness, or expressing anger, are important milestones for moving toward healing. I have also heard teens confess their sins at the grave, asking God to forgive them for the way they treated the one who is now gone. Releasing this weight through prayer can be symbolized by floating a leaf on a stream or throwing a stone. Small group care, ongoing adult prayer support, a text or call, or inviting teens to go shopping are all ways to extend care. These simple acts of kindness could make a significant difference for a teen who might otherwise choose unhealthy ways to cope.

One of the most helpful things you can do in the first year is to help teens find resources that they find meaningful. One of the best resources I have used for helping people through the first year of loss is the four-booklet series by Kenneth Haugk called *Journeying through Grief*.[27] The idea behind the booklets is that people need different things as they move through the first year of loss. A booklet is given at three weeks, another at three months, another at six months, and the last one at eleven months. They are short and easy to read, and the people I gave them to tended to read them multiple times.

One last thing before moving on. The most important date within the first year is the anniversary of the death. I like to put a reminder in my phone the week of the death so that I can respond in a way that the individual will find meaningful. I don't guess at this. I ask the teen how he would like to spend that special day and what kind of support he would find meaningful. There are few things more important, more compassionate, and more caring for a youth worker than honoring the memory of a teen's loved one by making it a top priority to remember and to be present.

Nurturing Teen Resilience

In this chapter I have helped you understand the nature of grief and the way people might move through specific stages. As I have mentioned, the stages are not static; they do not happen in order, and they are not neat and tidy. Grief is messy. It takes as long as it needs to take, and although if follows similar patterns in all of us, it's different for each of us. Understanding that teens are going to experience grief, either personally or through a friend's loss, it would seem useful to have a few tools related to grief in your tool belt. Nurturing resilience in the teenager's life will provide a foundation for those moments when the winds blow hard against the structure of that life. The idea of resilience might be unfamiliar, so let's look at how you can help to strengthen teens who are experiencing emotional or spiritual crisis because of grief.

"Resilience is the process of managing stress and functioning well, even when faced with adversity and trauma."[28] Teens are resilient when they're able to call on inner strengths to positively meet challenges, manage adversity, heal from trauma, and thrive, given their unique characteristics, goals, and circumstances.[29] In his recorded presentation on developing resilience, Michael Ungar highlights nine ways to help teens thrive, including: structure, consequences for actions, parent-child connections, strong relationships, powerful identity, a sense of control, a sense of belonging, rights and responsibilities, and safety and support.[30] When a teen is grieving a loss, it's normal for a caring youth worker to feel powerless, and yet, if you look at Ungar's list, you'll notice that youth ministry often excels in several of these areas. The rhythms of a weekly youth night provide structure and consistency when other areas of a teen's life might feel chaotic and out of control. Youth ministry programming and caring youth workers also typically excel at maintaining meaningful connections and nurturing strong relationships, while other teens in the youth group will often ensure teens in pain experience a sense of belonging. These are natural by-products of healthy youth ministry, but they are aspects that may get less attention when you're evaluating an evening of programming.

Instead of basing evaluation on attendance, how many things got broken, or how well the group engaged in the music, you might consider asking yourself, "Did I create space where teens could connect?" "Did I look students in the eye, call them by name, and invite them to participate?" "Did I do my best to create a safe place, free of insults, bullying, and aggression, where teens could be vulnerable and feel a sense of belonging?" "Did the program provide opportunities for teens to grow in their relationship with Jesus?" With this kind of an evaluation, you can look through a different lens and recognize that youth ministry is nurturing both personal resiliency and faith resiliency. Teens are faith resilient when they can consistently call on God's strength to help them manage challenges and adversities. They are faith resilient when they learn to prayerfully call on the power of God's Spirit for healing from the effects of grief and trauma and learn to trust in God's goodness, receive God's peace, and orient their lives around the call to follow Jesus—even in suffering.

The Ministry of Presence

While in seminary, I got to know a few people who worked at a funeral home. During a conversation with the funeral home director, I discovered that there were people who wanted a Christian burial but who had no connections with a church. Typically, these were people who knew little of the Christian faith yet had memories of a religious childhood. The director of the funeral home never quite knew how to serve these people, and I found the need intriguing. I volunteered to be on call should a family need to "rent a pastor for a day," and God gave me some interesting ministry opportunities.

One of the funerals I officiated involved a newly married couple. He had passed away in an accident quite suddenly, leaving behind a young bride in shock. I worked with the family to organize the funeral, and on the night of the closed-casket visitation, I sat near the young woman, providing quiet support. We prayed, even though I wasn't confident that prayer was even important to her. I replaced an empty Kleenex box, gathered a plate of sandwiches, and filled her water cup several times as people strolled by to pay their respects. Her pain was so intense that you could feel it hovering in the air like a moist fog. I felt helpless and useless, and at times I had to fight the urge not to shout, "Everybody go home!" The young bride was heroic in her pain, but her eyes were vacant and distant; I could tell she just wished it would all be over. She wanted to go home, go to sleep, and wake up to discover it was all just a bad dream.

The next day, I honored her husband's life, gently encouraging the room full of non-religious attendees to turn to Jesus for strength. I prayed and read from the Bible, and I finished the service by speaking final words of hope at the graveside. Driving home after the funeral, I felt depleted and disappointed. My caregiving seemed hollow and empty. What was the point? I thought to myself. There was really nothing I could do to help.

Weeks later, I received a card from the widow. I am a serious packrat, but for some reason, I no longer have the card in my folder reserved for special memories. Yet I recall the card rather vividly, because it was like a slap in the face. In the card she wrote, "Thank you for all you did for me at the funeral. I can't imagine this experience without your presence." Those brief words have given shape to my grief support to this very day, and I leave them with you as you consider how you might support the grieving teen in your life. Take care not to underestimate the healing power of your silent presence. It may very well be the greatest gift you ever give to a teen living with the pain of loss.

Ideas for Discussion and Reflection

1. You're the program director at a camp when there is a fatality. Understanding the stages of grief and knowing how my pastor friend helped kids work through the grief of a suicide, describe how you would respond.

2. Describe the ways teens might respond to a death. List how you think a teen's response might be different, contrasting anticipated versus unanticipated death.

3. After a youth group meeting one Wednesday night, fourteen-year-old Lily asks to speak with you. You know she has recently lost her mom, so you ask how she is doing. "Grief is sadness," Lily replies. "It's kind of like you have this hole in your chest. Like this missing part of you." What would you say or do next? Write out the rest of your conversation, using some of the ideas from this last chapter.

4. A seventeen-year-old Christian young man who attends youth group faithfully has a father living with terminal cancer. His dad was recently hospitalized, and doctors don't expect him to live out the week. Looking at the Discipleship Triage Model in Appendix A and back at the chapter you just read, list five things you could do as a youth worker to provide support for this young man.

5. Describe faith resiliency. How can you help nurture faith resiliency in teens, even when they are experiencing grief due to loss?

1   Michael Thom, "Bible camp asks for prayer after tragedy," CHVN Radio, July 2017. Available online at https://www.chvnradio.com/news/bible-camp-asks-for-prayer-after-tragedy

2   Kelly Soifer, "Limping Through the Valley of the Shadow of Death: Lessons from One Who Is Acquainted with Grief," *Youth Worker* 2018, https://www.youthworker.com/articles/limping-through-the-valley-of-theshadow-of-death-lessons-from-one-who-is-acquainted-with-grief/

3   Kimberly Chriscaden, "More than 1.2 million adolescents die every year, nearly all preventable," News Release, *World Health Organization*, accessed February 24, 2018, http://www.who.int/mediacentre/ news/releases/2017/yearly-adolescent-deaths/en/

4   Ibid.

5   "Table 5.5 Leading causes of death of children and youth, by age group, 2006 to 2008," *Statistics Canada*, accessed February 24, 2018, http://www.statcan.gc.ca/pub/11-402-x/2012000/chap/c-e/tbl/tbl05-eng.htm

6   Arialdi M. Minino, "Mortality among teenagers Aged 12–19 Years: United States, 1999–2006," Centers for Disease Control and Prevention, NCHS Data Brief No. 37, May 2010, accessed February 24, 2018, https://www.cdc.gov/nchs/products/databriefs/db37.htm

7   Kenneth Doka, "Did You Know: Children and Grief Statistics," in Children's Grief Awareness Day, accessed February 24, 2018, https://www. childrensgriefawarenessday.org/cgad2/pdf/griefstatistics.pdf

8   Melinda Smith, Lawrence Robinson, and Jeanne Segal, "Coping with Grief and Loss: Understanding the Grieving Process and Learning to Heal," *HELPGUIDE.ORG*, last modified October 2017, https://www.helpguide.org/articles/grief/coping-with-grief-and-loss.htm

9   Kenneth C. Haugk, *A Time to Grieve: Journeying Through Grief* (St. Louis: Stephen Ministries, 2004), 3–4.

10   "Grief Out Loud: Teens Talk About Loss," (video), *Hospice of the Chesapeake* (August 10, 2016) https://www.youtube.com/watch?v=qgrRoJyljeQ

11   "bereave (v)," *Online Etymology Dictionary*, accessed February 15, 2019, https://www.etymonline.com/word/ bereave

12   "Grief Out Loud"

13   Lani Leary, "Grief Is Like a Fingerprint." *Psychology Today*, posted August 22, 2013, https://www.psychologytoday.com/blog/no-one-has-be-alone/201308/grief-is-fingerprint

14   "Grief Out Loud"

15   Kübler-Ross, Elizabeth. *On Death and Dying: What the Dying Have to Teach Doctors, Nurses, Clergy, and Their Own Families* (New York: Scriber, 1969), 264.

16   Psalm 34:18

[17] Julie Axelrod, "The Five Stages of Grief and Loss," *Psych Central,* accessed February 21, 2018, https://psychcentral.com/lib/the-5-stages-of-loss-and-grief/

[18] Ibid.

[19] Ibid.

[20] David Kessler, "The Five Stages of Grief," *Grief.com,* accessed February 6, 2019, https://grief.com/ the-five-stages-of-grief/

[21] K. Doka

[22] Kessler

[23] "Grief Out Loud"

[24] K. Doka

[25] See Appendix A, "Discipleship Triage Model"

[26] Comfort Zone Camp. https://www.comfortzonecamp.org/locations

[27] Kenneth C. Haugk

[28] "Youth Resilience: Protective and Promotive Factors," *Center for the Study of Social Policy,* accessed March 10, 2019, https://www.cssp.org/reform/strengthening families/practice/ body/HO-3.1e-YT Youth-Resilience.pdf

[29] Ibid.

[30] Michael Ungar, "Nurturing Resilience: Nine Things Children Need," *Heart-Mind 2016,* accessed March 5, 2018, https://www.youtube.com/watch?v= gXALq7SZU7U

CHAPTER 4
Unhealthy Dependence:
Finding Freedom through Surrender

*God became incarnate to save the addicted,
and that includes all of us.*
—Gerald May

Once upon a time, there was a little girl who loved adventure. Her name was Cayenne, but her friends called her Cay. She was the kind of rough-and-tumble girl who loved to climb tall trees while her friends stood and watched in awe. She would tease the guard dog chained by the town garage. Often she'd pick fights with girls twice her size, even though she seldom won. Fearless and reckless, Cay often caused her friends concern that she would one day find herself in trouble.

Every year in June the carnival came to her small Midwestern town and set up rides not far from her elementary school. There were bumper cars, a Ferris wheel, music, and food; it was a playground for adventure. One year the carnival brought an animal show to town. Four young Bengal tigers were drawing crowds, as people gathered to see these wonders of creation. The mother tiger had died, leaving the four cubs to be hand-fed by the trainers. Cay was mesmerized by the creatures and stood for hours watching them play, listening to their little cries and growls. *If only I could have one for my own,* she thought to herself. *It would be fun, and I'm sure I could take care of it. No one would have to know.* Cay's mind began to scheme and plot. There must be a way!

One night, as the fair was winding down and the workers were preparing to move to the next town, the little thrill-seeker slipped into the animal tent and found the keys to the cage hanging on a hook. The keepers had gone for supper, so she quietly made her way to the enclosure, opened the gate, lifted a small male cub, and placed it inside her backpack.

This will be my best adventure ever, Cay thought as she made her way down alleys and to her home on the other side of town. Her bedroom was in the basement of her house, so she knew it would be easy to hide her new friend without getting caught. She fed him dog food and grabbed the old litter box her dead cat had used.

The next few days were more fun than she could have imagined. She faked the flu so she could stay home, and her bond with her little friend strengthened. As weeks turned into months, she started to notice how large and strong her little tiger was getting. It was more demanding. Bottled milk was no longer good enough, so Cay had to steal meat from the freezer—so much meat! It seemed the tiger was constantly eating. She missed the days when she could hold him in her arms and control his eating and sleeping.

Now, after a year, her "little" tiger weighed over one hundred pounds, was demanding and controlling, and scratched and bit her regularly. The true wild nature of the tiger had become obvious. In just a short period of time, her life had become overwhelming, unmanageable, painful, and chaotic. Yet she still craved his attention. All day long she sat in her desk at school watching the clock, her thoughts on that moment when she could be with him again. She loved her tiger, and she knew he loved her, too. They just needed more time to learn to live together. All she'd wanted was a tiger cub to love, an adventure to experience. But her adventure had become a nightmare she could no longer hide or control.

She thought about telling a friend or her parents, but then she'd have to face the shame of her foolishness. Instead, she decided she had no choice but to live with her secret. Maybe things would get better. She promised herself that she'd learn to control him, to make him do what she wanted. But one day her tiger escaped up the stairs and ripped apart the living room. He was destroying her life, yet she kept telling herself, "I can make this work; I can control him if I just have more time." Cay was helpless to make it stop. She now had to endure the pain as her family was confronted by a tiger they'd never known was living in their home.

I created this rather unrealistic fictional tale to describe how a substance or behavior can take hold of a life. Cay's story demonstrates that addictive behavior is progressive, often involves denial, and can create a great deal of pain. It highlights the distinguishing features of any addiction: compulsion, preoccupation, impaired control, persistence, relapse, and craving.[1] One problematic issue with this tale is the way it puts the full weight of the responsibility on Cayenne. The story suggests that if she'd only made better choices, she would not have created such a problem for herself.

Choice always plays a role in addiction, but painful life experiences, trauma, lack of resources, mental illness, and other life issues can make it harder for some people to make healthy choices. There is always a story that puts into context an unhealthy attachment to behaviors or substances. Listening to teens as they tell their stories and empathizing without judging are important tools for helping those trapped in addictive behaviors to discover freedom through a relationship with Jesus.

Telling Cayenne's tale when I speak to adolescent audiences gives me the opportunity to use a little humor while teaching a serious topic. Sometimes I snuggle a small stuffed tiger as I'm talking, just to emphasize the point that this animal is truly harmless. I've often asked students, "What would a full-grown tiger do to your bedroom?" When the group debriefs the story, students will give me a hard time, asking how on earth it was possible that Cay's parents didn't know she had a tiger in her room for a full year.

Okay, so the story has a few flaws, but how close is it to reality? Addiction begins with a desire to manage pain or simply to meet an emotional need. The substance or behavior takes control over time, and denial makes it difficult to see the danger. Addiction often thrives in secret (like a tiger living in the basement), and yes, people in the same house often don't know what's happening until the "tiger" breaks loose and creates chaos. The person caught in the addiction often experiences shame and must give an account for a behavior that has brought pain into the family system.

Fundamentals of Addiction

"An addiction is an unhealthy relationship between a person and a mood-altering substance, experience, event, or activity which contributes to life problems and their recurrence."[2] Teens, like adults, can develop unhealthy relationships with behaviors or substances. Much like substance addiction, behavior addictions are marked by the failure to resist an impulse, a drive, or a temptation to perform an act that's harmful to the person or to others.[3] Some people have described substance addiction as the loss of control over the intense urges to take a drug, even at the expense of adverse—and even catastrophic—consequences.[4]

As Cay discovered, loss of control is progressive; the individual increases both the frequency and amount of the stimulant in order to experience intoxication. An unhealthy relationship with a behavior might include binge eating, gambling, gaming, or sex using pornography. Failure to resist the impulse or temptation is how one might describe Cay as she stands in front of the tiger cub's cage. The temptation seems irresistible and may be thought of as a reasonable solution to pain or trauma. For many teenagers tempted by a behavior or substance, it's hard to imagine how anything painful could come of this one seemingly harmless decision.

Blinded Eyes

As you read about addiction, you'll find two competing schools of thought. Some will call it a disease, while others will refer to addictive behavior as a choice. Followers of Jesus are often hesitant, as I was at first, to use the language of disease. It seems to imply that the individual is not responsible for her actions but is merely a victim of circumstances. And yet, a disease is not always separate from personal responsibility. Smoking is still a major cause of cardiovascular (heart) disease in Canada[5] and the United States,[6] killing thousands every year. Heart disease due to smoking is then *both* a choice and a disease. For the youth worker who is discipling teens, addictive behaviors are often the same. Poor choices lead to compulsive behaviors that turn into large tigers, destined to tear lives apart. What begins as a choice will at times become a disease. As you love teens trapped in addictive behaviors, you'll witness chaos and pain, and on occasion you'll find yourself mystified by the continuation of actions that are clearly devastating to an individual's life. Once addiction has a hold on a person's life and mind, there is blindness to behavior that sustains the lifestyle.

The Apostle Paul could have been thinking about addiction when he wrote these words to the church in Corinth: "The god of this age has blinded the minds of unbelievers, so that they cannot see the light of the gospel that displays the glory of Christ, who is the image of God" (2 Corinthians 4:4). Sadly, when it comes to addiction to behaviors or substances, it's not only non-Christians who are blinded. James says that the pathway to sinful action is not random. People are not helpless victims of a disease called "addiction." James explains that people are "tempted when they are dragged away by their own evil desire and enticed. Then, after desire has conceived, it gives birth to sin; and sin, when it is full-grown, gives birth to death" (James 1:14–15). The results of a methamphetamine addiction certainly look evil, and yet, as you'll see, the choice to use a narcotic once looked about as evil as taking a little tiger home from the zoo. It's important to understand that an unhealthy attachment to a behavior or substance will often begin as a solution to a problem that a teen had no other solutions for at the time.[7]

Addiction as Sin

Sin is a biblical idea that's often misunderstood. Sitting in a university class, I listened as a professor spoke about caring for people. She was passionate about social work and clearly wanted her students to treat clients as people with potential, not primarily as problems to be solved. Even though she'd done her doctoral research in a shelter for female abuse survivors and brought firsthand knowledge of pure evil into her lectures, she still held to the idea that people were essentially good. At one point in the lecture she directed her anger toward Christians who believed in the idea of sin. She became quite animated when she described how ridiculous and judgmental Christians could be, daring to refer to human beings as "sinful." Her point was clear: People who act in evil ways are not *sinners*; rather, they simply lack the resources needed to live healthy and productive lives. The people in my class have come to understand that to be a sinner is to be a bad person, which is the way the word is often used in popular culture. They have also come to believe that sin—*bad behavior*—is avoidable, if people are healthy, supported, and given equal opportunities to succeed.

As you think about addictions, it would be biblically appropriate to describe the problem as sinful. But what does that mean? Does it mean that we're to think of people experiencing the catastrophic consequences of compulsive behavior as bad, evil people? How do you disciple teens living with addiction, addressing the problems associated with sin while continuing to value them as people cherished and loved by God? How do you avoid shaming people who have made choices you yourself might have made, had you shared similar life experiences? To answer these questions, I'm going to take a few moments to think about the biblical concept of sin.

In the New Testament, acts of sin always stem from a problem between God and people. In Romans 1, the Apostle Paul writes about the wrath of God that people will experience due to godless and wicked behavior. Although Paul acknowledges the behavior as problematic, he recognizes the deeper problem in the relationship between God and humanity when he writes in Romans 1:20–21,

> For since the creation of the world God's invisible qualities—his eternal power and divine nature—have been clearly seen, being understood from what has been made, so that people are without excuse. For although they knew God, they neither glorified him as God nor gave thanks to him, but their thinking became futile and their foolish hearts were darkened.

The problem of sin is summarized even more clearly when Paul writes, "All have sinned and fall short of the glory of God" (Romans 3:22–24). Karl Barth understood *unbelief* as the core problem of sin. "It is true enough that unbelief is *the* sin, the original form and source of all sins, and in the last analysis the only sin, because it is the sin which produces and embraces all other sins."[8] Unbelief then becomes the foundational internal problem from which stems all of humanity's violence, addiction, trauma, and pain.

Although Jesus didn't talk much about sin, he did tell a story about a lost son that helps us understand what sin does (Luke 15). The young man demanded his inheritance from his father. Typically, an inheritance was money or land that was only transferred after death. In asking for his inheritance, the young man was telling his father, "You're dead to me." In the Jewish mind, to take your inheritance and wish your father dead was a grave insult, and the father would be justified in responding with severe discipline. Instead, the father gave his inheritance to his son. The boy left home, squandering his wealth in wild living. When famine hit the land and food was scarce, the young Jewish prodigal found himself feeding pigs and even longing to eat the pig's slop. Jewish people are not permitted to eat pork, and even to touch a pig is vile. To them, this is a sickening story about sin. The relationship with the father is severed, and out of this disconnection, life begins to spin out of control. As the young man returns home, full of remorse, the father runs to him, embracing him. The story helps explain that the problem is not the pig slop or the parties; the problem is the broken relationship with the father.

The central theme in the story is not the problem of sin but the love of the heavenly Father. It's not a story about a lost son but of a longing father who is eager to show mercy and to be restored with his wayward son. Telling the story in this way, Jesus drives the point home: God the Father forgives sin. In the New Testament, the word most commonly translated as *sin* comes from a Greek word meaning "to miss the mark." Although the word takes several forms, it's usually a matter of offence in relation to God, with emphasis on guilt.[9] You might think that the lost son only becomes a sinner once he's in a far-off land, but that's not what the Bible teaches about sin. It's not the actions that make sinners but sinful nature that results in sinful thoughts, words, and actions.

To put it plainly, the young man in the story, like all of us, had a serious heart problem long before he asked his dad for the cash. Jesus once said,

> But the things that come out of a person's mouth come from the heart, and these defile them. For out of the heart come evil thoughts—murder, adultery, sexual immorality, theft, false testimony, slander. These are what defile a person, but eating with unwashed hands does not defile them (Matthew 15:18–20).

Here, Jesus points to the core of the human problem. "Scripture distinguishes between sin and sins, the one the nature, the other the expression of that nature. Sin is present in everyone as a nature before it expresses itself in deeds."[10]

John teaches about the two realities of sin as both nature and behavior when he writes, "If we claim to be without sin (*nature*), we deceive ourselves, and the truth is not in us. If we confess our sins (*behavior*), he is faithful and just and will forgive us our sins and purify us from all unrighteousness" (1 John 1:8–9). Sin is, therefore, both a principle—a reality within each human being—and an act. It flows out of a heart that is either disconnected from the Creator or connected through faith but actively refusing to be transformed to the image of Christ, by the renewing of the mind (Romans 12:1). To say that addiction is a sin, then, is to say two things at once. The existence of addiction is itself the result of human beings searching to find satisfaction in behaviors or substances that were never intended to satisfy the longings of the heart. It's misplaced worship.

Gerald May writes, "Addiction makes idolaters of us all, because it forces us to worship these objects of attachment, thereby preventing us from truly, freely loving God and one another ... It is the absolute enemy of human freedom, the antipathy (or *hatred*) of love."[11] Second, to call addiction sin is to say that this behavior is the result of submitting oneself to evil. "But each person is tempted when they are dragged away by their own evil desire and enticed" (James 1:14). When teens choose to be dragged away by their own evil desire, they become trapped by behaviors and substances that steal their freedom, negatively impact their potential, destroy their peace of mind, and often ruin their lives. May writes, "Sin, then, is not just ignorance or moral straying, but a kind of bondage or slavery from which one must be delivered into freedom. Freedom is possible through a mysterious, incarnational synthesis of human intention and divine grace."[12]

To find freedom from the sin of addiction, then, is not to build the internal strength to say no to an unhealthy relationship with a behavior or a substance. On the contrary, as step 1 of the twelve-step process used by Alcoholics Anonymous (AA) confirms, the most effective starting point is humility. AA's first step reads, "We admitted we were powerless over alcohol and that our lives had become unmanageable."[13] To face the reality of addiction as sin is to admit that the tiger has taken control, to become honest about feeling powerless, to rediscover freedom. It's not unlike the principle that Jesus taught his disciples when he said, "For whoever wants to save their life will lose it, but whoever loses their life for me will save it" (Luke 9:24).

In discipleship, we're not calling teens to self-mastery but to humility, as they bring their inability to manage life and addiction to Jesus. It is through the relationship with Jesus Christ that the power of addiction is broken, and teenagers experience true, lasting freedom. May writes, "For Christ, the way to abundant grace and forgiveness is through himself, away from all possible attachment ... Jesus came for the sinners who had missed the mark of responding to God's love. To put it bluntly, God became incarnate to save the addicted, and that includes all of us."[14]

If addiction is a choice, people need to be taught to make better choices. If it is a disease, teens need to be inoculated, or healed, or put into a treatment program. But if addiction is first and foremost a sin problem, then teens will only find freedom as they address their broken relationship with Jesus. This is not to say that forgiveness of sin is some kind of get-out-of-jail-free card like the one you find in the game of Monopoly. Leading teens to admit that they are helpless to make a change without God's help is only the beginning of what will often be a long and gruelling journey of recovery.

Shortly after becoming a follower of Jesus, I received a phone call from a close friend. He was not a Christian, and he thought I had gone crazy in leaving the party life. He was calling to ask for help. Addiction had blinded his ability to see that his "tiger" now weighed two hundred pounds and was destroying both his life and his home. After consuming a massive amount of LSD, he had held his mother to a wall with a butcher knife to her throat. Although he didn't cut her, his hallucination that she was a demon was so real, he easily could have taken her life. The experience was sobering for him, and his family members were afraid to have him living in their home. As we talked, he wondered how things had gotten so out of control. He honestly had not seen the progression. He felt trapped, afraid, and ashamed. I'll never forget what he said to me that night: "I need a psychiatrist, or I need Jesus." He likely needed both, but that night, we got started by bringing his addiction to Jesus.

As a disciple maker, you have this to offer—Jesus! I didn't apologize to him for not being a therapist, or a social worker, or a wise counsellor. Sometimes in youth ministry you might feel like you have little to offer because you're not the "professional" caregiver. It's wise to remember biblical passages like Acts 3. In this passage, Peter and John are standing in front of a lame beggar, and Peter, full of the Holy Spirit and boldness, says to the man, "Silver or gold I do not have, but what I do have I give you. In the name of Jesus Christ of Nazareth, walk (Acts 3:6). They gave what they had, just as God calls you to give what you have. Like Justin standing in the backyard with his arms open wide, you stand in the gap for those you love, and you offer the hope of Jesus.

Addictive thinking is not likely to disappear at the point of salvation. Some say Jesus has banished theirs, but it hasn't been my own experience or that of the teenagers I've worked with. Jesus sets people free, but they must learn to walk in his healing. Often they are living with the painful repercussions of their unhealthy actions. After my friend surrendered his life to Jesus, God began to open his eyes to the pain he had caused and the life-ruining evil of his addiction. Then, together, we began the long and difficult journey of putting the tiger back into his cage.

Addictions and Trauma

Dr. Gabor Maté left his family practice to provide medical care for people living with drug addiction. For twelve years he worked in Vancouver's Downtown Eastside, an area known for substance use and fatalities due to overdose. Christian youth ministers tend to like the simplicity of the theological foundation I've just described. Addiction is due to sin. Addiction is sinful behavior. One resolves the sin of addiction through faith in Jesus. Of course it's not that simple. Helping people who struggle with addiction is never easy, and many will never fully recover.

As you interact with professionals working in the addictions field, you won't find many who appreciate it being considered sin. To those outside of Christian faith the idea sounds cruel, like an unfair judgment toward a person who already has a significant problem. Dr. Maté encourages readers to look at addictive behavior through a different lens. From his extensive experience, he provides a perspective on addiction that can help you care for teens who have issues with a behavior or substance.

In an interview, Maté said, "Addiction is not a choice that anybody makes. It's not a moral failure. It's not an ethical lapse. It's not a weakness of character. It's not a failure of the will, nor is it an inherent brain disease. Addiction is a response to human suffering."[15]

Patrick, a man living with a heroin addiction, confirms this idea in an interview when he says, "It's wonderful, it's great—I love it. It's a beautiful, warm feeling; it's like being hugged by God ... I didn't feel all the troubles that I was carrying. And the next thing you know I'm addicted."[16]

Laurie doesn't consider herself a typical drug user. Suffering a deep depression due to the end of her marriage and separation from her children, she tried heroin for the first time at age 37. "The guilt of leaving my children and my family, that's really what brought me down. [Heroin] made me feel like nothing could touch me and I was okay. I didn't have that deep pain anymore."[17]

Calling addiction a response to human suffering reorients the thinking of Christian disciple makers. Maté believes it's important to get to the reason the individual turned to a behavior or substance in the first place and understand that behavior meets needs. "The addiction came along to help you solve a problem that you had no other solutions for at the time."[18] Development of unhealthy dependence on a behavior or substance begins with a need for pain relief. After years of engaging in conversation with people living with drug-dependency, Maté concludes, "What people need in response to their addiction is not judgment and symptom control; they need to be helped to heal from their trauma— 'cause it's all about trauma."[19]

Connecting addiction and trauma changes everything about the way the word *sin* is applied. I wonder how your approach to discipleship might be different if you understood addictive behavior as a painkiller—a response to trauma and not just an act of disobedience or sin. "The object, form, and severity of addictions are shaped by many influences—social, political and economic status, personal and family history, physiological and genetic predispositions—but at the core of all addictions there lies a spiritual void."[20]

As I mentioned in the first chapter, trauma comes from a word that means "wound." How does your understanding of unhealthy behavior change when you consider that unhealthy actions, or ones you might think of as evil, flow from a state of woundedness? The idea reinforces the biblical message that the greatest need of human beings is not to be addiction free but rather to be healed from the "spiritual void"—the wound of a broken relationship with the Creator.

This Is a Football

It was July 1961, and the Green Bay Packers football team was gathered for its first day of training camp. The previous season had ended with a heartbreaking defeat, and for months, the team had been thinking about that loss. As the players gathered for their first practice, they were eager to develop new skills that would help them win more games. Instead of giving them new ideas, their coach, Vince Lombardi, gave a speech that's become famous in the football world. In his book *When Pride Still Mattered: A Life of Vince Lombardi*, David Maraniss writes, "He began a tradition of starting from scratch, assuming the players were blank slates who carried over no knowledge from the year before. He began with the most elemental statement of all. 'Gentlemen,' he said, holding a pigskin in his right hand, 'this is a football.'"[21]

In youth ministry, you'll get tired. You'll love most of the teenagers God brings into your life, but at times you'll hate their behavior. When faced with the pain of teen addiction, your heart may sometimes feel as though it's literally breaking. When the tiger of addiction begins to roam, it doesn't care much whose home it destroys. The greater your empathy, the more vulnerable you will be, and the more deeply you will feel the betrayal of deception. Addiction often thrives in secrecy and promises that things will change. At times you will struggle with anger, and you may even wonder whether Jesus has gone on vacation. It's during times like these that you'll need to remember Vince Lombardi's lesson: "This is a football."

The equivalent for you and those who serve with you in youth ministry is this: "Ladies and gentlemen, we need Jesus!" Saying these words to a bunch of Christian youth workers would probably be received with the same sort of unimpressed, slack-jawed response that Lombardi got from players who were hoping to hear something profound. In the introduction I wrote about discipleship. I explained that a disciple is a learner, or an apprentice, who imitates the teacher. The apprentice learns by use and practice, for the purpose of acquiring a custom or habit. Remember Christopher Adsit's words: "A disciple is a person-in-process who is eager to learn and apply the truths that Jesus teaches, which will result in ever-deepening commitments to a Christ-like lifestyle."[22]

In my discussion on discipleship in the Introduction, I described the purpose of youth ministry using words written by Andrew Root. "The purpose of youth ministry is to invite both young and old to participate in God's action. Youth ministry, like all ministry, seeks in humility to be swept up into God's own action, and therefore to participate in God's activity in our world."[23] Refocusing on the basics of discipleship in ministry is to remove the superhero cape, admit that we're not the life-changing Messiah, and find creative ways to look for and participate in God's action already underway in the lives of the teens we serve. Discipling teens in pain will involve the practice of helping young people form new habits that will act as guardrails for a healthy, godly life.

Serving people is messy, and things seldom turn out the way we'd like, but in Jesus there is grace, there is mercy, and there is hope. When I feel overwhelmed by the power of sin and the pain caused by my broken relationship with God, I feel comfort in reading the words penned by the Apostle John. John is teaching the reader how to discern evil from good when he writes, "You, dear children, are from God and have overcome them, because the one who is in you is greater than the one who is in the world" (1 John 4:4).

Turn Up the Pain

Gary is in his fifties, and over the last two years his drinking and drug use have slowly increased. For the longest time his wife made excuses for him, but eventually she'd had enough. Not long ago, Gary came home drunk and found that his key no longer fit in the lock on his front door. His wife and kids were gone for the night, staying with her parents, and for the first time in his married life, Gary found himself completely alone. The experience of standing on his own front lawn with no family and unable to enter his own house shook him to his core. It was a wake-up call. As I write, Gary is in the Winnipeg Teen Challenge program, a ministry that uses discipleship as their primary ministry tool to combat addiction. Speaking in our church recently, Gary said, with tears streaming down his face, "The best thing my wife ever did for me was change our locks. That's when I started to think that I might have a problem."

In an article detailing the *Community Reinforcement Approach* to alcoholism, the authors explain that it's important to "rearrange the person's life so that abstinence is more rewarding than drinking."[24] In my introduction, I suggested that discipleship is not removing pain but rather teaching people to follow Jesus, even as they experience suffering. Discipleship may even at times require increased pain, to create the kind of clarity that leads to repentance and behavior change. A line in the *Community Reinforcement Approach* article caught my eye when I read, "What then would make a dependent drinker want to give up drinking? One common approach is to 'turn up the pain'—that is, to confront the person with the unpleasant and costly consequences of drinking."[25]

Mia, a 17-year-old girl, came home drunk and lost her stomach on her kitchen floor. She was aggressive and foul-mouthed, and her mom and dad were not impressed. This was new and confusing behavior, not a pattern they'd noticed; it was inconsistent with the Mia they'd known. I didn't know Mia, but the family sporadically attended our church, so her mother called to see if I could help. I agreed to meet with Mia, but it became clear early in our conversation that she didn't think she had a problem. She laughed at my suggestion that she might consider speaking to an addiction counsellor. In her mind, her parents were overreacting, and being forced to speak to the youth pastor was an embarrassment and a total waste of time. Her tiger had been secretly living in the basement, while Mom and Dad, both working professionals, had not realized there was a problem. Mom was a strong, straightforward woman and she made it clear, in front of me, that Mia would be getting help. The confrontation wasn't pretty. Within a few weeks their daughter had been removed from school and admitted to an addiction treatment center. The parents had provided a motivational ultimatum: "If you want our money for your university education, you'll get help."

Mia wanted to ignore the problem, but her wise parents understood that the only way to deal with her alcoholism was to turn up the pain. A few months into her treatment program, I went to visit Mia. She was in a better head space and said, "I'm glad my parents didn't believe me when I told them I didn't have a problem with alcohol." The social workers and the other participants in the small group sessions had pressed her to be honest about the controlling power of alcohol in her life. They, too, had turned up the pain, making her look honestly at her behavior and dependence. For a time Mia had denied what they were saying. She had raged at the participants and workers for attacking her and refused to participate in their programming. She was resistant to any suggestion that she had a problem. It would take weeks before her hard exterior softened. Although Mia would find this experience to be the most painful of her young life, facing the tiger of her addiction would become the pathway to freedom and a completely new way of living.

Sometimes, like the skilled surgeon removing a cancerous tumor, you must inflict pain, under controlled circumstances, to bring about life-saving healing. In discipleship, this may be as simple as an honest conversation that risks the loss of a relationship—speaking hard words of truth. Jesus demonstrates this kind of severity when he says to Peter, "Get behind me, Satan! You are a stumbling block to me; you do not have in mind the concerns of God" (Matthew 16:23). I'm not suggesting you start quoting this text in your conversations with teens, although I expect these words have crossed your mind at times. Rather, I'm suggesting that you don't need to be afraid to turn up the pain to help teenagers experience the freedom Mia found through supportive relationships.

The Journey toward Wholeness

Youth workers dream of encounters like the one in John 1:29. Jesus is out for a walk, minding his own business, and John yells, "Look, the Lamb of God!" It's a funny text. Two disciples hear John say these words, and they begin to walk behind Jesus. He turns around and asks, "What do you want?" As the chapter proceeds, Andrew, one of the disciples who had followed Jesus, now finds his brother, Peter. Verse 42 reads, "And he brought him to Jesus." The next day Philip follows Jesus, then Nathanael.

At the beginning of his story, John makes gathering disciples look easy, but as the Gospel unfolds, there's a religious leader seeking truth at night, a woman with a complicated past, and people hated by the Jews and thought to be cursed by God—the Samaritans. As unlikely as it would seem, each of these begins to show interest in Jesus.

The Bible teaches that the greatest problem humans face is not addiction. The story of the people of Israel, as told in the pages of the Old Testament and this story of the New Testament both describe wayward independence. From the opening chapters of Genesis, the pressing problem with humanity is autonomy. It's captured in the story of Adam and Eve when they disobey God's only command: "You must not eat from the tree of the knowledge of good and evil" (Genesis 2:17). In the creation story, human beings are made in the image of God and made to depend on God, even for breath. Old Testament scholar Henri Blocher writes that "being an image stresses the radical nature of dependence."[26]

To be truly human, functioning by the Creator's design, is to live aware of your own need to depend on God for life, for love, and for health, and to carry out God's desire for you to oversee and manage all that he has created. Instead, the story of humanity is a story of independence. To touch the tree of the knowledge of good and evil is to make the claim that humans are all-knowing. To turn away from the one who gives breath is to reject healthy dependence and to depend solely on one's human capacity for survival. This is the sad biblical story, and this is the problem that creates the possibility of unhealthy dependence: religious, relational, behavioral, or substance.

Father Sam Portaro, the former Episcopalian chaplain to the University of Chicago, once said, "The heart of addiction is dependency, excessive dependency, unhealthy dependency—unhealthy in the sense of un-whole; dependency that disintegrates and destroys."[27] As you think about discipling teens living with addiction, you must resist the urge to attack behavior through either persuasive conversation or fear. The only way to heal and make whole is to change in whom (or in what) you place your dependence, so that disintegration becomes reintegration into the life of the Creator. Helping teens change their dependence stands at the very heart of this disciple-making mission.

Discipleship and Healthy Dependence

After five years of heavy marijuana and hashish use, along with escalating LSD and alcohol consumption, I'd developed a dependence on intoxication. It's true that unhealthy attachments often begin as a solution to a problem that you had no other solutions for at the time. Intoxication provides escape, even if the user can't quite remember what it is he or she is trying to get away from. Trauma and sexual violation in my childhood, family conflict and violence in my teen years, a lack of positive adult support, an inability to thrive at school, grief due to relocation, and poor social skills all worked to create the perfect internal context for medicating behavior. Unhealthy dependence often becomes the painkiller for debilitating, unsolvable problems. Trusting Jesus with my life would lead to significant behavior-change and a new ability to resist the pull of the unhealthy dependence. But it has been a brutal and agonizing process, which still requires conscious daily choice. You can help teens living with unhealthy dependence take a similar journey, by inviting them to experience dependence on Jesus.

Narcotics Anonymous is a twelve-step recovery program, much like Alcoholics Anonymous. Step one of the twelve steps is to admit that you are powerless over your addiction and that your life has become unmanageable. I've heard many in the program refer to this as the hardest step. Admitting you have a problem is often referred to as surrender; this idea stands at the heart of the entire process. "At the point of this surrender we are generally in a physical, emotional, and spiritual state that precludes the ability to choose. Indeed, it can be said that we surrender precisely because we have no choice. We have truly run out of options."[28]

The first step in discipling teens in pain is to invite them to surrender. Sounds easy enough, but think for a moment about your own experience with painkillers. Perhaps you've had an injury, after which the doctor prescribed Tylenol 3 with codeine, or maybe you've been given morphine. Used properly, these drugs are a welcome reprieve after surgery. How might you respond if that same doctor took away your pills while you still needed pain relief? What if you were asked to "surrender" your medication while you were still experiencing discomfort? It's likely that you would resist and put up a fight.

I remember when I surrendered my smoking habit. I had only been a follower of Jesus for a short time. I was standing in the smoking area of my high school, sharing a cigarette with a few friends, when a girl walked over to me and said in a self-righteous tone, "I thought you were a Christian." Up to that point it hadn't dawned on me that smoking and faith in Jesus might be incompatible. I wasn't sure how she knew that the two didn't go together, but I felt foolish. The last thing I wanted to do was embarrass Jesus with my behavior. As I look back on my thought process, it dawns on me that I didn't quit smoking; rather, I surrendered my habit to Jesus. I gave it to Jesus as a sacrifice of obedience.

When you challenge teens to discontinue nurturing unhealthy dependence, you don't call them to quit: you call them to surrender to Jesus. Teens are very familiar with the idea, and many practice surrender with remarkable conviction. Those involved in athletics will surrender time, money, personal priorities, and relationships to pursue their sport. When I choose to quit a behavior, my willpower is typically the only thing that determines my success, but when I surrender, I admit to Jesus that I am weak and in need of his strength. I give him my inability to quit and my desire to continue. I surrender my love for an unhealthy behavior or substance as an act of love for someone I value far above the addiction that is destroying my life. This is discipleship. It means calling teens to surrender to the life-altering, life-sustaining, healing Spirit of Jesus, who reorients their way of thinking so that they begin to desire what Jesus would desire and live the way Jesus himself would live.

Spiritual Friendship

There's no magic recipe for helping teens surrender unhealthy attachments. As a matter of fact, it's not uncommon for youth workers to feel frustrated with their inability to help them surrender attitudes, behaviors, or substances that are obviously creating disruption, chaos, and pain for them and their families. The good news is that God uses youth ministry and youth workers to help teenagers discover freedom in Jesus! Here are a few ideas that you can use in your own youth ministry setting. I would suggest that you choose one, share it with a few youth leaders, and consider how you might use it in your discipleship ministry.

1. Acknowledge Your Limitations

Richard Dunn writes, "To be authentic, spiritual caregivers must begin by acknowledging that there is no foolproof method for making an adolescent develop the moral self we desire. Spiritual caregivers, if they are honest with themselves, realize this foundational truth: adults are not ultimately in control of the process of an adolescent's moral development. In the end, as in all of life, we are left with mystery and faith."[29] Parenting has taught me that there is no obedience button that I can push to make my child choose healthy behavior. That is not to say that I don't have considerable influence, but as kids grow into young adults, the way I influence needs to transform from an emphasis on instruction to a new emphasis on negotiation.

2. Inspire Vision

I recently got braces. I'm fifty-four years old. For many years I was told by dentists that braces would be challenging for me. My jaw would have to be broken. I'd drink through a straw for four to six months, and then we would see if braces would work. After I saw what braces did for my son, I called the orthodontist to see what he might be able to do for me. I already knew it wasn't possible for me to have braces, but seeing my son's incredible smile made me wish for the same kind of results.

When I met with the orthodontist, I explained my fears and told him I would understand if there was nothing he could do. He laughed at me. Then he said, "Years ago we broke jaws. Today you're just another day at the office." I booked my next appointment, arranged my finances, and now I'm six months into a process that will one day change the structure of my face and my smile. My orthodontic process reminds me of the process of spiritual transformation and finding freedom from addictions.

Describing spiritual formation, Dallas Willard writes, "If we are to be spiritually formed in Christ, we must have and must implement the appropriate vision, intention, and means. Not just any path we take will do. If this *V-I-M* is not put in place properly and held there, Christ simply will not be formed in us." [30]

My son's smile gave me a concrete *vision* for how crooked teeth could become a beautiful smile. Based on my non-personal experience of a new reality, I decided to make an appointment, spend some money, and endure pain and inconvenience for a time: this is called *intention*. Finally, I am relying on the resources available to me, including my finances and the expertise of the orthodontic staff. I am being responsive to my role in the process—cleaning my teeth properly and wearing elastics consistently to pull my teeth into place. This part of the process is called the *means*.

You can't just demand that teens make better choices. You can't use spiritual language to guilt them into breaking ties with their unhealthy dependence. Youth ministry provides a context for adult followers of Jesus to become the vision for a healthy, growing relationship with Jesus. When the Apostle Paul writes to the church in Thessalonica, he describes their discipling relationship like this: "Just as a nursing mother cares for her children, so we cared for you. Because we loved you so much, we were delighted to share with you not only the gospel of God but our lives as well" (1 Thessalonians 2:7–8).

In youth ministry, you'll do your best to provide a *vision* of freedom from unhealthy dependence by sharing your life with teens and giving them opportunities to hear stories about the transforming power of Jesus. Like me seeing my son's straight teeth, discipling teens caught in addiction is often as simple as sharing life with them so that they can see that freedom in Christ is possible.

As a teen begins to catch this new vision for life in Christ, the youth leader can help them become *intentional* about change. To quit smoking cigarettes, I took small intentional steps. I told my friends I was quitting. They were pleased to help me, as this meant they would no longer be giving me cigarettes from their own packs. Although I could not quit, I could begin to do things within my *means*. I could choose not to visit the smoking area at my school. I could stop buying cigarettes. I could carry toothpicks to give me something to do with my fingers. On occasion I had a cigarette, but my general orientation was toward complete freedom from the addiction.

Relapse can lead to overwhelming feelings of guilt, and it's important to help teens realize that relapse is a part of the process and not a failure to recover. Relapse is not a sin, and it's not letting God down. Relapse is just part of the addiction reality for the walking wounded; it's a normal part of the ongoing struggle for freedom. Relapse can be painful, and it often clouds the vision that was once so clear. To continue through relapse, teens need a fresh vision, including stories, music, testimonies, small groups, a place to be honest, and prayer support—anything that will help to reignite hope.

3. Put Systems in Place

Addictions can't be immobilized through willpower alone. At the Christian college I taught at for years, students would often complete assignments in the computer lab. When the lab was first built, the people in the computer department noticed that students were often accessing pornography on school computers. Instead of relying on human willpower to stop the behavior, the computer department decided to try an experiment. The computer monitors faced away from the only door into the room, providing students with privacy but also contributing to the secrecy required for viewing porn. Instead of turning all the screens toward the door, two large mirrors were placed on the back wall of the computer lab. To anyone walking into the room, every screen was immediately visible. Pornography use in the computer lab dropped by 90 percent overnight, and the change had little to do with willpower.

In youth ministry discipleship, consider helping teens find freedom from addictive behaviors through systems that take decision making out of the equation. Mirrors in the classroom don't remove the temptation, but the risk of public shame *turns up the pain* and empowers teens to make healthy choices. For me, entering the smoking area at my high-school triggered my desire for a cigarette. Choosing to avoid such a location made it easier for me to distance myself from my addiction. I couldn't say no to a cigarette, but I could say no to the lesser temptation of stepping out into the courtyard.

4. Disciple through Assets

When I was fourteen, I found myself standing in a courtroom in front of a rather stern-looking judge. I'd been arrested for being drunk and disorderly in a public place. I'd gotten into a fistfight with a guy in the downtown core of our town and was now facing disciplinary action. The judge decided I would benefit from an eight-week substance-abuse education. On the first night, I found I knew most of the other teens mandated to be at the workshop. Soon we were gathering before class to smoke pot together. During the class we'd goof off and giggle uncontrollably as a social worker with the patience of a saint tried to help us understand the dangers associated with drugs and alcohol. Today I place a high degree of value on education, but in that instance education didn't solve the problem.

It's important to note that the education didn't fail because the material was poor or because the presenter wasn't well-educated. It didn't fail because the students were stupid or even because we were stoned. None of the students experienced a change in behavior because the focus was on *substance use,* instead of *asset building.*

The Search Institute has identified forty positive supports that teenagers need in order to succeed in life. These assets, as they're called, represent common wisdom about what teenagers need. Research suggests that teens with fewer assets are more likely to engage in high-risk behaviors, while those experiencing a higher number of assets are less likely to engage in high-risk behaviors. [31] Increasing assets then decreases high-risk behavior. Common practice in youth ministry is to focus on the negative behavior, but as was the case with my substance-use education, focusing on the problem of addiction seldom leads to change.

As you address addictive behavior with a teenager in your discipling ministry, add assets first. Visit the Search Institute's webpage and print off the list of assets. Bring the list with you as you engage in conversation with the teen you hope to disciple. Read it over together. Explain that you want to help him or her find freedom in Jesus. Ask the teen what kind of support would be most meaningful. Invite him or her to identify specific items on the list of forty and apply *vision, intention,* and *means.* As you partner with the teen to build an asset base, he or she will feel empowered and supported and will discover hope and joy, along with a decrease in the controlling power of addictive behaviors and an increase in ability to self-manage. As hope increases, it's likely that relapse will occur. Normalize the relapse as part of the process, but keep the emphasis on the asset building, never treating relapse as a failure. Partner with the teen in prayer and spiritual disciplines, helping to see Jesus at work in his/her life.

Labelling teens is never helpful, but as I look back on my own teen experience, I've often labelled myself with words like "delinquent," "evil," and "rebellious." However, when I look at my life through the asset-building lens, I notice that these labels are unfair for a teenager who didn't have even one of the forty developmental assets at work in his life. Is it any wonder that some teens will find themselves unable to find freedom from controlling addictions?

May the Lord forgive you and me for unfair judgments and empower us by the Holy Spirit to be empathic toward those lacking the assets we've taken for granted.

Ideas for Discussion and Reflection

1. Consider Cayenne's tale of the tiger. Identify the key similarities between this story and the addiction process. What weaknesses have I identified with this story?

2. Gerald May writes, "Addiction makes idolaters of us all, because it forces us to worship these objects of attachment, thereby preventing us from truly, freely loving God and one another." Describe what May is getting at and how this quote influences your own understanding of addiction.

3. How does your understanding of unhealthy behavior change when you consider that unhealthy actions, or actions you might think of as evil, flow from a place of woundedness?

4. As I write about my addiction to cigarettes, I talk about the transforming power of surrender. Describe a time when you surrendered a habit or behavior to Jesus. What was that like for you? How is that different from simply quitting?

5. Study the forty developmental assets and the concept of asset building on the Search Institute website. Identity and describe the assets that youth ministries can contribute.

1. Gabor Maté, *In the Realm of Hungry Ghosts: Close Encounters with Addiction* (Toronto: Vintage Canada, 2008), 79.

2. Addictions Foundation of Manitoba, Fundamentals of Addictions (Course Manual), 19.

3. Jon E. Grant, et al, "Introduction to Behavioral Addictions," *American Journal of Drug and Alcohol Abuse* (2010) September: 36(5): 233–241, https://www.ncbi.nlm.nih.gov/pmc/articles/PMC3164585/

4. Charles P. O'Brian et al, "What's in a Word? Addiction vs. Dependence in DSM-V," *The American Journal of Psychiatry,* May 2006, 163, No. 5: 764–765, https:// ajp.psychiatryonline.org/doi/full/10.1176/ajp.2006.163.5.764

5. "Heart Disease – Heart Health," *Government of Canada,* Date Modified: 2017-01-30, https://www.canada.ca/en/public-health/services/diseases/heartdisease-heart-health.html

6. "Smoking and Cardiovascular Disease," *Centers for Disease Control and Prevention,* ahttps://www.cdc.gov/tobacco/data statistics/sgr/50thanniversary/pdfs/fs smoking CVD 508.pdf

7. Gabor Maté, "Why You Are Addicted (Part 1)," on *London Real,* posted July 16, 2017, https://www.youtube.com/watch?v=iKFJ3y0TdYI

8. Stephen D. Morrison, "Karl Barth's Revolutionary Doctrine of Sin," accessed January 22, 2019, http:// www.sdmorrison.org/karl-barth-s-revolutionary-doctrine-of-sin/

9. Ibid., 295.

10. Henry C. Thiessen, *Lectures in Systematic Theology* (Grand Rapids: Wm. B. Eerdmans Publishing, 1983), 173.

11. Gerald G. May, *Addiction and Grace* (New York: Harper and Row Publishers, San Francisco, 1988), 4.

12. May, 114.

13. "The Twelve Steps of Alcoholics Anonymous," *Addiction Center,* last modified March 22, 2018, https://www.addictioncenter.com/treatment/12-step-programs/

14. May, 115.

15. Maté

16. Rafferty Baker, "City on Drugs: The Dark Pull of Vancouver's Downtown Eastside," *CBC Radio,* August 1, 2017, http://www.cbc.ca/radio/ondrugs/city-ondrugs-the-dark-pull-of-vancouver-s-downtown-eastside-1.4229455

17. Ibid.

18. Maté

19. Ibid.

20. Maté, *Hungry Ghosts*, 79.

21. James Clear, "Vince Lombardi on the Hidden Power of Mastering the Fundamentals," accessed April 14, 2018, https://jamesclear.com/vince-lombardi fundamentals

[22] Christopher B. Adsit, *Personal Disciple-Making: A step-by-step guide for leading a Christian from new birth to maturity* (San Bernardino, CA: Here's Life Publishers, 1988): 31–32.

[23] Root, 38.

[24] William R. Miller, Robert J. Meyers, and Susanne Hiller-Sturmhöfel, "The Community-Reinforcement Approach," Alcohol Research & Health, Vol. 23, No. 2, 1999: 116.

[25] Ibid.

[26] Henri Blocher, *In the Beginning: The Opening Chapters of Genesis* (Downers Grove: InterVarsity Press, 1984), 82.

[27] Maté, 131.

[28] Living the Spiritual Disciplines and Virtues in 12-Step Recovery: Surrender, accessed March 3, 2019, http://practicetheseprinciplesthebook.com/surrender 311. html

[29] Richard Dunn, *Shaping the Spiritual Life of Students: A Guide for Youth Workers, Pastors, Teachers & Campus Ministers* (InterVarsity Press: Downers Grove, 2001), 121–122.

[30] Dallas Willard, *Renovation of the Heart: Putting on the Character of Christ* (Colorado Springs: NavPress, 2002), 85.

[31] "The Developmental Assets Framework," *The Search Institute*, accessed February 5, 2019, https://www.search-institute.org/our-research/development-assets/developmental-assets-framework/

CHAPTER 5
Creating Space:
Sexual Discipleship in a World with No Limits

Above all else, guard your heart,
for everything you do flows from it.
—Proverbs 4:23

The phone in the hallway was ringing as I rubbed the sleep from my eyes. It was midnight. The parent on the other end of the phone was irate and afraid, demanding that I explain why her sixteen-year-old son had not returned from the youth group meeting—a meeting that had ended two hours earlier. She was a single mom with several kids at home, and her son had recently come to faith in Jesus.

I said I would make some calls and get back to her. None of Colin's friends knew where he was, but they did tell me that he'd planned to spend some time with his new girlfriend. On a hunch, I drove to a park not far from my house. Sure enough, his little black sports car was parked under some cedars. *Now what?*

I got out of my vehicle and made my way over to his car, wondering why I hadn't listened to my father and become a welder or a plumber. I knocked on the glass. Colin rolled down the window, his face red with embarrassment as his girlfriend frantically worked to adjust her clothing. *Awkward* doesn't even begin to capture the feelings we all experienced.

Colin and I would meet later in the week to discuss our uncomfortable encounter. It has been years now since we had that conversation, but I can still vividly recall his tears of repentance. He had lost his virginity that night, right after a wonderful night of prayer, worship, and Bible study.

When we met, we didn't speak much about sexual behavior. Rather, Colin wanted to talk about his strong sense that he'd disrespected his non-Christian girlfriend and acted in a way that he believed was contrary to his new faith. He was overwhelmed by the sense that he'd disappointed Jesus. We spent time in prayer together that afternoon, and I listened as this young man poured out his aching heart to God.

In those moments when teenagers hit the wall of regret regarding their sexual decisions, it's important for you to remember that you're being called by Jesus to make disciples. This might include ministering with words of absolution, as you hear a confession and feel the deep regret associated with irreversible decisions. At times God will use you to speak words of healing, forgiveness, and truth, like those found in Psalm 103:8: "The Lord is compassionate and gracious, slow to anger, abounding in love." At other times your role might be educational, as you teach about purity, holiness, and respect for both self and others. Wherever you find yourself on the spectrum of conversations about sexual behavior, your goal will always be the same—to help teens follow Jesus.

Warning: Mature Audience(S)

In the Telecommunications Act of 1996, the United States Congress asked the entertainment industry to establish a rating system that would provide information about material in television programming.[1] On February 29, 1996, all segments of the entertainment industry joined together and voluntarily pledged to create a system. By 1998, television programming would fall into one of six new ratings, including TV-MA (Mature Audience), with content descriptors, like (S) for sexual content. There are at least four reasons that it might be wise to apply an MA(S) rating to any youth ministry brave enough to engage in conversations about sex, sexual behavior, or sexual orientation.

First, any time an adult engages in conversations about sexual behavior with a minor, it's wise for other adults to consider motives for the protection of the child or teen. As a youth worker engaging in sex education on a youth night, Bible Study, or in private prayerful conversations like the talk I had with Colin, you need to be prepared to have your motives questioned. Those not present for the education or conversation might be suspicious or even angry, wondering why an adult is having a conversation with a minor about sexual behavior.

This takes us to the second reason for a Mature Audience(S) warning. Not only will your motives face scrutiny, but some people will disagree with the content of your teaching or your approach to discipleship in these conversations. Using this chapter as an example, some of you will not see any disparity between premarital sexual intercourse and following Jesus. You might be troubled that Colin was experiencing remorse for actions that, in your estimation, were not the result of disobedience to God but simply a normal adolescent response to sexual curiosity and changes in the flow of testosterone.

As a youth ministry intern, I taught my first Bible study on sexual purity. It was a difficult study for me, as I'd been sexually active as a teen and young adult, both before and after becoming a follower of Jesus. Although I felt like a hypocrite, I wanted to engage in the kind of sexual discipleship that I thought might help teens avoid the pain I'd caused others and myself through my unwise and unhealthy sexual intimacy.

Soon after the study, I attended a church leadership meeting during which one of the church leaders asked me what I'd been teaching. When I mentioned sexual purity, I added that I'd been teaching teens not to live together before marriage and to commit themselves to purity in dating relationships. Ironically, the teenagers responded well to the lesson, but one adult church leader didn't take kindly to the content of my teaching, referring to my lesson as "unreasonable." He wasn't interested in using scripture to form a biblical theology for healthy sexual practice, and thus he clearly didn't see any value in my content. Disagreement with content is a literal minefield that, if not anticipated, can create conflict, confusion, and unemployment for the youth worker.

The third reason this topic needs an MA(S) warning is to remind youth leaders that how *you* teach about sexual behavior also matters. You might have heard stories of youth leaders acting unprofessionally or teaching about sexual behavior in a way that others find offensive.

While I was teaching at a college in Southern Manitoba, a furious student stormed into my office. Her anger was well-founded. She'd been in a class in which two professors—one a theologian and the other a sociologist—were working together to help students think about the theological-sociological implications of pornography. The concept was brilliant. Although she had no issue with the motivations underlying the lecture, she found the content and methodology to be inappropriate for a Christian college. The professors thought it was important to show the class a documentary explicitly detailing the making of a pornographic movie.

I'll never forget the student's words: "I didn't expect to see a man's genitals for the first time in a Bible college classroom." Those were painful words for me to hear from her. It's important not to miss the lesson here. The methodology used by the teachers was so disturbing to the student that the important learning was completely lost. The student dropped the course and left the school at the end of the semester, and so we lost the opportunity to help her develop critical thinking skills as a follower of Jesus.

Finally, I might give this topic a Mature Audience(S) rating because of the sexualization of our culture. Founder of the ministry Authentic Intimacy, clinical psychologist Dr. Juli Slattery observes that the secular world is doing a fine job of discipling teens according to a secular understanding of sexual norms. She concludes that if people want to know what *sexual discipleship*™ looks like, they need only observe how the world operates. With their own "great commission," secularists are doing a fine job of converting people into disciples of their sexual agenda.[2] In addition to experiencing a barrage of sex-related information, teens in this image-sensitive culture have unprecedented access to increasingly violent pornography. They face challenges associated with sexting, virtual reality, sexual addiction, and choice of sexual identity.

I recently attended a workshop about creating safe spaces for transgender teens. The presenter discussed the responsibility of religious organizations to provide safe, private bathroom stalls for people not desiring to choose between bathrooms designated only for men or for women. The presenter was clearly naïve regarding the social upheaval this would create in most churches. This represents some of the challenges that churches, Christian camps, and youth ministries will need to process as they think together about the implications of sex, sexual behavior, sexuality, sexual identity, and discipleship. If these varied topics are not enough to make you feel a bit nervous about leading your first "sex talk," you might also add to the list important and relevant topics like same-sex attraction, masturbation, transgenderism, intersex, the sexual life of the single person, and the increase in Christian premarital co-habitation.

Cohabitation among Christians barely registers as an important sexual issue, considering the more contentious debates raging over same-sex attraction and sexual identity. Yet Christian cohabitation resulting in sexual relationships outside of marriage is one of the most important sex-related issues facing the church today. There's plenty to think about, but before turning to current research regarding sex and the *screenager*, I want to take a few moments to ground this thinking in biblical and theological reflection.

Finding a Place to Stand

Florida is the sinkhole capital of the United States. The peninsula is made up of porous carbonate rocks that help move groundwater. Over time, these can dissolve, creating a void beneath the limestone and leading to a collapse.[3] Sinkholes occur naturally, but they can be triggered by outside events like heavy rainfall or human activity.[4] When a sinkhole forms, people find they have no place to stand. Homes and vehicles simply sink into the ground, without warning.

Likewise, with a weak biblical-theological foundation, discipleship conversations about sexual behavior will be based on opinion, political affiliation, human rights, or your own personal sexual history or orientation. There's no need for you to pretend that you don't have personal opinions or political affiliations, but the theological sinkhole threatens to collapse the ground beneath your feet when these things take priority over a solid, thoughtful, biblical-theological foundation.

"Christian theology is the reflective and obedient response of the Church to the Word that God speaks about himself in Jesus Christ. But theology is also concerned with human response to this Word spoken by God alone."[5] It's not enough to say that the Bible is your firm foundation. The reality is that your foundation is not the Bible itself but *the way you think about the truths* you find in the Bible. Your foundation is formed by the ideas you embrace as a result of biblical reflection and by your obedient response to the way in which God has revealed his character and mission, in the person of Jesus Christ. For your discipleship to be Christian, your conversations and teaching concerning sexual behavior must be saturated in ongoing biblical reflection and a commitment to Jesus Christ. Here are a few foundational theological ideas for you to think about as you engage teens in conversations about sexual behavior.

1. God invites you to build your life around worship.

    In Exodus 20, the commandments begin by calling the people of God to remember. God does not begin a relationship with a group of people by giving them instructions on how to behave. God acts first, extending mercy and grace, initiating rescue, and demonstrating love and compassion. "I am the Lord your God, who brought you out of Egypt, out of the land of slavery" (Exodus 20:2). God has acted on behalf of this people and out of these actions; God now expresses expectations: "You shall have no other gods beside me" (Exodus 20:3). In Psalm 29:2, the Psalmist will write, "Ascribe to the Lord the glory due his name; worship the Lord in the splendor of his holiness."

    In the Book of Psalms, worship is not a weekly activity but a moment-by-moment orientation. Steeped in Old Testament worship-theology, the Apostle Paul wrote these words about Jesus: "Therefore God exalted him to the highest place and gave him the name that is above every name, that at the name of Jesus every knee should bow, in heaven and on earth and under the earth, and every tongue acknowledge that Jesus Christ is Lord, to the glory of God the Father" (Philippians 2:9–11).

    When the worship of Jesus, as the revelation of God, is the foundation of your theological convictions, discipleship conversations with teens about sexual behavior might include questions like, "How does your desire to build your life around the worship of Jesus impact your thoughts and actions concerning sex?"

2. Human beings are created in God's image.

    It's a bit ironic that Genesis 1:27 reads, "So God created mankind in his own image, in the image of God he created them;

male and female he created them," when the Old Testament explicitly outlaws any images that aspire to represent God. Exodus 20:4 reads, "You shall not make for yourself an image in the form of anything in heaven above or on the earth beneath or in the waters below." Brueggemann writes, "There is one way in which God is imaged in the world and only one: humanness! This is the only creature, the only part of creation, which discloses to us something about the reality of God."[6] The generally accepted idea of the image here has to do with a king who places statues of himself all over his kingdom to assert his sovereign rule.[7]

God gives to the image bearer the role of dominion over creation, but the word is not coercive. "The human creature attests to the goodness of God by exercising freedom with and authority over all the other creatures entrusted to its care."[8] Jesus, the shepherd-king and servant-leader, is the perfect example of what it means to be an image-bearer, as he honors God with his life in every way and lays his life down for his sheep (Mark 10:43–44 and John 10:11).

As you read Genesis 1:28 back through the cross and the life of Jesus, you'll better understand what it means to reflect the likeness of God in your world. As Jesus was the image of God, those in Jesus are now his image bearers, increasingly reflecting his character (Romans 8:23 and 1 Corinthians 15:49). As this thinking becomes a part of your biblical-theological foundation, discipleship conversations about sexual behavior might include questions like, "How does your sexual behavior impact your ability to represent Jesus as his image in the world?"

3. The Bible sets limits on sexual behavior.

Les Parrott writes that "going through puberty is like exchanging a Volkswagen bug for a red Corvette and being told you can't drive over 30 miles per hour until you're married. When it comes to sex, most adolescent curiosity is in high gear."[9] Curiosity is healthy, but sexual curiosity without limit setting can result in decisions that create wounds unlike anything else you experience. The challenge in discipleship is creating space for teens to remain curious about their developing bodies, sexual feelings, and relationships while communicating the limits the biblical writers place on sexual behavior. There's just one complication. As the biblical story unfolds, from the garden of Eden, through the Prophets, and down through the ages, there is one strong message, loud and clear: people don't like God's limits!

Believing that your Creator has set limits on your sexual expression will help keep you from falling into the sinkhole of personal preference. As you prepare to teach teenagers about the limits that God's Word sets on sexual behavior, take some time to study the Bible. Think about the godly limits you practice with your own sexual behavior. How did you come to set these limits? Are your convictions firmly rooted in your study of scripture, or do your limits come from your family, your church, or your favorite authors? How has sexual woundedness or guilt shaped your opinion of God's limits?

As you understand the formation of your own convictions, you may find that you have some pain to address. As I've already written in this book, it's often the case that God will transform your place of deepest injury and use your healing wound as an oasis from which others find nourishment and life. As you heal and grow and are transforming in your relationship with Jesus, you'll engage in discipleship conversations with teens. In those moments when teens back you into a theological corner with questions like, "How far is too far?" you might consider a biblical study that begins with a question such as, "If Jesus were living his life in your body, how might *he* answer that question?"

The Days of the Magazine

Hardy's Variety Store was on a corner near our house. It was where we got our candy, baseball cards, and if we had a note, packs of cigarettes for our parents. Hardy's also had pornographic magazines high up on a shelf behind the counter, but you had to be an adult to buy one. For my friends and me, the magazines with images of naked men and women were alluring, mysterious, and magnetic, drawing our little eyes to the upper shelves every time we entered the store and igniting in us strange new feelings of arousal and desire.

As children, my friends and I had access to pornography in most of our homes, but the dad of one of my friends owned a substantial collection. He kept his pornography magazines in the bedroom closet. In a cardboard barrel the size of a 40-gallon oil drum, he stored hundreds of pornographic magazines. As he and his wife were seldom home after school, my friend and I were able to view thousands of nude images before we entered puberty—women and men in every conceivable sexual situation, captured in full color.

I share this story of my own sexual history for three reasons. First, to acknowledge that this massive image-based childhood research project was responsible for some of my earliest learning regarding heterosexual and homosexual behavior. This same kind of learning is currently taking place with some of the teens you care about, and it will affect the way in which you need to engage in discipleship. Research indicates that viewing pornography shapes attitudes about sexual behavior and can influence the age of a young person's first sexual encounter.[10]

The second reason I tell this story is to highlight the need in youth ministry for not only salvation but for sanctification. It's true that I needed God's salvation, or regeneration, through faith in Jesus Christ, but I also needed sanctification. In the Old Testament, sanctification refers to the process of making something holy; dedicating something or someone to God.[11] Leviticus 20:8 reads, "Consecrate yourselves and be holy (sanctified), because I am the Lord your God. Keep my decrees and follow them. I am the Lord, who makes you holy." It is clear in this text that God is the one who makes people holy. You'll find the same theology in the New Testament, but there you'll discover that God *makes* people holy ("set apart") through faith in Christ and then calls Christians to *become* holy, not through personal effort alone but as a result of the indwelling of God's Spirit. Wainwright writes, "It is clear that sanctification is God's gift before it is our goal."[12]

Once God's Spirit has done the work of regeneration, the believer has an obligation—literally a debt. Followers of Jesus no longer owe a debt to the desires of the body, but instead, those who have been rescued by Jesus are obligated to holiness. The Apostle Paul writes, "Therefore, brothers and sisters, we have an obligation—but it is not to the flesh, to live according to it. For if you live according to the flesh, you will die; but if by the Spirit you put to death the misdeeds of the body, you will live" (Romans 8:12–13).

Discipleship calls teenagers to a life of sanctification, set apart by new obligations because of the love of Jesus. Pornographic images began to shape my mind when I was just seven years old. By my teen years, the desire for sexual images had become as controlling as drug addiction. Like me, the teens you call to follow Jesus will need your help finding freedom and learning to say no to desire. They will need someone to teach them what it means to lead a holy life.

Finally, I share this story of my own sexual history to draw attention to the needs of today's teens. It's laughable to think about a magazine with thirty images when any teen with a phone and a wireless internet connection now has access to an *unlimited number* of pornographic images. If you're going to call teenagers to follow Jesus in the age of screens, you'll need to have a discipleship approach that includes a theological foundation for holiness, online safety and accountability, and mind-renewing Christian education that takes seriously the need for spiritual transformation.

Sex and the "Screenager"

The small town of Bridgewater sits on the southwestern shore of Nova Scotia, not far from the coast of Maine. Bridgewater doesn't often make the national news, but when six adolescent boys were charged for sexting images of girls, the little town became famous for all the wrong reasons. The young men pleaded guilty for sharing nude photos of young women after creating an online group in which they housed and exchanged the photos. The boys persuaded girls ages thirteen to seventeen to send them nude images, and as the crown attorney stated, they used the images "like bartering chips and baseball cards."[13]

Young Canadians in a Wired World is an ongoing research project that studies child and adolescent online behavior. In addition to focus groups, over five thousand children and teens participated in a national survey.[14] The research began by defining sexting (or "sex texting") as the sending or receiving of sexually explicit or sexually suggestive images, messages, or video via a cellphone or the Internet.[15] Examples of sexting include sending "selfies" of nude or nearly nude persons; videos that show nudity, sex acts, or simulated sex; and text messages that propose sex or refer to sex acts. This Canadian research found that 8 percent of kids in grades 7 to 11 had sent a sext, 24 percent in grade 7 to 11 had received a sext, and 15 percent of those in grades 7 to 11 who had received a text had forwarded it to someone else.

A larger international study of adolescent sexting behavior that is currently receiving considerable attention reviewed findings from 39 studies, surveying over 110,000 adolescent participants from around the world. The study, released in 2018, found that one in seven teens reported sending sexts while one in four reported receiving sexts.[16] The study also found that boys and girls were equally likely to participate in sexting, debunking the myth that boys are more likely to request a sext while girls are more likely to send one. Stephen Asatsa sampled a much smaller population of high school students in Kenya, but his research findings are notable. He found that 65 percent of the two hundred students he studied were sending or receiving sext messages daily, while 25 percent were sending or receiving sex messages weekly.[17]

The One Thing

In youth ministry discipleship, it's important to have conversations about online safety, but it's also a good idea to talk about the relationship between commitment to Jesus and the way in which phones are used. You may have noticed by now that I'm a bit hung up on this idea of discipleship. If you don't keep this biblical mandate in the forefront of your mind, you'll find it easy to shift into social-work mode, especially when you're talking about phone safety. Or you might find yourself teaching as a public health nurse, a therapist, or a physical education teacher in a health class would. These professions are important, but youth ministry professionals and volunteers invite teenagers not only to *wellness* but also to *holiness*.

Your primary role is to not to challenge teens to a life of sexual purity or safety but to live life, moment-by-moment, in worship to God, fully committed to being God's image in the world. Calling teens to join you as you commit to living according to these core theological values will result in their setting limits in every aspect of life.

According to Jesus, setting limits for those who follow him is a full-life and full-body experience. He once said, "Whoever wants to save their life will lose it, but whoever loses their life for me will save it" (Luke 9:24). This involves sexuality, but the call of Jesus here refers to a commitment extending far beyond sexual behavior. In his beautiful prayer called "To Will One Thing," Danish theologian and philosopher Soren Kierkegaard wrote about this full-life commitment to God:

> Father in Heaven! What are we without You! What is all that we know, vast accumulation though it be, but a chipped fragment, if we do not know You! What is all our striving, could it ever encompass the world, but a half-finished work if we do not know You: You the One, who is the one thing and who is all![18]

Ministry on Both Sides of the Law

According to research into adolescent sexting behavior, teens can experience shame, regret, and humiliation as a result of sexting.[19] Terms like "sexual exploitation" or the newly coined "sextortion" and "revenge porn" are now being used to describe the dangers associated with this growing problem. Some are using images as bribery, coercing, and extorting additional pictures, favors, or money, while others use sexted images as an act of revenge after a relationship ends or to humiliate after a betrayal or fight. Other serious repercussions of sexting might include sexual harassment, cyberbullying, sexual assault, and criminal charges.

Sexting creates a context for sexual shame that can result in a traumatic response, not unlike sexual assault. Humiliation can be experienced by the one sending the image, but in youth ministry you may also have the opportunity to care for the guilty—like the boys from Bridgewater, Nova Scotia, who were convicted for distributing sexual images. There can be pain and shame on both sides, and as you've found in this book, teens who are humiliated because of an image or due to criminal behavior may also suffer emotions associated with trauma; this can result in medicating or self-destructive behaviors like addiction, self-mutilation, and even suicide.

In Luke 4, Jesus says that he comes into the world to set captives free—those imprisoned by humiliation, shame, bitterness, and rage. At times you will walk with the pain on both sides of the law, just as Jesus did, calling people to surrender themselves to The One Thing—the only One that gives life meaning.

Accountability

"Internet-enabled devices have indiscriminately allowed people of all ages to encounter, consume, create, and distribute sexually explicit content, and a growing body of data reveals that these phenomena are increasingly common for adolescents worldwide."[20] Not long ago, pornography referred to sexually explicit images or videos, but today these are quickly being replaced by interactive chat rooms where participants can watch, speak to, and interact with people stripping, masturbating, or engaging in sexual acts. This is the new pornography, and the sites are easily accessible to anyone with an internet connection.

Here are a few ideas that will help you care for teens who want to set new limits. Some teens will want to avoid contact with pornography before it becomes a problem. Others may feel trapped by compulsion, or even addiction, feeling unable to simply "will" themselves to stop.[21] Freedom *is* possible, but it will require systems that result in complete abstinence. In order to manage this, teens will experience some discomfort. Sanctification is typically a painful process, which is why Jesus uses the metaphor of crucifixion when he calls people to follow him (Luke 9:23).

As a youth leader you demonstrate, with the way you live, what it means to be set apart to Jesus. As you do, you invite teens to walk with you on this journey of faith. Taking up a cross daily and denying some of your strongest passions and urges feels unnatural. The sinful nature is like a toddler running loose in a grocery store, ripping open bags of cookies and chips, fully consumed with self-interest and desire. Eventually the kid's parent catches him with the cookie bag and says, "Enough!" I've been in a similar situation, and I can tell you what happens next. When you say no to the sinful nature, all hell breaks loose! Junior screams and stomps, throwing himself on the floor. The sinful nature doesn't want to be denied, and it will resist any efforts to restrict its insatiable appetite.

Here are a few ideas to help you address pornography from the perspective of a disciple maker. First, encourage teens to honor Jesus, making abstinence a matter of surrender, rather than as giving up a behavior. Pray consistently and honestly, demonstrating compassion and understanding while communicating the place of spiritual warfare in the struggle with temptation (Ephesians 6:10–20). Second, remove the secrecy. Have teens move their computer to a public area in the house and commit to not using technology in the bedroom at bedtime. Finally, increase accountability. This is where it would be helpful to involve parents and caregivers, but doing so could intensify the embarrassment and shame for the teen. Encourage teens to use online accountability software like www.x3watch.com, www.accountable2you.com, or www. covenanteyes.com. Accountability is relatively inexpensive and easy to use. Each week, a full report of the individual's internet use is sent to accountability partners of his own choosing. Images and sites with pornography are blocked; however, if a teen should find him/herself on a site with pornographic content, a text is immediately sent to the accountability partner's phone, with a warning that the partner needs assistance.

As I use *accountable2you* for my own safety, I had to warn my accountability partner that I'd be engaging in research about adolescent sexuality. My wife has asked me several times in the last few days about the "warning" texts she's receiving regarding my online activity. It's good to be able to look together, without shame or guilt, at my internet record, sent from accountable2you. Your willpower will never be strong enough to fight temptation on its own, but the reduction in access and complete accountability take the will completely out of the conversation. Reports can include phone numbers called and a complete list of websites visited, including all social media. It's important to note that the software does not report content viewed on apps like Instagram; however, the report does include time spent daily on social-media applications.

It's not always comfortable speaking about sex, let alone talking about sexting or pornography, but normalizing the conversation and the associated temptations might make it easier for teens to engage in conversations with you. The hope is that teens will see that they can talk with you about sexuality, even as you help them follow Jesus. When you teach about sexual behavior, be approachable, taking care to speak about sexual interest and desire as both healthy and normal—part of God's original design. Paul tells the Colossian Church that they are "holy and dearly loved" (Colossians 3:12). Jesus is not asking you or the teens you serve to accomplish the impossible on your own. Saying no to sexual temptation that leads to pain and despair is possible only because Jesus is fully committed to making us holy, because of love.

Using the Bible for Your Sex Talk

Frank was in my office to talk about same-sex attraction. It was one of his favorite "sin topics." I was his pastor, and for some reason he felt the need to be angry with someone about gay marriage—often. During one conversation, Frank blurted out, "I believe in biblical marriage!" This phrase is often used when a Christian wants to affirm that God is on his side. What Frank didn't realize, I suspect, is that he was fighting for *his own understanding* of marriage from the perspective of a white, heterosexual, middle-class, twenty-first-century Mennonite male. In other words, he had not considered the role culture had played in the shaping of his biblical interpretation.

When this happens, Christians often assume that their personal worldview and reading of the Bible align perfectly with biblical theology and the will of God. In his book, *Sweet Surrender: How Cultural Mandates Shape Christian Marriage*, sociologist Dennis Hiebert writes about the interplay of culture and biblical interpretation. "To grasp adequately how cultural mandates shape Christian marriage requires both biblical and cultural literacy sufficient to read well the texts of both culture and the Bible."[22]

As you prepare to teach teenagers about sex using the Bible, think about the ways your ideas have been shaped. How has your family shaped your ideas about sexual behavior? How did the youth groups or churches you've attended shape your thinking? What about the books you've read, the schools you've attended, or the speakers you've heard? What about the culture you live in? How has media shaped your ideas about sex? Has sexual violation or wounding influenced your thinking and feeling?

As you're honest about your own learning, you'll begin to recognize that some of the things you've come to believe about sexual behavior are not actually found in the Bible. You may also discover that you have closely held convictions that are rooted in fear and come from pain. Some of your ideas will reflect wisdom shared from friends, while others come directly from your study of the Bible and are grounded in Christian theology. Let's take some time now to think about how to use the Bible for a youth talk on sexual behavior.

The Hidden Lesson

Eisegesis means reading your own ideas into text that you are reading. *Exegesis* is drawing the meaning out of the text. My friend, Frank, was engaging in eisegesis. He knew what he believed. In his eyes, he was right. Therefore, his reading of the Bible had to confirm his beliefs— no additional thinking required. For Frank, there simply was no other option.

Christians will never rid themselves completely of eisegesis, nor is it necessary. Instead, you should practice humility, understanding that you need the Spirit of God to teach, rebuke, correct, and train you in holy living, "so that we might be equipped for every good work" (2 Timothy 3:16–17). Eisegesis can happen when a group of teens challenges you on sexual limits. They press you with a question like, "How far is too far?"

Your reply could be this: "1 Corinthians 6:18 tells us to run from sexual immorality." Therefore, you conclude, "anything other than holding hands before marriage is sexual immorality."

You might laugh at this eisegesis, but running away from immorality, as the text suggests, might very well mean refusing to place yourself in situations in which you need your will to control your passion. "Nothing more than holding hands before marriage" seems like a decent conclusion to you, so it can easily pass as biblical wisdom, even though it's not what Paul is teaching in this text.

With eisegesis one asks, "What do I believe?" In exegesis one asks, "What was the Spirit of God teaching the original reader?" While this is difficult to assess, this is the work of biblical study and interpretation. Once you have a sense of what God was saying to the original reader, you can use this understanding to teach on biblical sexuality, acknowledging in humility that you may not yet understand all that the text is teaching. Exegesis requires attention to context and asks questions such as these:

- Who wrote this text?
- When was it written?
- To whom was it written?
- What's the dominant theme of the entire document?
- What's the context of the text itself?

Good exegesis means paying close attention to context, to biblical words, and to the social setting of the text. We must remember that these words were written to real people, living in a unique culture, and experiencing challenges unique to their setting.

Let's go back to our example. A group of teens challenges you on sexual limits. They press you with a question like, "How far is too far?"

You reply, "Let's take a few moments to look at 1 Corinthians 6 together and see what the Bible has to tell us." As you read the text together, one of the sharper teens in the group notices the context. "Hey! This isn't about sexual limits in dating. This is about sleeping with a prostitute!" *Awkward silence.* You let the silence hang in the air for a moment, and then you say, "Well … yes and no. Let's take a closer look."

You've spent some time studying Corinth, so you know the people were obsessed with pleasure, sports, and money.[23] Paul writes the letter to the Church in Corinth to help them understand how the people of God can be faithful to Jesus in this kind of setting. You open your *Disciple's Study Bible* to 1 Corinthians and read about the theological setting. "The prevailing philosophy in Corinth encouraged people to indulge their desires, whatever they might be. Greed, dishonesty, drunkenness, impurity, lust, and selfishness of every kind flourished in Corinth. The Corinthians recognized no law but their own lusts and desires and no god but themselves."[24]

From the text itself, it's known that some of the content of this letter is a response to questions asked by the Corinthian Church (7:1). As young believers in an affluent, violent, sexualized culture, they were trying to figure out how to be holy—set apart. But instead of growing in faith, chapter 3 tells us, they were constantly fighting. Ironically, there the text leads us to believe that they were fighting about the exact same question the teens are asking: "How far is too far?" But it's not just about sex—food, alcohol, sports, lawsuits, and every conceivable passion! And the answers they were coming up with were pretty messed up. It makes sense that Paul would describe them as "worldly," and "infants in Christ" (3:1–2). My exegetical study has included a reading of 1 Corinthians, looking at the commentary in my study Bible, and studying words, phrases, and culture in a biblical commentary.[25]

With this bit of exegesis, the teens in your study might be surprised to discover that the culture of Corinth was not that different from their own. In *The Expositor's Bible Commentary*, W. Harold Mare writes that these new believers didn't accept that matters of the body had any bearing on matters of the spiritual life.[26] In verse 13(b), Paul challenges them to change the way they think when he writes, "The body is not meant for sexual immorality, but for the Lord, and the Lord for the body." In verse 15, Paul writes, "Do you not know that your bodies are members of Christ himself?" This leads him to his conclusion at the end of the chapter, "Therefore, honor God with your body." Although the context of Paul's argument has to do with food and sexual relations with prostitutes, this conclusion can be applied to all areas of life.

Exegesis of this text teaches us that Paul wasn't asking the question posed by the teens in your Bible study, nor was he asking the same questions the immature Corinthian believers were asking. This would be a great time to ask the group, "What question was Paul asking?" To answer this, turn back to chapter 1:2, where you'll read, "To the Church in Corinth, to those sanctified in Christ Jesus and called to be holy, together with all those everywhere who call on the name of our Lord Jesus Christ—their Lord and ours."

Paul's question is not How close I can get to the electric fence before I get shocked? Paul's question is How I can answer the call of Jesus to be holy. He wants the believers in Corinth to think about the "one thing"— growing closer to Jesus. To Paul, everything else is a distraction. The entire letter is about living out the sanctified life we already have because the Spirit of Jesus has set us free from the obligations that once held us captive.

As you engage in Bible study with teens, remember that helping them grasp the content of your lesson is only one-third of what you want to achieve. One-third of the lesson is developing a safe relationship, one-third is teaching them how to read the Bible, and one-third is helping them apply the teachings of scripture to their daily lives. Learning to read the Bible is kind of like getting a driver's license. There's the written part of the test, but then there's the road test. Getting 100 percent on the written portion doesn't mean you're a safe driver. When you take teens to the Bible, the lesson must always include methods of biblical interpretation so that they can learn to read the scriptures on their own. It's the hidden lesson within the lesson.

Communication and Transparency

Dr. Dow was the president of the Bible college I attended. He also taught the Old Testament. One day, while teaching from that erotic poem in the Song of Songs, our seventy-year-old professor looked up from his reading and, with a gleam in his eye, said, "Maybe I'll go home for lunch today and have a little visit with my wife." His face immediately changed to a deep shade of red, and it took some time before the young students could pull themselves together. We laughed until we cried. It was a great moment.

As I bring this chapter to a close, I'm reminded of this joyful moment in the classroom and of the deep and profound love our professor had for his best friend, his wife. He truly cherished her and was not afraid to speak of intimacy with a twinkle in his eye. I've rarely seen such humility and love from a man, and I hold this memory with fondness. It's no sin to acknowledge the enjoyment of sex; it is, however, a problem if you're too open and detailed with minors in sharing about your own sexual relationships or history.

If I were to return to youth ministry as a pastor, I'd be careful to inform parents and caregivers of my content before teaching about sexual behavior. I'd give my teaching material to my senior pastor and to a few parents for their feedback before I taught it. I'd look carefully at our church doctrines and the statement of faith of the denomination.

Gathering this information and feedback, I'd craft a series of youth talks, and I'd teach essentially the same lesson, year after year. I would also aim to teach my lesson on sexual behavior around the same time that the local schools were teaching on similar topics. I encourage you to communicate well and to be appropriately transparent as you teach teens how to live their lives set apart for Jesus.

Ideas for Discussion and Reflection

1. Think back to the opening story about Colin. If you were the youth worker meeting with Colin or his girlfriend, what would you hope to accomplish?
2. What were the reasons for an MA(S) rating for this topic? Which of these reasons concerns you the most?
3. In my section on forming a biblical-theological foundation, I suggest three ideas. List the ideas and write out the questions at the end of each section. Using your Bible, create your own biblical-theological foundation for sexual behavior.
4. Engage in your own research by asking a few teens about phone safety. What concerns do they have? Do they practice setting limits? How do they protect themselves from unwanted images or solicitations?
5. Describe how *eisegesis* and *exegesis* are different. Why is humility important when reading and studying the Bible? What's the hidden lesson?

1   The TV Parental Guidelines (2004), accessed December 15, 2018, http://www. tvguidelines.org/history.htm

2   Juli Slattery, "The Importance of Sexual Discipleship," *Authentic Intimacy,* February 3, 2016, https://www.authenticintimacy. com/resources/2641/the-importance -of-sexual-discipleship

3   Mike Schneider, "Sinkholes: Why So Frequent in Florida?" *Associated Press,* posted August 13, 2013, https://weather.com/ science/news/sinkholes-why-so-frequent -florida-20130813

4   Ibid.

5   J. Daane, "Theology," in *The International Standard Bible Encyclopedia* Vol. 4 (Grand Rapids: Wm. B. Eerdmans, 1988), 827.

6   Walter Brueggemann, Genesis: *Interpretation: A Biblical Commentary for Teaching and Preaching* (Louisville: John Knox, 2010), 32.

7   Ibid., 32.

8   Ibid., 32.

9   Les Parrott, *Helping the Struggling Adolescent: A Guide to Thirty-Six Common Problems for Counselors, Pastors, and Youth Workers* (Grand Rapids: Zondervan, 2014), 341.

10 Eric W. Owens, et al, "The Impact of internet pornography on adolescents: a review of the literature," in *Sexual Addiction and Compulsivity* (Taylor & Francis, 2012), 107, accessed January 3, 2019, http://psych.utoronto.ca/users/tafarodi/ psy427/ articles/Owens%20et%20al.%20(2012).pdf

11 R.E.O White, "Sanctification," in the *Evangelical Dictionary of Theology,* edited by Walter A. Elwell (Grand Rapids: Baker Book House, 1984), 1051.

12 Geoffrey Wainwright, "Sanctification," in *The Westminster Dictionary of Christian Theology,* Alan Richardson & John Bowden, eds. (Philadelphia: The Westminster Press, 1983), 521.

13 Alison Auld, "Nova Scotia teens treated girls' intimate photos 'like baseball cards,'" The Canadian Press July 31, 2017 at *The Globe and Mail,* https://www. theglobeandmail.com/news/national/ nova-scotia-teens-treated-girls-intimate- photos-like-baseball-cards-crown/ article35841245/

14 Valerie Steeves, *Young Canadians in a Wired World, Phase III: Sexuality and Romantic Relationships in a Digital Age* (Ottawa: MediaSmarts, 2014).

15 "Sexting." *Internet Safety* 101, accessed May 3, 2019, https://internetsafety101.org/ sexting

16 Sheri Madigan and Je Temple, "One in seven teens are "sexting" says new research," *The Conversation,* posted February 26, 2018, https:// theconversation.com/one-in- seven-teens-are-sexting-says-new-research-92170

17 Stephen Asatsa, "Cell phone sexting and its influence on adolescence sexual behavior in Nairobi County, Kenya," *Research Gate,* posted February 2017, https://www.researchgate.net/publication/313655458_Cell_Phone_Sexting

_And_Its_Influence_On_Adolescence_Sexual_Behavior_In_Nairobi_County_Kenya

18   Ibid., Kierkegaard, 353.

19   "Self/Peer Exploitation: It's Not OK: A Resource Guide for Families Addressing Self/Peer Exploitation," *Canadian Centre for Child Protection* (2017), accessed February 2, 2019, https://www.cybertip.ca/app/en/internet safety-intimate images

20   Eric W. Owens, 100.

21   Judith K. Balswick and Jack O. Balswick, *Authentic Human Sexuality: An Integrated Christian Approach*, 2nd ed. (Downers Grove: InterVarsity Press, 2008), 281.

22   Dennis Hiebert, *Sweet Surrender: How Cultural Mandates Shape Christian Marriage* (Eugene: Cascade Books, 2013), 10.

23   The Disciples Study Bible, New International Version (Nashville: Holman Bible Publishers, 1988), 1444.

24   Ibid.

25   A biblical commentary is a detailed study of a portion of the Bible. In this case, I'm using *The Expositor's Bible Commentary* edited by F. E. Gaebelein and published by Zondervan. Consulting a commentary will help you understand things like Jewish culture, Hebrew and Greek words, ancient history, and the meaning of your text.

26   W. Harold Mare, 1 Corinthians in *The Expositor's Bible Commentary*, Vol. 10, ed. F. E. Gaebelein (Grand Rapids: Zondervan, 1976), 224.

CHAPTER 6
Wounds of the Body:
Spiritual Formation for those Who Self-Harm

Self-harm will lose some of its appeal
when the lightness of gracious acceptance
transforms those we love.[1]
—Jerusha Clark

Inspired by the asceticism of St. Anthony, Benedict became the father of Western monasticism and the author of the first organized system for faith formation: The Rule of St. Benedict.[2] Born in Nursia (now Norcia), Rome, around 480 AD, he left civilization to live in solitude and discomfort in a cave. After three years on the mountainside, St. Benedict formed small religious communities called monasteries, where men and women could step away from the temptations of the world to fully surrender themselves to Christ. By the Middle Ages, more than fifteen thousand Benedictine monasteries dotted the landscapes of Europe.[3]

St. Benedict was serious about holiness, and there's a rather unique story that captures his commitment. In *The Life of St. Benedict*, Pope Gregory writes of sexual temptation more powerful and all-consuming than anything Benedict had ever experienced.[4] The memory of a woman suddenly filled his mind, inflaming him with desire. Gregory writes, "Suddenly assisted with God's grace, he came to himself; and seeing many thick briers and nettle bushes … off he cast his apparel, and threw himself into the midst of them, and there wallowed so long that, when he rose up, all his flesh was pitifully torn: and so, by the wounds of his body, he cured the wounds of his soul."[5]

Before I begin writing a chapter for Christian youth workers about adolescent self-injury, I think it's important to be honest about the history of self-injury in the Church. St. Benedict threw himself into a bush of thorns to break the power of sexual temptation. The self-inflicted pain is "assisted with God's grace" and it *saves* him from temptation.

For many serious and devout Christians, self-injury has been the primary tool for managing the sinful nature and growing in holiness. The spiritual practices of St. Benedict, and others like him, became a model for thousands to follow. St. John of the cross called this spiritualized self-injury *mortification of the appetites*, by which he means, "All the things we outwardly or secretly love and desire, which prevent us from setting our hearts on God, like creature wealth and selfish sensual pleasures, need to be put to rest, as if entering a dark night where they are no longer seen, so that the soul can advance unhindered towards the love of God."[6]

Engaging in the spiritual act of mortification, third-century religious scholar Origen reportedly castrated himself.[7] Saint Rose would place ceramic shards between the planks of her bed, to increase her discomfort while she slept.[8] She would injure herself physically to diminish the power of desire and temptation. Catherine of Siena wore a tight metal chain around her waist, whipped her own back, and starved herself.

The words of the Apostle Paul provide biblical motivation for self-injury, as a necessary tool for faith formation. "No, I strike a blow to my body and make it my slave so that after I have preached to others, I myself will not be disqualified for the prize" (1 Corinthians 9:27). Since the writings of Paul, self-injury and self-denial have played a significant role in faith formation for those serious about overcoming the power of sin and increasing in holiness. Wounds of the body to cure the wounds of the soul.

Non-Suicidal Self-Injury

Abraham was a teenage cutter. It seemed odd to me at first that no matter what the temperature outside, his arms were covered with sleeves. It wasn't until we spent a weekend together at a youth retreat that I finally learned his secret. The upper portions of his inner biceps were lined with scars and fresh reddish wounds. It was his preferred place to cut. In those days, it was typical to think that people who cut also wanted to die—it was considered a kind of preamble to suicide. Discovering knife wounds on a teen's arms would send an adult youth worker into a tailspin and have him or her moving quickly into suicide intervention and trips to the hospital. It was difficult to believe a teen who regularly cut or burned his skin but said that he didn't want to die. It was baffling to youth workers and parents. What exactly was the teen trying to do if not die?

Today the term *non-suicidal self-injury* helps people recognize that those who self-injure are not typically attempting to kill themselves. However, once you start reading on the topic, you'll quickly notice that there's no consistent terminology.[9] It's common to find terms like *parasuicide, self-injurious behavior, self-mutilation, self-wounding,* and *deliberate self-harm,* in addition to *non-suicidal self-injury*—just to name a few.[10] To make matters worse, multiple terms means multiple definitions. For the purpose of this chapter, *teenage self-injury* will mean that people hurt themselves *on purpose* but don't intend to end their lives.[11]

Self-injury might include cutting or burning the skin or any variety of practices used to inflict pain.[12] Although it isn't a mental illness, self-injury shows that a teenager could use help. It's an indication that there is unmanageable pain. It also means that the teen needs to experience the life-saving, mind-changing, healing power of Jesus.

The Library and the Street

As an adult youth worker, you might experience anger when you learn that one of the teens you love is cutting or burning her body. You might also be afraid. When you're afraid, it's common to think or say things you might regret; for instance, you might minimize self-injury by seeing it as attention-seeking or even manipulation. When faced with self-injury in youth ministry, I've felt overwhelming panic and cried tears of despair, facing into my own feelings of inadequacy.

I've discovered that there's no special button you can push or spiritual quick fix that will make a teen discontinue self-harm. But there is your presence. Remember, you stand in the gap, arms outstretched, noticing and responding to the pain you see, while reaching for Jesus—your source of hope. The Psalmist writes, "May your unfailing love be with us, Lord, even as we put our hope in you" (Psalm 33:22). Hope is critical for life and wellness, but hope is not only a supernatural gift of God. Sometimes hope comes through study.

I've never had an energy drink. I like the idea of energy; I'm just not crazy about getting it from a can. Learning is my energy drink. As I walked away from the college campus after completing my undergraduate degree, I remember thinking to myself, "I'm not reading another book for a year!" I was a bit burned out on education. But I quickly discovered that effective youth ministry requires a youth worker to have one foot in the library and the other on the street. Learning will energize you, help you grow in wisdom, and increase your effectiveness in youth ministry. The library I'm speaking of may have four walls and shelves of books, but you'll also learn on the street. (*On the street* is a phrase referring to everywhere that's not the library.)

Effective youth workers pay attention to teen culture, listening carefully to language and noticing changes in slang, clothing, behavior, and relationships. Youth ministry isn't a weekly program; rather, it's a continual qualitative research project. Like those serving in cross-cultural missions, your ultimate goal is to help people grow in their relationship with Christ. But to accomplish this, it can't be your first goal. The first goal is to build a relationship with the people you want to reach. To hear their stories. To understand their worldview. To know their history. Then, when there is friendship and trust, there will be opportunities to speak about Jesus.

Listening to Learn

In preparing to write this chapter, I've been deeply moved by the direct quotations I've come across. Let the words of those who hurt themselves shape your thinking and adjust your bias.

Listen, as Daphne describes her experience:

> I mostly do it when I'm angry. But whenever I'm mad, I find myself to be at fault, so I punish myself. The anger builds up, higher and higher, until something has to happen—and for me, that something is self-injury.[13]

Fiona also speaks of anger and release:

> If I was sad or angry—for me, 99.9 percent of the time it
> was about anger—I could hear this voice saying, 'Just let
> it out.' Or if I was cutting to feel empowered, it would
> tell me, 'You have more power than anybody. You are
> invincible.' Then, I would sigh. And almost in unison, I
> would hear the voice inside my head sigh with complete
> relief.[14]

Although these teens are not harming themselves to grow in holiness, there are similarities in the motivation. Like Christians practicing mortification of the appetites, it's important to recognize that these teens injure themselves to *accomplish something.* They cut to cleanse, to punish, to purge, to experience the sigh of relief, to calm their racing thoughts and overwhelming emotions. In a very real sense, these are wounds of the body intended to cure the wounds of the soul.

Deciphering the Secret Code

"To non-cutters, self-mutilation appears to be either self-destructive, masochistic, or simply irrational. But cutting has great meaning for those who do it. The meaning, however, is often kept hidden and unspoken because of the secrets it reveals and the shame it attracts. It is like a secret code known only to those who speak its language, or those who take the time to listen carefully."[15]

As I mentioned earlier, for many years parents and youth workers have found it difficult to understand self-harm, assuming cutting or burning to be failed suicide attempts or perhaps attention-seeking. To many in youth ministry, it does indeed seem like irrational behavior, but listen as fifteen-year-old Lindsay describes the day she started cutting. It was a day after a difficult week in which depression and family pressure worked to create the perfect context for self-harm.

> I stood in the bathroom, looking in the mirror, and I
> didn't recognize myself. It was my face looking back at

me in the mirror, but my soul wasn't there. It was just a body to me, and I didn't feel part of it anymore. I felt I had lost control of my thoughts, my emotions, and my actions. And when you've lost control of everything, what do you have left? I saw the box of razors my parents kept in the medicine cabinet. It just seemed to make sense at the time, though I didn't know exactly why. I was only scared and searching.[16]

As you read Lindsay's story, you begin the work of deciphering the code of her internal world, understanding the irrational—yet, at the same time, incredibly rational—thought process that led to cutting.

Teens self-harm to accomplish something, although the reason is not always clear—even to those who hurt themselves. Some find injury a welcome distraction from emotional pain, while others use harm as punishment. But make no mistake: to the one who cuts, the action is entirely rational. As you listen to those who self-harm and read about those who study their behavior, you'll notice that *self-soothing* seems to be a common theme. Self-soothing might seem like a strange choice of words to those who don't self-injure, as the phrase makes cutting and burning sound more like a warm bath.[17]

Like Lindsay, this self-soothing is using "pain to interrupt a downward spiralling chain of thoughts, providing a release from feeling trapped in distressing memories. Pain from a self-inflicted cut or burn can provide a concrete physical focus, providing a distraction from inner psychic pain or symbolically converting it into something that feels more tangible."[18] For some it's a way to feel when life is numb, while for others cutting may be a form of punishment for unwillingly experiencing sexual arousal during an abusive act. It can be a way to cope with sadness, depression, or other mental illness. Self-harm can also be a tool used to control or as payback, aimed at making someone suffer.[19]

Non-suicidal self-injury thrives in secret, so it's difficult to know how many teenagers like Lindsay use self-harm to cope with life. Some studies have shown that one-third to one-half of adolescents in the US have engaged in some type of non-suicidal self-injury,[20] while other studies reveal that 14 to 21 percent of adolescents self-injure at least once in their lives, with 25 percent self-injuring repeatedly.[21] Typically, self-harming behavior begins at the onset of adolescence, between the ages of twelve and fifteen, with girls ages fourteen to seventeen *four times more likely* than boys to be hospitalized.[22] You and I might not know for sure how many teens are engaging in self-harming behavior, but Canadian provincial Kids Help Phone impact reports reveal that for every region of Canada, suicide, suicide-related issues, and/or self-injury make the list of top five reasons that kids call for help.[23]

An Act of Self-Help

In the stories told above by Daphne and Fiona, sadness and anger play a role in creating a context for self-harm. If you were to look closely at their lives, you might discover painful childhood experiences, like sexual abuse, loss, trauma, torture, neglect, or assault. You might discover that there was a parental death, family substance abuse, negative body image perceptions, or lack of impulse control.[24] "Because the combination of pain, shame, and grief from these experiences often remain unresolved, feelings of dread and emptiness can build up and quickly grow to unbearable proportions."[25] Dr. Armando Favazza writes that cutting gives people a way to manage their inner world, converting chaos to calm and powerlessness to control; it's a morbid act of self-help.[26] Some stumble into this odd form of self-help spontaneously, with little forethought. Oddly, one young man describes the spontaneous burning of his arm as feeling like the opening of a safety valve.[27]

Unless you've engaged in intentional self-harm, you likely have some difficulty understanding how burning your skin with a lighter can feel like opening a safety valve. In youth ministry there will be times when you connect with a teen naturally, but at other times you might find it difficult to understand their behavior. In my chapter about addictive behavior, I referred to an interview with Dr. Gabor Maté and to this quote: "Addiction is a response to human suffering."[28] At first glance, self-harm might appear to be unnecessary—and even irresponsible—injury, but Maté provides an alternative lens through which to look. How might it change your discipleship efforts if you began to think of non-suicidal self-injury as a response to suffering instead of as an act of sin? Listen again, as Mate speaks: "The addiction came along to help you solve a problem that you had no other solutions for at the time."[29] How might your discipleship efforts—and your opinion of a teenager—change if you began to look at cutting or burning as an unhealthy way to solve a problem?

Faint Tappings

Recently I had lunch with some teenagers at a youth retreat. The youth worker running the retreat asked the teens to eat their lunches while wearing blindfolds, to increase their empathy for those who don't have the use of their eyes. It was a frustrating lunch for some but a powerful lesson. It's one thing to *say* you understand what it must be like to be blind, but it's quite another to put on a blindfold and share in the experience of eating in complete darkness.

Doctor Carl Rogers was a psychologist who believed it wasn't enough to hear a client tell a story about pain. To be effective, the therapist had to engage, using empathy. Rogers believed that there were several facets to an empathic way of being with another person. Empathy in a helping relationship means "entering the private perceptual world of the other and becoming thoroughly at home in it. It involves beings sensitive, moment by moment, to the changing felt meanings which flow in this other person, to the fear or rage or tenderness or confusion or whatever he or she is experiencing."[30] For Rogers, empathy means temporarily living in the other's life and moving about in it delicately—without making judgments. It means that for a time you put aside your own values and views in order to enter this other world without prejudice.[31]

Empathy means walking around in another person's shoes. It's attempting to understand their experience by listening carefully without judgment and asking questions for clarification. Practicing empathy decreases the possibility that you'll make incorrect assumptions about self-injurious behavior (e.g., "She just wants attention!"). It's also correlated with self-exploration and growth. Studies show that when empathy is present early in the forming of a therapeutic relationship, it increases the potential for positive outcomes. This means that empathy—not just biblical content—needs to be a key ingredient in helping teens follow

Jesus.[32] Listen again, as Rogers describes the positive effects of empathy from a counselling perspective:

> I have often noticed that the more deeply I hear the meanings of this person, the more there is that happens. Almost always, when a person realizes he has been deeply heard, his eyes moisten. I think in some real sense he is weeping for joy. It is as though he were saying, "Thank God, somebody heard me. Someone knows what it's like to be me." In such moments I have had the fantasy of a prisoner in a dungeon, tapping out day after day a Morse code message, "Does anybody hear me? Is anybody there?" And finally, one day he hears some faint tappings, which spell out "Yes."[33]

Teenagers who self-injure are tapping out a Morse code that adults find difficult to understand, but you don't have to understand every word in the secret code before you're able to tap out your own message. *I hear you. I am with you. You are not alone.* Just as in my story of sitting with the young widow in the funeral home, your nonjudgmental, loving presence might be the most important, life-changing gift that you have to offer, as you invite the self-injuring teen away from self-hatred and into the arms of the Healer.

The Cycle of Self-Harm

I remember what it felt like to see the blood," recalls Lindsay of her first cutting experience at age fourteen. "It's weird to say this, but it was beautiful. It was as if the entire outside world had closed and everything was calm and quiet and peaceful. For a few moments, it seemed as if the poison in my blood was leaving—calmly, submissively. I was in control of it. It felt like rain. After the tranquility wore out, I was terrified at what I had just done. It scared me, and I thought I was crazy. But I knew that those few moments had released me from the chaos in my head. And I knew that I could do it again.[34]

After cutting herself, Lindsay felt calm and tranquil. Again, this quote comes to mind: "Wounds of the body to cure the wounds of the soul."

Earlier in this chapter, Lindsay spoke of seeing a body in the mirror but not perceiving that the refection was her own. These stories together provide a glimpse into the self-injury cycle.[35]

The trigger can be self-loathing, anger, self-criticism, failure, panic, feeling overwhelmed, or—as is often the case with adolescents—anxiety related to performance or friendships. The trigger could be associated with unmanageable feelings, depression, and real or perceived loss or abandonment. Self-harm then becomes a rather effective solution to a problem. "Cutting is really a remarkable, ingenious solution to the problem of 'not existing.' It provides concrete, irrefutable proof that one is alive."[36] The self-harming behavior takes place to reduce the chaos and the tension, resulting in feelings of calm—the opening of the pressure valve. Guilt and shame often follow, reinforcing the self-loathing and the trap of hopelessness. Self-disgust brews, causing the pressure to build until a trigger event, or feeling, leads to another episode. Disrupting the pattern before self-injury occurs is key to breaking the cycle and is critical for helping a teen make better choices when faced with overwhelming feelings.

Suicide and Self-Injury

You're crossing a bridge on your way home from a party when you notice a teen standing on the railing, looking down at the water far below. She's holding on to a support beam, crying. You stop to help but are not sure how to begin. You ask her name, but she's nonresponsive. You ask her to come down, but she refuses. You ask what's wrong, and she tells you it's none of your business. You stand in silence, present, but not sure how to help.

During the Applied Suicide Intervention Skills Training course, the instructor climbs onto a chair in front of the class and pretends to be this person on the bridge railing.[37] Calling on participants to talk her down, she demonstrates to the class how hard it can be, when faced with a real-life situation, to provide meaningful assistance. Thankfully, by the end of the two-day workshop, students in the class feel better prepared, having learned and practiced the six-step intervention model.

Although suicide is the ultimate form of self-injury, self-harm in itself is not an attempt to end one's life. The Centre for Suicide Prevention (Calgary, Alberta) provides a useful graphic for thinking about the relationship between suicide and self-harm. With non-suicidal self-injury, the intent is not to die but, as discussed, to manage strong emotions by locating the pain, opening a safety valve, and reducing chaos. The image below illustrates how intent to die is critical for determining whether a person is engaging in self-harming behavior or is intent on suicide.[38]

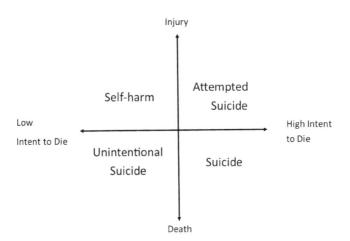

To say that self-injury is not a suicide attempt is not to imply that it's safe. According to the Centre for Suicide Prevention, even though the majority of those who self-injure don't have suicidal thoughts when self-injuring, self-harm can escalate into suicidal behaviors. Familiarity with inflicting personal pain can make suicide seem less intimating and perhaps an easy next step. According to one study, nearly half of people who self-harm reported at least one suicide attempt.[39] Practicing empathy means hearing teens who self-injure when they tell you that they don't want to die. The truth is, they're just trying to find a way to *live*.

No Free Rent

The winds picked up, thunder clapped overhead, and the guards grew nervous as the man on the cross prayed, "Father, forgive them, for they do not know what they are doing" (Luke 23:34). Jesus was betrayed by a friend, sold out by his community of faith, humiliated, assaulted, and crucified on a cross like a criminal, and yet his final prayer was a request for God's forgiveness for those who did not understand.

As a survivor of childhood sexual abuse, I have raged at the idea of forgiving my assailants. In those moments, I've often come back to these powerful words: "Forgive them." Right when I thought I'd come to an age when I'd made peace with those who'd violated me, my wife and I had children. Watching our beautiful little ones grow, and seeing their vulnerability, opened the floodgate of hatred in my heart, and for years I struggled with feelings of bitterness all over again. "Father, forgive them"? How could anyone truly come to forgive brutal acts of violence?

Jesus takes a cross of shame to break the power of sin and make a way for teens to be in a relationship with God. As the story goes, Jesus will rise from the dead and call his followers to make disciples of his kingdom (Matthew 28:16–20). As teens repent and receive what Jesus has done for them, by taking their punishment for sin, the Bible says they will be reconciled to God and become new persons—literally new creations (2 Corinthians 5:17). As new creations, teens will need to begin thinking, living, and acting as Jesus would think, live, and act if he were living his life in and through them. With worship of Jesus as the King of Kings and Lord of Lords at the center of their lives, they will learn to follow the leading of God's Holy Spirit, dying to selfish inclinations and keeping in step with the Spirit's priorities (Galatians 5:25). This will result in the fruit of the Spirit forming character through surrender.

The quote by St. John that appeared at the beginning of this chapter (reprinted below) is appropriate here as you think about participating with the work of God's Spirit when you encounter teens who injure themselves.

St. John believed that living as God's new creation would require you to put to death those parts of the old nature desperately holding on in your life. "All the things we outwardly or secretly love and desire, which prevent us from setting our hearts on God, like creature wealth and selfish sensual pleasures, need to be put to rest, as if entering a dark night where they are no longer seen, so that the soul can advance unhindered towards the love of God."[40]

St. John says you will need to rid yourself of things that you love or desire that prevent you from setting your heart on God. As you heard from those who injure themselves, you can love self-hatred. You can love bitterness. You can learn to find rage and murderous thoughts comforting. But these things will prevent you from setting your heart fully on God and will become a barrier, making it difficult for you to experience God's love. Forgiveness may be an important healing step for the one who engages in self-injury—not to excuse the violence but in order to break the power that perpetrators hold over those who continue to relive the pain. People often allow those who cause them pain to live rent-free in their brains. Forgiveness is a way to say, "No more free rent!"

Finding a Fit

While I was teaching a class on family ministry one afternoon, I noticed that a young woman sitting near the back had started to cry. She hid her tears well, and at the close of class she lingered to speak with me. I'd been teaching about ministry to families with adopted children and touched on the life of Jesus, as one adopted by Joseph. I spoke of 1 John 3:1, which reads, "See what great love the Father has lavished on us, that we should be called children of God! And that is what we are!" In talking about the lecture, the young woman told me that she had been adopted. She said that this was the first time she'd thought about being adopted into God's family. She could barely hold back the tears of joy as she recounted her feelings of abandonment as she was growing up.

In her book, *Inside a Cutter's Mind*, Jerusha Clark writes of the healing that takes place over time as teens learn to trust Jesus and consistently live in biblical truth. Clark writes, "Self-harm will lose some of its appeal when the lightness of gracious acceptance transforms those we love."[41] The young woman mentioned above was practically skipping out of class that day, because she realized for the very first time that God had adopted her. In language that made sense to her, she knew where she fit. Years later, I met this student with her husband and children, and sure enough, she mentioned the transformative power of that lecture, thus validating Clark's comment that the lightness of gracious acceptance does indeed transform people's lives.

As you've read the words of teens who hurt themselves in the first half of this chapter, you've come to appreciate the intensity of their anxiety. When teens come into a relationship with Jesus, through empathy, wisdom, and biblical study, you can begin to help them understand that they're loved by God, adopted into God's family, alive with purpose, and filled with God's Spirit—a new creation! As you walk in Christ together, you can then gently begin to challenge them to put to rest those things that distract—even self-harm—so that their souls can advance, unhindered, towards the love of God.

Worship with a Faith Community

Three teenage girls new to faith were standing in the front row one Sunday morning, giggling. They were trying to sing from the hymn book. The problem was, they didn't know how to read a hymn that was divided into four stanzas. Everyone around them knew that you sang the first line of stanza one, the first line of stanza two, and so on down the page. It took them a few minutes to catch on. I wish I could remember the name of the hymn. All I can remember is the line that said, "At your feet, we hurl our crowns." That was the moment they began to lose their composure, laughing uncontrollably. To them, to "hurl" had more to do with throwing up than surrendering your all to Jesus. I can still see the people around them glaring as the girls enjoyed their worship experience.

It's a great memory. The adults around them were gracious after the service, once they understood the reason for the laughter. There is simply nothing more powerful or effective in discipling teens through pain than consistent worship with a faith community—even if the church uses organ music, or the people all have gray hair, or the preaching is just plain awful. Engaging teenagers in worship is key to life-sustaining change. In their groundbreaking research for their book *Sticky Faith: Practical Ideas to Nurture Long-Term Faith in Teenagers*, Kara E. Powell, Brad M. Griffin, and Cheryl A. Crawford describe a faith that sticks for a lifetime. It is both internal and external, something that's part of a teen's inner thoughts, emotions, and actions. "Sticky" faith is also personal and communal, celebrating God's care for people while locating faith in the community of the church. Finally, they describe a faith that sticks while maturing and growing.[42]

The Hebrew word most commonly translated as "worship" literally means to bow down or prostrate oneself. For the Christian, worship is a sign of inner and outer homage to God, a token of awe and surrender.[43] Biblical worship is a response to all that God has done in both personal and corporate worship. It shapes the worldview and character, as you practice remembering the work of God in your life, anticipating God's future acts, and celebrating God's goodness and love.[44]

Worship in the book of Deuteronomy consistently partners the ideas of remembering, obedience, and worship. "Observe the commands of the Lord your God, walking in obedience to him and revering him" (Deuteronomy 8:6). The Psalmists call upon the congregation to give praise to God, even in spite of enemies, desperate circumstances, lamentation, and calamity. Psalm 34:1–3 reads, "I will extol the Lord at all times; his praise will always be on my lips. I will glory in the Lord; let the afflicted hear and rejoice. Glorify the Lord with me; let us exalt his name together."

Over the centuries, worshippers have found their own feelings and thoughts in the pages of the Psalms. They have used these poems to express their own prayers, praises, and complaints to God in private and public worship. As you disciple teens through the heartache and anxiety associated with self-injury, invite them to experience worship in a faith community. Invite them to find their words in the pages of the Psalms and learn to pray these thoughts and feelings back to the God who loves them.

Disrupting the Cycle

Practicing mindfulness meditation has become a popular way of addressing stress and increasing one's sense of personal wellness, without any of the religious baggage associated with a god or prayer. Christians have been practicing meditation and silence for hundreds of years, but they've chosen to focus their attention during their stillness on the Creator. The Psalmist writes, "Be still before the Lord and wait patiently for him; do not fret when people succeed in their ways, when they carry out their wicked schemes" (37:7). Psalm 46:10 advises, "Be still, and know that I am God; I will be exalted among the nations, I will be exalted in the earth." Stillness gets mixed reviews among Christians. For some it's frustrating and disruptive, while others find the practice healing and refreshing.

In his book, *Helping Teens Who Cut*, Michael Hollander has devised a way to short-circuit the self-injury cycle featured above. He suggests something he calls the "Stop Skill." It works like this:

1. Stop when you notice emotions rising,
2. Take a step back,
3. Observe what's happening, and
4. Proceed to mindfully appraise the situation in a new way.[45]

This Stop Skill is excellent and useful, but I want to adjust it slightly to suit a disciple-making context. For Christian disciple-makers who value prayer as a way of interacting with God, I suggest you use this with teens who self-injure:

1. Stop when you notice emotions rising,
2. Take a step back,
3. Observe what's happening, and
4. Prayerfully appraise the situation in a new way.

Prayerfully appraising a situation is recognizing, at that moment, that God is in the space with you. God's presence and love are supporting and empowering you, and God's Spirit is giving you power at that moment to say no to controlling habits. Prayerful appraisal leads to surrender and to the experience of freedom from overwhelming emotions. It takes time, but practicing this new habit will reinforce your need to depend on God and enhance your ability, in the power of God's Spirit, to manage overwhelming feelings that were once crippling and controlling.

Ideas for Discussion and Reflection

1. Describe how your discipleship efforts might change if you began to think of non-suicidal self-injury as a response to suffering instead of an act of sin.
2. How might your discipleship efforts change if you began to think of self-injury as an unhealthy way to solve a problem?
3. Look again at the Cycle of Self-Harm. Interrupting the cycle before the teen begins to self-harm is the goal. Write down three discipling ideas that you think might help disrupt the cycle long enough for the teen to make a better choice.
4. Forgiving abusers is controversial. Do you think this is a wise suggestion? Why or why not? Contrast the dangers of making this suggestion with the potential benefits. What does the Bible teach about making peace with one's enemies?
5. Worship radically reorients worldview. Describe the potential life-shaping power of worship on the one engaged in self-harming behavior. What biblical texts help you understand the importance of putting God first in your life?

1. Jerusha Clark, *Inside a Cutter's Mind: Understanding and Helping Those Who Self-Injure* (Colorado Springs: THINK, 2007), 193.

2. "St. Benedict of Nursia," Kevin Knight (ed), *New Advent* (2017), accessed January 15, 2019, http://www.newadvent.org/cathen/02467b.htm

3. "Benedictine," *New World Encyclopedia,* last modified June 1, 2016, http://www.newworldencyclopedia.org/entry/Benedictine

4. Stephen Beale, "Saints and Sexual Temptation," *Catholic Exchange,* posted March 20, 2012, https://catholicexchange.com/saints-andsexual-temptation

5. Ibid.

6. "Oh Blessed Night of Pure Faith: A Bird's-eye View of the Spirituality of St. John of the Cross," *Catholic Strength,* accessed January 16, 2019, https://catholicstrength.com/tag/a-summary-of-the-spirituality-of-saint-john-of-the-cross/

7. "Origen: Biblical scholar and philosopher." *Christianity Today,* accessed January 15, 2019, https://www.christianitytoday.com/history/people/ scholarsandscientists/origen.html

8. "Saint Rose," *Providentia,* posted January 23, 2011, https://drvitelli.typepad.com/providentia/2011/01/saint-rose.html

9. Shana Ross and Nancy Heath, "A Study of the Frequency of Self-Mutilation in a Community Sample of Adolescents," *Journal of Youth and Adolescence,* Vol. 31, No. 1, February 2002: 67, http://citeseerx.ist.psu.edu/viewdoc/ download?doi=10.1.1.414.4759&rep=rep1&type=pdf

10. Ibid., 67–68.

11. "Youth and Self-injury," *Canadian Mental Health Association* (2019), accessed January 16, 2019, https://cmha.ca/documents/youth-and-self-injury

12. Ibid.

13. Marilee Strong, *Bright Red Scream: Self-Mutilation and the Language of Pain* (New York: Penguin Books, 1998), 9–10.

14. Ibid., 115.

15. Marilee Strong, Ibid., 36.

16. Ibid., 36.

17. Michael Hollander, *Helping Teens Who Cut: Using CBT skills to end self-injury* (New York: The Guilford Press, 2017), 18.

18. Digby Tantam and Nick Huband, *Understanding Repeated Self-injury: A multidisciplinary approach* (New York: Palgrave Macmillan, 2009), 28.

19. Ibid., 28–29.

20. John Peterson et al, "Nonsuicidal Self injury in Adolescents," *Psychiatry* (Edgmont), Nov; 5(11): 20, posted November 2008, https://www.ncbi.nlm.nih.gov/pmc/articles/PMC2695720/

21. Tina Hu and William Watson, "Nonsuicidal self-injury in an adolescent patient," *Canadian Family Physician,* March 2018, 64 (3) 192–194, http:// www.cfp.ca/content/64/3/192

22 "A Suicide Prevention Toolkit: Self-Harm and Suicide," *Centre for Suicide Prevention*, accessed January 5, 2019, https://www.suicideinfo.ca/self-harm-suicide-toolkit/

23 Impact Report, *Kids Help Phone*, accessed January 18, 2019, https://apps. kidshelpphone.ca/ImpactReport/en

24 Ibid.

25 Marilee Strong, Ibid., 43.

26 Ibid., 43.

27 Ibid., 36–37.

28 Gabor Maté, "Why You Are Addicted (Part 1)," on *London Real*, posted June 11, 2017, 1https://www.youtube.com/watch?v=iKFJ3y0TdYI

29 Ibid.

30 Carl R. Rogers, *A Way of Being* (Boston: Houghton Mifflin Publishing, 1980), 142.

31 Ibid., 143.

32 Ibid., 146–147.

33 Ibid., 10.

34 Marilee Strong, Ibid., 55.

35 Sinead Smithson, Sharon Pearce, and Laurie Potter, "Understanding Self-harm in Children and Young People," Primary Mental Health Team: Community CAMHS, Nottinghamshire, accessed March 2, 2019, https://slideplayer.com/slide/12486357/

36 Marilee Strong, Ibid., 55.

37 Workshop information is available through Living Works at https://www. livingworks.net/

38 Ibid., "A Suicide Prevention Toolkit: Self-Harm and Suicide."

39 Ibid.

40 "Oh, Blessed Night of Pure Faith: A Bird's-eye View of the Spirituality of St. John of the Cross," *Catholic Strength*, accessed January 16, 2019, https://catholicstrength. com/tag/a-summary-of-the-spirituality-of-saint-john-of-the-cross/

41 Jerusha Clark, Ibid.

42 Kara E. Powell, Brad M. Grffin and Cheryl A. Crawford, *Sticky Faith: Practical ideas to Nurturing Faith in Teenagers* (Grand Rapids: Zondervan, 2011), 21.

43 Robert E. Webber, *Worship Old and New* (Grand Rapids: Zondervan, 1994), 29.

44 Ibid.

45 Michael Hollander, 52.

CHAPTER 7
Truth That Transforms:
Dispelling the Lies that Feed Disordered Eating

We become fully alive and free when
God's truth informs, forms,
and reforms our lives. Truth matters.
—Gordon T. Smith

We sat in black leather chairs in my tiny church office, staring at one another.

"Uncomfortable" doesn't begin to capture the experience. No doubt we were both wondering how this chat might proceed. The girl's mother sat in the foyer, waiting for results. I'd gotten the call from her a few days earlier; she was clearly angry and determined to make her daughter "shape up." Although they didn't attend our church, Sasha came regularly to our worship nights.

Her mom came in like a storm through the front doors of the church. She shook my hand firmly, and informed me, "Sasha doesn't have her period anymore. She hardly eats. She won't listen to anything I say. If she doesn't start eating, she's going to kill herself. You need to fix her." This is no exaggeration. While I can't recall her exact words, I do remember the gist and my feeling of shock when she told me I needed to "fix" her daughter.

At the mention of her period, Sasha turned crimson and looked away, not wanting me to see the tears welling up in her eyes. It was an awful moment, and it immediately occurred to me that the mother might be the one in need of help. Thankfully, I kept that thought to myself. Mom sat on a chair outside my office door while Sasha and I went in to the office to have a nice conversation about her period. Imagine! She was fourteen, and I was an unmarried twenty-five-year-old youth pastor. Could things get any worse? I can't remember a single word we said, but I do know that it was the beginning of a friendship that would last for many years. I tell you this story here because it was my first experience of helping someone with food-related issues to follow Jesus, eat enough to stay alive, and not get kicked out of the house. I didn't have a *clue* what to do!

Later that week, feeling completely unprepared for our next meeting, I drove to the nearest university library, where I began to read. As I sat studying disordered eating, I kept praying, "Lord, what can I do? How can I help her experience your love in this situation?" I knew she was a follower of Jesus, yet she was making choices that were leading to slow self-destruction. As I read, my mind kept drifting back to Sasha's sad eyes, her frail frame, and the determined set of her jaw. With the onset of adolescence, she'd gained new confidence in herself, a desire to be in control of her life, and the power to decide if—and when—she would eat. It was going to be a long and painful journey, and Sasha would need to look death in the face from a hospital bed before she would get honest about the severity of her illness.

In this chapter, you'll have the opportunity to think about discipling teens as they live with the daily pain of disordered eating. I've provided firsthand accounts and poetry to humanize the struggle. The danger with discipling teens through crisis is that the issue can dominate your attention. It's good to sit in a library and study, but the goal is not to become an expert in crisis issues. The goal is to help the teen follow Jesus. At the end of the chapter, you'll find some practical suggestions regarding the use of food in youth ministry. My prayer is that this chapter will be a resource for you when you find yourself praying, as I have, "Jesus, what can I do to help?"

A Netflix Springboard

Eating disorders have become a part of mainstream culture, thanks in part to the movie industry, the internet, and social media. For example, *To the Bone* is a Netflix movie starring Lily Collins as Ellen, a young woman living with anorexia nervosa. After multiple attempts at inpatient treatment programs, she agrees to live in a group home run by an unconventional doctor, played by Keanu Reeves. The 2017 film was criticized for glamorizing eating disorders, but Collins, who has had real-life struggles with these, disagrees, stating that the writers didn't want to encourage disordered eating but hoped the movie would start conversation about a serious illness.[1]

Commenting on the film in their article in *Psychology Today*, psychiatrists Eugene Beresin and Jennifer Derenne write, "It seems intended to significantly raise awareness, educate viewers, and open conversations about these psychiatric disorders."[2] Although critical of the level of care provided by the "medical professional" in the film, the article concludes with a rather soft endorsement: "When supplemented by trustworthy material curated by adults who are experienced with the trajectory of eating disorders, the film may be used as a springboard to discuss the nature, course, and treatment of eating disorders. Watch the movie with teens and ask them what they think."[3]

Thankfully, there are celebrities who've chosen to use their public platform to draw attention to the painful reality of eating disorders. Demi Lovato has recently been open about her ongoing struggle with bulimia and anorexia. Others, including Paula Abdul, Elton John, and Lady Gaga, have spoken publicly about their own struggles, working to address the stigma, provide resources, and get people talking about a subject that's often a closely guarded secret.

You might find it helpful to draw attention to celebrities like these, or to music or movies, in order to help teenagers begin what is often a difficult and even shame-filled conversation.

Burn the Body Down

As with some of the other issues in this book, you might find it difficult to understand why a person with anorexia nervosa would deliberately refuse to eat. However, it's important for you, as a youth worker, to suspend your judgment and begin asking questions. As we've seen, it's also important to practice empathy and to put on the shoes of someone with an eating disorder and walk around for a bit. Sit through a communion service, listening as Jesus is called the "bread" of life, and think about how someone with a love-hate relationship with food might hear those words. Practicing empathy means trying to listen, to feel, and to understand.

One of the ways you might do this is to read poetry, listen to music, or look at art created by teens living with disordered eating. I recently discovered this moving poem written by Katie DeVries. In her writing, she's able to capture some of the deeper emotions and magical thinking that are associated with disordered eating. Listen as she writes about her eating disorder (ED) as "slow suicide." As you read these few lines, pay attention to the emotions associated with what she's expressed.[4]

> My ED tells me so many lies
> When really, it's just slow suicide.
> ED said you will finally be skinny; pretty enough for a husband,
> Maybe even children will follow; your own happy dozen.
> You will have stature; respect in society;
> Being thin will cure your social anxiety.
> Doctors will listen because health you achieved;
> Your physical symptoms finally believed.

In her poem, "Diagnosis," Cynthia Cruz powerfully describes the battle raging in the mind, including the shame and self-hatred, with graphic and compelling lines like, "burn the body down." Listen as these few lines provide a tiny peek into the internal chaos that is far more complicated than simply a problem with food:

> Miles, counting
> Calories of everything put
> Into my mouth—desperate to ward the onslaught
> Off. Until I am nothing
> But a body.
> Burn the body down
> And, with it, out goes the pilot
> Blue light of the mind.[5]

Reading poems like this with young people and having them reflect on what they're experiencing through the thoughts and emotions of the authors is a powerful way to engage them. How might poems like this aid you in your ability to help teens follow Jesus? How might poetry, music, and art influence people with no experience of eating disorders? Can you imagine how attitudes, prayer ministry, and caregiving in the youth group might change?

Life Is Messy

There are three main types of eating disorders: anorexia nervosa, bulimia nervosa, and binge-eating disorder. "Eating disorders are not just about food. They're often a way to cope with difficult problems or to regain a sense of control. They're complicated illnesses that affect a person's sense of identity, worth, and self-esteem."[6] For teens living with an eating disorder, body weight becomes the prime focus of life, including a preoccupation with calories, fat, and exercise that allows them to ignore the painful emotions or situations at the heart of the problem while providing a false sense of control.[7]

Canadian data suggests that more than one in five teenage girls is on a diet at any given time, and research indicates that these stats are consistent with findings in the US, Australia, and England.[8] These are not carefully regulated diets, as a significant percentage of teenagers engage in unhealthy behaviors to control weight. Recent Canadian studies reported that 8.2 percent of Ontario girls aged twelve to eighteen and 4 percent of British Columbian girls admitted self-induced vomiting as a weight-control strategy. "It's important to recognize the high prevalence of dieting among normal and even underweight teenagers."[9] Distortion of body image is common among teens, who feel fat even at a normal weight. It's clear that the *perception* of being overweight is a factor in a teenager's decision to attempt weight loss, regardless of whether they are actually overweight. It's critical for you, the youth worker, to understand that perception of body image is at the heart of disordered eating. It's also critical that you understand how dangerous disordered eating can become.

Before taking a closer look at the three types of eating disorders, it's relevant to acknowledge that most of the crisis issues covered in these chapters can be associated with *disordered eating*. Carolyn Costin, a specialist in the area of eating disorders and director of the Monte Nido residential treatment facility in Malibu, California, writes that "eating disorder clients (and/or their family members) are often diagnosed with other psychiatric syndromes—particularly affective, anxiety, obsessive-compulsive, and substance-use disorders."[10] A high percentage of those living with eating disorders also live with depression and/or anxiety.

There is also a relationship between sexual abuse, trauma, and eating disorders. "Clinicians across the country have encountered countless clients who describe and interpret their eating disorder symptoms as being connected to early sexual abuse or other victimization."[11] As you work at understanding behavior that might seem strange, unnecessary, or even foolish, consider the fact that people with anorexia have described starving and weight loss as a way of trying to avoid sexuality—a way to escape sexual experiences and avoid the attention of potential perpetrators.[12] Some living with bulimia describe their behavior as a way of purging the perpetrator, raging at the violator or themselves, and getting rid of the filth or dirtiness inside of them.[13] Binge eaters have claimed that overeating results in weight gain that armours them, keeping them "unattractive" and therefore safe from potential sexual assault.

Finally, there's a relationship between those who self-harm and those living with an eating disorder. One study of those who self-injure found that 61 percent reported a current or past eating disorder. Traumatic pain creates a multitude of injuries; unfortunately, seldom will you find a teen in an emotional crisis living with only *one* crisis issue.

Life is messy. When I spoke to a group of youth workers about trauma recently, I found one young youth pastor frustrated and exhausted. Overwhelmed by the pain he was experiencing with several teens, he couldn't sleep; he found himself constantly responding to crisis texts at 4 a.m. With tears in his eyes, he asked me, "What can I do?" We spoke for a bit and prayed together. After our conversation, I was reminded that when pastors and youth workers disciple teens, prayerfully pledging peace of mind, wholeness, and the newness of life promised by Jesus, they often put themselves into the mess by choosing to walk with teens through their valley of the shadow of death.

When you find yourself in that place, walking with teens and overwhelmed by their pain, remember that the story doesn't end in the shadow of death. Jesus is your Shepherd, and he wants to shepherd these teens you care about. His ministry—and his joy—is to lead those in crisis beside the still waters, where there is safety, restoration of souls, and hope.

Anorexia Nervosa

As you spend time discipling teens, you'll have a front-row seat to watch their lives play out. You'll hear stories, see changes in peer relationships, and witness shifts in behavior that other adults might not notice. Spending time weekly with teenagers means it's likely you'll be one of the first to notice when a teen engages in an unhealthy relationship with exercise, food, or weight management. You might be one of the few adults a teen will trust to share pain associated with bullying, low self-esteem, sexual assault, or any number of other issues that have caused them misery. You might have more than one teenager in your life, so it's reasonable to feel anxiety regarding your ability to spot the beginnings of an unhealthy relationship with food. There are a few things to watch for.

For example, while pastoring at a church in Sioux Falls, South Dakota, I got to know several athletes. A young man, a junior in high school, was into wrestling. One night at our youth group meeting, I noticed that he wasn't quite himself. For one thing, he hadn't eaten any of the snacks, something completely out of character. He looked exhausted, sick, and distracted. I took him aside to see if everything was all right. He said his coach had told him to lose weight before his match on Monday night, so my young, lean, and lanky friend had eaten nothing for several days. He told me he was just drinking water for a few days; then, after his wrestling match, he would eat a big meal.

I've also seen this kind of advice given to teenagers who are competing in gymnastics—terrible advice that could lay the foundation for anorexia. As a youth worker, you need to pay attention to teen athletes and advocate for their health, even if it means speaking to parents or coaches about unhealthy expectations in competition.

If a teenager is needlessly dieting, refusing food, or complaining about body image, you could be witnessing the onset of anorexia nervosa.

Anorexia is a life-threatening mental illness marked by weight loss and the refusal to maintain body weight at or above a minimal weight for age and height.[14] You might also see teens avoiding food due to a deeply intense fear of becoming fat.

"People living with anorexia fear that they will become fat, weak, undisciplined, and unworthy. With the progression of the illness, there are eventually no fattening foods but simply the dictum that food is fattening."[15] It's not our job to diagnose an illness but to be part of a team of adults who are paying attention and responding, preferably before teens find themselves in crisis. With the onset of anorexia, you may also witness distortions in body perception, as teens complain about being fat or express hatred toward their own body. Constantly wearing baggy clothing, avoiding mirrors, and leaving when food is served could all point to a growing problem with body image. As in the story of Sasha at the opening of this chapter, the presence of amenorrhea (absence of menstruation) may also be an indicator of a lack of nutrition, and there may be reason for concern if a teenage girl has missed at least three consecutive menstrual cycles.[16]

One of the most damaging things a youth worker can do is publicly remark on a female's food consumption. Statements like, "Wow, you sure eat a lot for a small girl!" or "C'mon, eat up. You've hardly touched your food," may not even register as problematic for the average young, male youth leader. Statements like these could be experienced by some teens as terrifying and humiliating, sending them spiraling out of control and severely damaging your credibility as a safe caregiver. Be wise, and exercise some caution when speaking to teens about food.

Costin writes,

> People with anorexia are afraid of food and of themselves. What often (but not always) begins as a determination to lose weight progresses and transforms into a morbid fear of gaining weight—even when it is necessary to maintain life. A relentless pursuit of thinness takes hold. These individuals are literally dying to be thin. Being thin, which translates to being in control, becomes the most important thing in the world.[17]

As a method of losing weight or to prevent weight gain, people with anorexia severely restrict how much they eat. They may control calories by purging after eating or by misusing laxatives, diet aids, diuretics, or enemas. They may also try to lose weight through excessive exercise. Regardless of how much weight is lost, the individual will continue to fear weight gain.[18]

There are plenty of excellent books and websites available to help you learn more. As you research, you'll notice characteristics common to those who are susceptible to anorexia.

The disease is more common with women, and risk factors include perfectionism, need for control, depression, rigid thinking, and having a close family member or friend with an eating disorder.[19]

If control and fear are central to disordered eating, what challenges might you experience as you engage in discipleship? How might a person living with anorexia hear a challenge to give Jesus control? What you witness as resistance might be terror; what you see as serious discipleship could be unhealthy perfectionism. How might this influence the way you engage in conversations about surrender when helping teens follow Jesus?

Bulimia Nervosa

Bulimia is a word that comes from the Latin meaning "hunger of an ox."[20] It's a funny image, but the disease is no laughing matter. Bulimia is a life-threatening mental illness in which a person restricts his or her food consumption and then engages in a binge-eating episode.[21] Large amounts of food are consumed in a short period of time, typically leaving the individual feeling helpless and out of control. Binge eating is followed by behaviors that prevent weight gain, including self-induced vomiting; excessive exercise; fasting; and the misuse of laxatives, diuretics, or enemas. For the person to be diagnosed as bulimic, the restricting, binging, and purging cycle will occur at least once a week for three months. Due to intense shame, teens living with bulimia may go to extremes to hide their behavior, including eating alone, hiding food, weight-management practices, and lying about the amount of food consumed during a binge. It may be difficult to see that a teen is in crisis, as his or her weight may appear to be normal—and yet the struggle continues in secret.

The binge-purge cycle is illustrated below, which is helpful in capturing both the process and the emotions.[22] For those unfamiliar with bulimia, overeating might seem like an easily managed behavior. Yet, as is the case with anorexia, food is only part of the problem. Costin writes, "The early behaviors in bulimia nervosa, which appear to be related to dieting and weight control, eventually become a means of mood regulation in general. Sufferers find solace in food and often in the purging itself."[23] Like self-injury, purging can have a calming effect, becoming addictive and helping teens cope with traumatic stress and overwhelming emotions. As you think about helping these teens follow Jesus, what passages of scripture come to mind? How might a commitment to following Jesus affect the "increased tension" and "feelings of shame" parts of the binge-purge cycle? Can you think of ways that the Christian faith might actually make things *worse* for a teen?

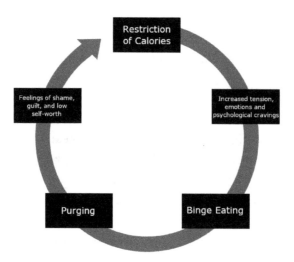

Binge-Eating Disorder

"There's a story of a Navajo grandfather who told his grandson, 'Two wolves live inside of me. One is full of greed, laziness, jealousy, anger, and regret. The other is full of joy, kindness, and love for the world. Always these wolves are fighting inside of me.'

'But grandfather,' the boy said, 'which one will win?' The grandfather answered, 'The one that I feed.'"[24]

In the WebMD video titled "Binge Eating," Robert Miller uses this story to describe the battle raging inside of him. Robert appears to be hundreds of pounds overweight and describes his feeling that people are constantly looking at him and making fun of him. You can hear the agony in his voice as he describes how overeating controls his life. He recalls being four years old and hearing his mother coming home from work. Instead of coming to see him or sitting down to share a meal with him, she would slide sandwiches under his bedroom door. In place of human comfort, little Robert would find comfort in food.

When he was a teenager, sandwiches became a problem for him. He would often find himself sitting alone in the garage, devouring several sandwiches before supper. He describes his binge eating as euphoric, not unlike a drug. However, when the food was gone, the voices would start (e.g., "You're such an idiot."). Guilt and remorse, self-hatred and shame would wear him down until he would turn again to the comfort of food. Near the end of the video, Robert says, "After a year in treatment, I now feel like that second wolf. I feel more gentle and giving. The tools I received in treatment have helped me to no longer feed that wolf."[25]

A teen might be living with binge-eating disorder if their consumption of food within a two-hour period is larger than most people would eat in the same period of time under similar circumstances. The teen with binge-eating disorder might also feel that he's unable to stop; he has no control over how much he's eating.[26]

Listen to the way one person describes his experience of the disease. "When I start eating, I can't stop. I don't know when I'm hungry or when I'm full anymore. I really don't know; I can't remember what it was like to know. Once I start, I just keep eating until I literally can't take another bite."[27]

Unlike those who struggle with anorexia and bulimia, those with binge-eating disorder don't purge or engage in excessive exercise or aggressive dietary restriction. But as with other eating disorders, patterns of food consumption may be less about hunger and more associated with stress, depression, or trauma. As you saw in Robert's story, food becomes a form of self-soothing and a way to medicate internal pain.

I was once in a prayer meeting in which a few adults were praying over a teenage girl. As we placed our hands on the teen and began to pray, the woman leading the prayer time felt led to pray against the spirit of obesity. I wasn't aware that there was a demon that fit that portfolio, but in her mind, fat was a "demonic problem." As you might imagine, the teenager left in tears. Instead of feeling closer to Jesus, the prayer experience left her feeling humiliated and ashamed.

What are the primary internal issues associated with binge-eating disorder? How might you have helped these adults understand the issues associated with adolescent overeating?

Youth Night

Consider this scenario. It's Wednesday night, and the junior-high program is in full swing. After a great night of games, music, study, and prayer, it's time for a snack. The boys hit the line first, and you watch as chips, cookies, and some nasty powdered juice mix is consumed in a frenzy. The girls are more reserved, but they, too, line up and fill their plates. There's laughter, things are getting spilled, and people are sitting in small groups, talking. It's controlled chaos. Scenes like this are common in youth ministry. But take a moment to look around the room, now that you've spent some time thinking about teens and disordered eating.

- Do you notice anyone *not* taking part in the snack?
- Has anyone left the room? Did this person also leave last week at snack time?
- How might your selection of food contribute to unhealthy eating?

The reason I encourage you to ask these questions is not so you can suddenly begin diagnosing eating disorders. This is not your role nor mine. Remember, your role is to help kids follow Jesus. If you know that a certain percentage of teens will develop problems associated with food, it seems wise that you would make it a priority to pay attention to the way teens are interacting with their food. The problem is, when it comes to youth ministry, most adults don't give food much thought.

Another scenario. It was my fourth thirty-hour famine. If you aren't familiar with this concept, my youth group chose to raise money for a local soup kitchen. We would all go without food for thirty hours and have people sponsor us by the hour. It's a great way to raise money for a local charity while teaching teens about the value of food. Each time I organized the event, I would invite teens to spend a night at the church—with adult chaperones, of course—and at the end of the thirty hours we would share a meal together.

One year, a nurse helped me plan the event, and for the very first time I began to think about adolescent health as it related to blood sugar levels, food consumption after a prolonged fast, and the type of foods best to eat after a prolonged fast. I felt a bit embarrassed that I'd never thought about food and teen health in this way before. Instead of sugary juice, we had water available. Instead of breaking the fast with my typical all-you-can-eat pizza bar with chips and pop, we each received a small bowl of rice with a few steamed vegetables and water. This food switch helped to reinforce the realities associated with world hunger and served as a gentle way to break the fast.

Lies that Kill

The wise story told by the Navajo grandfather is also found in the pages of the New Testament. The Apostle Paul doesn't talk about battling internal wolves, but he *does* describe an ongoing war between the fallen nature, which does not desire to please God, and the redeemed nature—that has been, is, and will be transformed into the likeness of Christ. These two natures, Paul tells us, are waging a war for control of the mind. Romans 8:5–8 reads thus:

> Those who live according to the flesh have their minds set on what the flesh desires; but those who live in accordance with the Spirit have their minds set on what the Spirit desires. The mind governed by the flesh is death, but the mind governed by the Spirit is life and peace. The mind governed by the flesh is hostile to God; it does not submit to God's law, nor can it do so. Those who are in the realm of the flesh cannot please God.

It's not *food* that feeds disordered eating, it's *lies*. Letting the sinful nature control your mind is believing lies that lead to self-destruction. Eating disorders are both created and sustained by lies. Through pain, some teens will come to believe that they're inadequate, that their bodies are ugly, and that to be accepted they must attain and maintain perfection. They'll believe lies that swarm like bees in the mind, nagging and pestering and destroying their hope for peace. Lies will tell them they're unlovable, defective, and disgusting until they come to believe that "burning the body down" is the only thing they deserve.

Truth that Transforms

In his opening words, John will introduce his readers to Jesus as the Word, as co-creator, as life, and as light. This word that God speaks becomes a person, and this person makes his dwelling among us. "We have seen his glory, the glory of the one and only Son, who came from the Father, full of grace and truth" (John 1:14b). In John 8:31–32, it says, "To the Jews who had believed him, Jesus said, 'If you hold to my teaching, you are really my disciples. Then you will know the truth, and the truth will set you free.'"

Jesus is the truth, and when he is trusted and followed and his teaching is known and embraced and lived out, the result is ever-increasing freedom and transformation. Gordon Smith reminds his readers that the Holy Spirit works in and through the truth and that life-change is possible. "We become fully alive and free when God's truth informs, forms, and reforms our lives. Truth matters. And the Spirit and the truth function in tandem."[28] This is exactly how Jesus rescues those living with disordered eating.

The Spirit *informs* through the scriptures, as well as through godly teachers, mentors, youth workers, parents, and friends. The wolves battle, and when there is even a speck of receptivity to the Spirit's work, the mind and life are *formed* by new truth, and the result is *reformation*.

Sasha is now married and has several beautiful teenagers. Jesus held her as together they walked through the valley of the shadow of death, and he became her truth, reorienting her attention, intention to self-harm, and self-perception. Thinking about her story reminds me that

Jesus promised he would send the Spirit of truth to guide us into all truth (John 16:13). Not all stories have a happy ending, and many followers of Jesus will live their entire lives struggling with food-related issues. This is not an indication of disobedience, sin, or resistance to God's Spirit; it may simply be that they still need the healing touch of Jesus.

God has placed you into the lives of teenagers to speak the truth, using the scripture and your life. You are a living demonstration of the life-changing power of Jesus. Your story. Your scars. Your losses. Your struggle with faith and your shining moments of faithfulness. God will use it all as you walk alongside of teens. The adolescent journey of self-discovery is hard enough without throwing in an eating disorder. Kids need champions in their corner who will speak the truth, pray truth, and consistently fight against the lies, always pressing to find a way back into the mind. Sometimes you'll feel like a lone fish swimming against the current, but God has called you to be the one to point teens to Romans 8:6, reminding them that a mind controlled by the Spirit of God will never lead to *slow suicide* but will result in the life and peace that so many crave.

Consider making a chart of lies and truths with a teen who suffers disordered eating. Have her use her own Bible as together you look at what God's Word says about the lies that she believes. A therapist had me create my own list of truths, which I had on my bathroom wall for years. I would read it every morning. Slowly, over time, these new ideas began to reform the way I thought about life, God, my identity, and my purpose in God's world. Soaking in truth is not a quick fix; change takes time. But as we wait for the return of Jesus, we hope that he will transform our bodies, so that one day they will be like his glorious body (Philippians 3:20–21).

The Lie	The Truth
"I'm not lovable."	"For God so loved the world that he gave his one and only Son" (John 3:16a).
"I'm alone."	"The Lord is near to all who call on him, to all who call on him in truth" (Psalm 145:18).
"Life is too hard."	"When I said, 'My foot is slipping,' your unfailing love, Lord, supported me" (Psalm 94:18).
"I'm ugly."	"I praise you because I am fearfully and wonderfully made" (Psalm 139:14a).
"I'm afraid."	"Do not be anxious about anything, but in every situation, by prayer and petition, with thanksgiving, present your requests to God. And the peace of God, which transcends all understanding, will guard your hearts and your minds in Christ Jesus" (Philippians 4:6–7).
"I want to die."	"Cast your cares on the Lord and he will sustain you; he will never let the righteous be shaken" (Psalm 55:22).

Ideas for Discussion and Reflection

1. If control and fear are central to disordered eating, what challenges might you experience as you engage in discipleship?
2. How might a person living with anorexia hear a challenge to give Jesus control?
3. How might a commitment to following Jesus affect the "increased tension" and "feelings of shame" parts of the binge-purge cycle?
4. Based on what you've learned in this chapter, review the way you're using food in your youth ministry programming. What changes might you want to make?
5. If you're going to ask teens to make a list of the lies they've believed, it's not a bad idea to do it yourself (first). Make a list of the lies you've believed and find scripture verses that provide the biblical truth.

[1] Hannah Orenstein, "We Just Want to Start a Conversation," *Seventeen* (July 14, 2017), https://www.seventeen.com/celebrity/movies-tv/ a10307840/lily-collins-responds-to-critics-who-say-to-the-bone-glamorizeseating-disorders/

[2] Eugene Beresin and Jennifer Derenne, "Two Psychiatrists Weigh in on Netflix's 'To the Bone': A Missed Opportunity to Understand Anorexia Nervosa," *Psychology Today* (July 21, 2017), https://www.psychologytoday.com/ca/blog/inside-out-outside-in/201707/two-psychiatrists-weigh-in-netflix-s-the-bone

[3] Ibid.

[4] Katie DeVries, "Slow Suicide," *Eating Recovery Center*, published November 29, 2017, https:// www.eatingrecoverycenter.com/blog/november-2017/slow-suicide-katie-jdevries

[5] Cynthia Cruz, "Diagnosis" in *The New Yorker* (February 1, 2010), https://www.newyorker.com/magazine/2010/02/01/diagnosis-10

[6] "Eating Disorders," *Canadian Mental Health Association*, accessed February 10, 2019, https:// www.cmha.ca/mental-health/understanding-mental-illness/eating-disorders

[7] Ibid.

[8] S. M. Findlay, "Dieting in Adolescence," *Canadian Pediatric Society*, accessed January 15, 2019, http://www.cps.ca/documents/position/dieting-adolescence

[9] Ibid.

[10] Carolyn Costin, *The Eating Disorders Sourcebook*, 3rd ed. (New York: McGraw Hill Books, 2007), 30.

[11] Ibid., 32.

[12] Ibid.

[13] Ibid.

[14] Ibid., 6.

[15] Ibid.

[16] Ibid.

[17] Ibid., 8.

[18] "Anorexia Nervosa," *Mayo Foundation for Medical Education and Research*, accessed March 30, 2019, https://www.mayoclinic.org/diseases-conditions/anorexianervosa/symptoms-causes/syc-20353591

[19] "Parent Toolkit," *National Eating Disorders Association* (2018), accessed March 31, 2019, https://www.nationaleatingdisorders.org/parent-toolkit

[20] Costin, 10.

[21] "Clinical Definitions," *National Eating Disorder Information Center* (2014), accessed March 31, 2019, http://nedic.ca/node/806#Bulimia Nervosa

[22] "Magnolia Creek: How to Stop the Binge-Purge Cycle of Bulimia Nervosa," *Eating Disorder Referral and Information Center* (2017), accessed March 31, 2019, https://www.edreferral.com/blog/magnolia-creek-how-to-stop-the-bingepurge-cycle-of-bulimia-nervosa-551

23   Costin, 12–13.

24   Jonathan Lacocque (ed), Binge Eating, *WebMD,* accessed January 6, 2019, http://www. coatofarmspost.com/portfolio/webmd-binge-eating/

25   Ibid.

26   Costin, 14–15.

27   Ibid., 15.

28   Gordon T. Smith, *The Voice of Jesus: Discernment, Prayer and the Witness of the Spirit* (InterVarsity Press: Downers Grove, IL, 2003), 110.

CHAPTER 8
The Monster under My Skin:
Pursuing Wellness despite Depression

Because of the Lord's great love
we are not consumed,
for his compassions never fail.
They are new every morning;
great is your faithfulness.
—Lamentations 3:22–25

In the early hours of the morning, he is with me. Although I can't see him, I feel the weight of his presence on my chest, and I find it difficult to breath. The "black dog" comes and goes as he pleases, letting himself in and making himself known.[1] He is depression, and he is my constant companion.

Lying in my bed, I force myself to sit and, after a few breaths, to stand. And then it begins. "You're weak. You're pathetic. You should just kill yourself and be done with it. No one would even know you were gone. Your life means nothing. You've accomplished nothing. You are nothing." The familiar voices greet me with the rising of the sun, and yet, as I wash my face, another quiet voice whispers in my ear: "This is the day the Lord has made; rejoice and be glad in it." I smile for a moment at the contrast. And so, my day of ministry begins.

But the black dog has a rival. *The Hound of Heaven* is a poem written by Francis Thompson in 1859. Thompson came from a wealthy family and, under parental duress, was set to become a physician, like his father.[2] He failed the medical exam three times and finally ran off to London.

Developing an opium addiction, he lived in extreme poverty and sickness till, in despair and sadness, he decided to end his life. A woman in the sex trade rescued him, inviting him to stay with her, and eventually a Franciscan community helped him overcome his addiction and restored him to health. His poem speaks of a God who chased Thompson throughout his life, even as the young man ran recklessly in the other direction. Although it is difficult to read, it is worth finding the poem online.

The sadness of the ancient Psalmist provides for you and for the teens in your life words to lament and to cry: "My God, my God, why have you forsaken me? Why are you so far from saving me, so far from the cries of my anguish?" (Psalm 22:1).

These words are familiar to any follower of Jesus who lives with the black dog. This canine companion has been living with me now for fifteen years, and although most days are not as dark as what I describe in the opening paragraph, there are days when going through the motions of daily living requires a great deal of effort. I am an avid dog lover, and yet I have little appreciation for a dog who tears my house apart, ignores my commands, and injures me at will. The black dog cannot be house-trained or taught to fetch or play nice, but I have learned that occasionally I can diminish his power if I refuse to feed him. Like the two wolves battling for your mind, the one you feed is the one that gets stronger. *The Hound of Heaven* is the Spirit of Jesus, chasing you and calling you to himself. As you respond in faith, daily submitting your life to Jesus, his Spirit becomes like a seeing-eye dog walking close by your side, gently nudging you with subtle cues, steering you away from danger, always being your friend, always paying attention, and always seeing what you cannot see.

How interesting that the Psalmist goes on to write, "But you, Lord, do not be far from me. You are my strength; come quickly to help me. Deliver me from the sword, my precious life from the *power of the dogs*" (Psalm 22:19–20) [emphasis mine].

It's not likely the Psalmist was thinking about the black dog, but that needn't stop you from writing in the margin of your Bible, "Jesus delivers us from the power of the black dog," as a reminder that depression will *not* have the last word.

In John's Revelation, he sees a new heaven and earth and the New

Jerusalem coming down out of heaven. John hears a voice say, "Look! God's dwelling place is now among the people, and he will dwell with them" (Revelation 21:3). John then describes what life will be like when God's dwelling place is among the people: "He will wipe every tear from their eyes. There will be no more death or mourning or crying or pain, for the old order of things has passed away" (Revelation 21:4).

The black dog dies in the end.

A Growing Problem

According to the World Health Organization, more than 300 million people in the world suffer from depression.[3] If this disease has never touched your life personally, you might find it shocking to read that "depression is the leading cause of disability worldwide and is a major contributor to the overall global burden of disease."[4] According to the National Institute of Mental Health (NIMH), in 2017 an estimated 3.2 million adolescents, aged twelve to seventeen, in the United States had had at least one major depressive episode. This number represented 13.3 percent of the U.S. population aged twelve to seventeen.[5] The 2012 Canadian Community Health Survey: Mental Health of just over four thousand respondents, found that people aged fifteen to twenty-four had the highest rates of mood and anxiety disorders of all age groups.[6] About 7 percent of them were identified as having had depression in the past twelve months, compared with 5 percent of people aged twenty-five to sixty-four and 2 percent of those aged sixty-five or older. The research did not include indigenous reserves or incarcerated teens, which means that 7 percent is a low estimate. These numbers tell us that well over 3 million fifteen- to twenty-four-year-olds in Canada are living with a mood or anxiety disorder—and that number does not include teens ages thirteen and fourteen.

Referred to as a "mood disorder," depression has been associated with things like suicide, self-injury, trauma, disease, mental illness, insomnia, disordered eating, violence, abortion, sexual assault, and diet. It's something we'll look at more closely later in this chapter. Research completed in the US found that mood disorders among teens are on the rise, with teen girls twice as likely to experience a major depressive disorder.[7] According to the 2017 Canadian Kids Help Phone Impact Report, depression and anxiety are two of the primary reasons that teens call for help.[8]

Tears on the Field

Major depressive disorder, also called clinical depression, is a common but serious mood disorder. The disease affects how you think, feel, work, sleep, eat, and engage with people—the black dog leaves nothing untouched. It is difficult to describe, even when the dog is sitting on your chest.

Depression comes and goes in episodes, with no warning. Episodes can last for weeks, months, or years, with stretches during which there are no symptoms at all.[9] An episode of major depression could be triggered by seasons of the year, as in the case of seasonal affective disorder, or childbirth, as in postpartum depression. For teens, depression can be situational, triggered by the loss of a friendship, getting kicked off a sports team, failure to pass an important exam, graduating high school, a breakup, moving to a new city, getting arrested, or parental divorce. Depression could be the result of sexting, sexual activity that goes beyond a teen's comfort level, a struggle with gender identity or same-sex attraction, addiction, or loss.

I still remember the final football game during the time I was chaplain for a high school team in Sioux Falls. I spent the year with the young athletes, but I did not expect the level of grief I would see at the season's final game. A few of the seniors sat on the field crying, grieving the fact that their football careers had come to an end. There was no need for this sadness to become major depression. But for some of those athletes the loss would bring on a depression that led to increased alcohol consumption, fixation on the past, and an inability to move on with life.

Dark Emptiness

Major depression is more than just a sad day. Teens living with depression will have multiple experiences of the things on this list—*every day*. Read the list slowly, and ask yourself, "How would I help a teen follow Jesus if this was their minute-by-minute reality, every single day?"

- Persistent sad, anxious, or empty mood
- Feelings of hopelessness, pessimism, and irritability
- Feelings of guilt, worthlessness, or helplessness
- Loss of interest or pleasure in hobbies and activities
- Decreased energy or fatigue; appetite and/or weight changes
- Difficulty concentrating, remembering, or making decisions
- Difficulty sleeping, early-morning awakening, or oversleeping
- Thoughts of death or suicide, or suicide attempts
- Headaches and/or digestive problems, with no clear cause[10]

In her 2013 article on depression, 16-year-old Elise Jamison expressed some of her frustration regarding the way other teens used the word "depressed."[11] She wrote the following:

> There is a humongous difference between temporary sadness and dissatisfaction with your life and the sinking desperation that is depression. It sucks when you don't fit in and you're lonely, but that isn't depression. Depression is the dark emptiness you feel that makes you believe you can contribute nothing to anyone or anything. You feel like your life means nothing to anyone."

Elise goes on to write of her personal struggle:

> I was diagnosed at age fourteen with depression, and I am so frustrated with all of the people around me who cannot differentiate between angst, PMS, and mental illness. I have worked so hard in the last couple years to overcome this illness, and it's still a daily battle. It took me years to even be able to acknowledge that I mattered and realize that people cared about me. There is nothing more frustrating than someone who says they are clinically depressed because they are feeling sad that day. It devalues the struggle that I and so many others have endured.

Elise wisely differentiates feelings of sadness with the "sinking desperation that is depression"; her point is well taken. In youth ministry we might disregard the intensity of a teen's depression by using the word as a synonym for sadness or disappointment. How do you use the word *depressed*? Does your use of the word in daily conversation diminish the painful, life-altering reality that you see in the list above?

Poetry provides a window into the soul. Listen to the way Katie Q. McKee, a teen poet living with depression, expresses her feelings in this piece of her poem titled "The Monster Called Depression."

> On the outside, I'm holding it together,
> But it's as unpredictable as the weather.
> "How are you?" "I'm fine."
> But the truth lies between the lines.[12]

Katie ends her poem with these words:

> Monsters don't live under our beds.
> They scream inside of our heads.
> Still, I live with the hope that one day I will win.
> I will defeat the monster that's under my skin.

In the Dust

The Bible is full of sadness, full of people in desperate circumstances crying out to God, asking, "Where are you?" "What's happening?" "Why does my life have to hurt so much?"

In her poem, Katie grapples with the monster under her skin, consuming her mind. She puts words to common feelings when she writes, "I live with the hope that one day I will win." Her words are a reminder that teens living in the darkness of depression need a seeing-eye dog to lead them in the darkness. As a youth worker, you will at times play that role, but you will quickly discover that you can't be *all* that teens may need. The Psalmist speaks of the Word of God as a light for your life when he writes, "Your word is a lamp for my feet, a light on my path" (Psalm 119:105). John writes of the hope we have in Jesus, the Light of the World: "In him was life, and that life was the light of all mankind. The light shines in the darkness, and the darkness has not overcome it (John 1:4–5). Depression is the darkness beneath, but Jesus is the light that shines, even in the darkness.

Lamentation first appears in Genesis 50:10, as Joseph mourns the passing of his father, Jacob. Here the word has the meaning of beating the chest in sorrow. In 2 Samuel 1:17, David laments the death of Saul, but here the Hebrew word refers to musical composition, like a ballad. The biblical idea of lamentation can include grieving, mourning, wailing, weeping, sorrow, crying, groaning, and more. It is an expressive idea, and there seems to be no guilt associated with anger directed towards God. In Jeremiah, Judah also *mourns*, but the word refers to clothing worn by those grieving and to the dust and dirt gathered from rolling on the ground.[13]

Approximately one-third of the 150 Psalms are classified as Psalms of Lament, and the sorrow you find in these pages can be a gift to those no longer able to find words to convey the depth of their despair. Consider the words of Psalms 44 and 142:

> Awake, Lord! Why do you sleep?
> Rouse yourself! Do not reject us forever.
> Why do you hide your face
> and forget our misery and oppression?
> We are brought down to the dust;
> our bodies cling to the ground.
> Rise up and help us;
> rescue us because of your unfailing love (Psalm 44:23–26).

> When my spirit grows faint within me,
> it is you who watch over my way.
> In the path where I walk,
> people have hidden a snare for me.
> Look and see, there is no one on my right hand;
> no one is concerned for me.
> I have no refuge;
> no one cares for my life (Psalm 142:3–4).

Rather than tell a teen that it is inappropriate to be angry at God or imply that they need to choose joy over sorrow, you might instead sit together and ponder the words of these Psalms or turn to the words found in Job 3. When teens see these texts about lament in the Bible, they are often surprised. In reading these biblical words, they are empowered to speak their own honest words to God in prayer. Listen as Job describes his feelings about his birthday:

> May the day of my birth perish,
> and the night that said, "A boy is conceived!"
> That day—may it turn to darkness;
> may God above not care about it;
> may no light shine on it.
> May gloom and utter darkness claim it once more;
> may a cloud settle over it;
> may blackness overwhelm it (Job 3:3–5).

Job's words are dark and dripping with self-loathing. How surprising that these words come from the Bible! Have you ever asked teens to write their feelings in lament? If these words from Job were written by a teen in your youth group, how would you respond? What are some ways you might help a teen transition from lament to hope?

The Way of Wellness

My wife, Heather, and I recently went to a Nordic spa. I had no idea what to expect, but the experience began as we slipped into our bathing suits and selected one of the comfortable bathrobes. It was winter, so the outdoor hot pools were bordered by snow and ice.

We soaked in the outdoor pools, sat in the fragrant steam rooms, and listened to pan flutes while sipping water filled with fresh fruit. We sat near a fireplace, wrapped in warm blankets and holding our warm herbal tea. To complete our experience, we sauntered into the restaurant, still in our robes, to end our relaxing time with a healthy plant-based meal. It was a healing experience.

After we left the spa, depression remained a part of my life, but the black dog was nowhere to be seen.

In youth ministry, you may not be able to take depression away from a teen, but perhaps you can find a Nordic spa—a place a teen can remember what it is like to feel joy, to feel connected to another person, and to feel the stress slip away.

I no longer look for ways to fight my depression. Instead, like my day at the spa, I look for ways to *increase my wellness*. The ministry and programming of the youth group can provide a wonderful resource for increasing wellness. It is not likely that your ministry will cover your expenses for weekly spa treatments, but you could think of your weekly discipleship as a part of a wellness strategy for teens living with depression. Remaining connected to a community is challenging for those who are sad and eager to be alone, but for most teens, friendships are the Nordic spa they crave.

Sharing the Snow

The Psalms of Lament have given the people of God a common language to express despair and hopelessness in the context of faithful worship. Psalm 22 might begin with "My God, my God, why have you forsaken me?" But as the Psalm concludes, the tone changes: "You who fear the Lord, praise him!" (22:23a, 24). "For He has not despised or scorned the suffering of the afflicted one" (22:23a, 24a).

For thousands of years the people of God have prayed these words in worship together, experiencing both the pain of apparent abandonment as well as the joy of the mercy, love, and goodness of God—all in the same Psalm! Hearing these words in the community of faith, you will find the strength to face the enemies from within and those that threaten from without.

Sometimes you read just the right book, at just the right time, and it connects with you and your situation. Around the time that I first started using the word *depression* to describe my own condition, I came across a wonderful book by Sue Monk Kidd, titled, *When the Heart Waits*. Writing about people's need for community, she reflects on a story told by Elie Wiesel of his time in a Nazi concentration camp.[14] The situation was dire, and the prisoners had gone without food for three days. They were forced to stand in a line in the cold and freshly fallen snow, not permitted to move while waiting for a train that would take them deeper into Germany. They had been standing all day, their legs cramped, their throats parched. Wiesel writes this:

> Finally, their thirst intolerable, one man suggested that they eat the snow; but they weren't allowed by the guards to bend over. The person in front of that man agreed to let him eat the snow that had accumulated on the back of his shoulders. That act spread through the line until there, in a frozen field, what had been individuals struggling with their separate pain became a community sharing their suffering together.

The author's conclusion is something I've come back to over and over again, as I have thought about the Church as a place where some find grace while others experience judgment and cruelty. This is what Monk Kidd wrote:

> The waiting heart arrives at the truth of compassion: that we'll survive as a human family only as we're willing, one by one, to become the place of nourishment for our brother and sister. We'll survive as we cease being individuals struggling alone with our pain and become instead a community sharing our suffering in a great and holy act of compassion.[15]

In your role as a youth worker, your teaching of biblical truth will always be more effective if the teens in your care know that you are not just their teacher but also someone who is willing to share in their suffering, and their humanity, as a holy act of compassion. How can you help teens follow Jesus, together? What examples of shared struggling have you seen in youth culture? I've suggested here that instead of *fighting* depression, you increase practices that support *wellness*. Can you think of ways you might help a teen accomplish this?

The Walking Wounded

I wish that people with major depression would agree to wear T-shirts, with MD on the front! It might make caregiving a little easier. The truth is, we do not always know the hard road a teen is walking until we take the time to hear his or her story. A teen might appear happy, even the "life of the party" at youth events, while carefully guarding a secret sadness.

I knew a teen just like this. Brock was a goof-off. He had memorized the words to several popular movies and enjoyed randomly reciting lines, whenever he thought it might get a laugh. He would dance around the room during snack time, visit small groups when he was supposed to be at his own, and sing in a high-pitched voice that drove the leaders crazy. Brock authentically seemed to love life.

One night, as we sat in a coffee shop together, he began to talk. His wealthy, successful parents were prominent members of our congregation and public figures in our community. But all was not as it seemed; his perfect family was falling apart. His mother's affair had infuriated his father, and the two had been fighting for months. His mom and dad did not think he knew what was going on, but the bedroom walls in their home were not thick enough to block the sound of the fighting. He knew the divorce was coming, and his anxiety overwhelmed him. Most nights he cried himself to sleep. Carrying the weight of the family secret was like dragging a steel ball.

Like so much of the pain that teens endure, his hard road was not of his own making. It was also not a road he could avoid. Looking from his dark cloud, he felt stuck in his family, stuck in his pain, stuck in inevitable shame, and stuck in a depression that neither of his parents had any energy for or interest in addressing. He was one of the walking wounded. His pain was invisible to anyone who did not want to see. He desperately needed help.

In chapter 3, I wrote about discipleship triage. There is *Critical Care*, for concerns that could result in death; there is *Crisis Care*, for problems that are severe; there is *Compassion Care*, for persistent, non-crisis pain; and there is *Companion Care*, for teens discipling friends. Your response will depend upon the type, duration, and intensity of the depression.

Perhaps I have not stressed it enough in this book, but one of the primary roles of the youth worker is to encourage teens in pain to understand and access available resources. A medical doctor can make an assessment, offer medication, and refer the teen to other assistance, such as a mental-health worker. Blood tests might reveal things like iron deficiency which, once corrected with supplements, could make a world of difference regarding mood. A school guidance counsellor, a coach, or a therapist are all excellent resources that you can encourage the teen to access.

Discipling a teen through pain doesn't mean that you are always talking about Jesus. Most of the time discipleship conversations begin with real-life situations, just as they did with Jesus. From a teen's expressed needs, a wise youth worker will do his or her best to lead the conversation to the presence of *The Hound of Heaven*, whose love is relentless.

The Devil in the Pasta

It is not uncommon for Christians to pray about depression, either for themselves or for those they love. In 1 Thessalonians 5:17, Paul encourages the Church to "pray without ceasing" and in Philippians 4:6 he writes, "Do not be anxious about anything, but in every situation, by prayer and petition, with thanksgiving, present your requests to God."

In the past twenty years I have heard my share of Christians praying about depression. Some pray for deliverance from demonic oppression; others pray for healing, or peace; while others agonize, in lament. You might find this odd, but there are times when prayer might not be the best answer.

Two years ago I discovered that I could manage my depression with my diet. In conversation with a professional nutritionist, I found that my consumption of dairy and gluten were making my depression worse. Although prayer was an important part of my journey, reducing my sugar intake, eating less bread and pasta, and discontinuing my use of dairy products has made a remarkable difference. I've also increased my vitamin D, B12, and probiotics, and I now exercise daily. This mix of supplements and exercise has dramatically increased my overall sense of wellness. In other words, it was not demonic oppression or lack of faith that was at the heart of my depression—it was my food and activity level.

In an article titled "Nutritional Medicine as Mainstream in Psychiatry," the authors state that "evidence is steadily growing for the relation between dietary quality (and potential nutritional deficiencies) and mental health."[16] They go on to make some striking statements about the relationship between teen depression and food. "In view of the early age of onset for depression and anxiety, these data suggest that diet is a key modifiable intervention target for prevention of the initial incidence of common mental disorders."[17] Translation: What we eat makes a difference in how we feel.

As a youth worker, you may have noticed some troubling things about teen diets. Tom Warshawski, chair of the Vancouver-based Obesity Foundation, believes that almost everyone is eating unhealthy levels of sugar.[18] According to data from the most recent Canadian Community Health Survey, kids consume 33 teaspoons of sugar a day, far above the World Health Organization's recommendation that sugars ideally make up 5 percent of a person's daily calories. The health consequences are serious, including an increased likelihood of everything from high blood pressure to heart disease, Type 2 diabetes, and depression."[19]

When it comes to teen health, be the kind of youth worker who values holistic wellness, not just spiritual growth. Go ahead and pray against the power of the black dog, but when the prayer meeting is over, make sure the kids you love are sitting down to a table spread with veggie sticks, hummus, and non-sugared drinks. That way you will not be feeding the pain that you just asked God to take away.

A Downcast Soul

Another young man I know just took his life. I spoke with his mom on the phone as she stood rock solid in the Intensive Care Unit, near the bed where his body was trapped in a coma. She spoke with hope-filled words, confident that God would rescue her son. The young man had recently been to our retreat center, enjoying a weekend with his dad. But when he got home, the black dog had met him at the door, situations had overwhelmed his capacity to respond with wisdom, and he had tried to kill himself. With his brain starved of oxygen, he'd slipped into a coma, and within a few days, the precious sixteen-year-old follower of Jesus had died.

In Lamentations, Jeremiah is overwhelmed by sorrow at the devastation of Jerusalem. Lamentations is full of mourning over the loss, as Jeremiah remembers the pain of the past. "I remember my affliction and my wandering, the bitterness and the gall. I well remember them, and my soul is downcast within me" (Lamentations 3:19–20). It would make perfectly good sense to stop right there. Life is full of pain, things have not gone my way, my enemies have conquered me, and there is no hope.

When parents lose a teen to suicide, the feelings are the same. Life is over. God has let them down. What's the point in living? But the child of God, in the midst of despair, is still able to say, with tears streaming down their cheeks, "This I call to mind, and therefore I have hope: Because of the Lord's great love we are not consumed, for his compassions never fail. They are new every morning; great is your faithfulness" (Lamentations 3:22–23).

Teens walk the hard road in the way of sadness and despair, trauma and abuse, loss and addiction—and yet, there is another road called hope, a road that Jesus walked with a cross, to demonstrate that God's faithfulness cannot be crucified. God's love cannot be murdered; it cannot be snuffed out by violence; it cannot be conquered by darkness. Even in the sorrow, even when the weight of life is suffocating, God remains faithful. This is the heart of our message as we sit with teens in the coffee shops, stand at the basketball games, chat in the malls, and walk the halls of the high schools.

God is faithful in your darkness. God is faithful in your feelings of hopelessness. God is faithful in Jesus, and this God will always be with you.

Ideas for Discussion and Reflection

1. How do you use the word "depressed"? Does your use of the word in daily conversation diminish the painful, life-altering reality seen in the list above?
2. What are some ways you might help a teen transition from lament to hope?
3. How can you help teens follow Jesus within community?
4. What examples of shared struggling have you seen in youth culture?
5. Instead of fighting depression, I've suggested that you encourage teens to increase wellness practices. Can you think of ways you might help a teen do this? What spiritual practices might you encourage them to integrate into their wellness plan?

1   Matthew Johnstone, "I Had a Black Dog": Video (1997), *World Health Organization,* posted October 2, 2012, https://www.youtube.com/watch?v=XiCrniLQGYc

2   Francis Thompson, "The Hound of Heaven," *Amazing Discoveries,* Winter 2016, posted April 4, 2016, https://amazingdiscoveries.org/the-hound-of-heaven

3   "Depression: Key Facts," *World Health Organization,* last modified March 22, 2018, https://www.who.int/en/news-room/fact-sheets/detail/depression

4   Ibid.

5   "Major Depression," *National Institute of Mental Health,* last modified February 2019, https://www.nimh.nih.gov/health/statistics/ major-depression.shtml

6   "Perceived Need for Mental Health Care in Canada: Results from the 2012 Canada Community Health Survey/Mental Health," *StatsCan,* last modified November 27, 2015, https://www150.statcan.gc.ca/n1/pub/82-003-x/2013009/article/11863-eng.htm

7   Kathleen Ries Merikangas, "Lifetime Prevalence of Mental Disorders in US Adolescents" in the *Journal of the American Academy of Child and Adolescent Psychiatry,* October 2010, Vol. 49, Issue 10, pgs. 980–989, https://www.ncbi.nlm.nih.gov/pmc/articles/PMC2946114/

8   "It Starts with Me: 2017 Kids Help Phone Impact Report," *Kids Help Phone,* accessed January 18, 2019, https://apps.kidshelpphone.ca/ImpactReport/en

9   J. Raymond DePaulo Jr. and Leslie Alan Horvitz, *Understanding Depression: What We Know and What You Can Do About It* (New York: John Wiley & Sons, 2002): 10.

10 "Depression," *National Institute of Mental Health,* last modified February 2018, https://www.nimh.nih.gov/health/topics/depression/index.shtml

11 Elise Jamison, "This is What Depression Really Feels Like," *HuffPost,* last modified March 2, 2014, http://www.huffingtonpost.com/elise-jamison/teen-depression b 4518746.html

12 Katie Q. McKee, "The Monster Called Depression," *Family Friend Poems,* accessed April 10, 2019, https://www.familyfriendpoems.com/poem/the-monster-14

13 J. E. Hartley, "Lament; Lamentation" in *The International Standard Bible Encyclopedia* Vol. 3, G. W. Bromiley, ed. (Grand Rapids: Wm. B. Eerdmans Publishing, 1986): 64.

14 Sue Monk Kidd, *When the Heart Waits: Spiritual Direction for Life's Sacred Questions* (New York: HarperSanFrancisco, 1990): 203.

15 Ibid.

16 Jerome Sarris, "Nutritional medicine as mainstream in psychiatry," *Lancet Psychiatry* (2015), 2:271–74, posted January 26, 2015, http://dx.doi.org/10.1016/S2215-0366(14)00051-0

17 Ibid.

18 Dave McGinn, "Canadian children consuming 5 times more sugar," *The Globe and Mail,* posted June 5, 2017, https://www.theglobeandmail.com/life/health-and-fitness/ health/canadian-children-are-consuming-five-times-more-sugar-than-they-should/ article35207835/

19 Ibid.

CHAPTER 9
Life Where You Least Expect It:
Speaking Peace in Violence

We all have a choice. We can give in and surrender,
or we can fight and move forward ... Don't surrender.
Move forward because you never know what
you'll be able to do with it, you never know
the lives you'll be able to touch.[1]
—Elizabeth Smart

The Rwandan genocide was a massacre, the slaughter of over eight hundred thousand people in one hundred days. In 1994, Theoneste Bagosora, a retired colonel and chief of staff in Rwanda's defence ministry, gave the order for the Hutu ethnic majority to take up arms and exterminate the country's minority population, an ethnic group called the Tutsis.[2]

That year, two million displaced Rwandan Tutsis crossed the border, fleeing into what was then Zaire but is now called the Democratic Republic of Congo. Rwandan militia would follow the Tutsis into Zaire, and fighting would spread across the country. Many followers of Jesus found themselves in grave danger, as they spoke publicly against the violence and cared for the needs of the refugees.

In 1997, a Presbyterian pastor in the Democratic Republic of Congo stood in his pulpit and opened the scriptures to his congregation. Immediately following the worship service, a high-ranking official in the military told the pastor that his life was in danger and that members of the militia were planning to attack his church and kill him and his family—that afternoon. Somehow, that very day, the pastor and his two teen children were put on a plane, and eventually they found themselves in the US. His wife, who was home with their two younger children, was also rescued, but for some reason, she and the children were put on a flight to Italy.

One Sunday, following our worship service, I was walking to my office in our church in Sioux Falls when I noticed a tall, dark man standing in the foyer. I asked him if I could help, and he said, "I am here to claim asylum in the United States." It was the Presbyterian pastor from Zaire. I had no idea what he was talking about, but we quickly found people in our church who could help. That afternoon, I began a relationship with his teenagers, and our community of faith became their family. It was a difficult two-year journey before husband, wife, and children were joyfully reunited.

I do not recall taking a class in my youth ministry training that addressed the issues related to discipling teens from war-torn countries. As a matter of fact, you would be hard-pressed to find even a single chapter written on the topic, and yet one 2018 estimate suggests that over 357 million children live in war zones.[3] Millions have been displaced, and hundreds of thousands have been killed or injured. Many have carried weapons and engaged in murderous acts themselves. You will encounter these children and teens as you travel the world, but you might also encounter them when they arrive at your church, traumatized and desperate for help.

In this chapter, you and I will take some time to think about discipling teens through the pain associated with violence. In addition to thinking about issues related to immigration, you will also have a chance to think about discipling teens who have experienced abuse and those who have been bullied.

Culture Clash

Teens commonly begin to pull away from the family as they enter adolescence, placing a greater value on the peer group. A growing need for independence and privacy can create tension for the family, as teens begin to develop a life separate (and sometimes secretive) from their parents. Parents noticing this new emphasis on the peer group may experience pester power from a teen attempting to get permission to engage in activities or behaviors that make the adult uncomfortable.

On occasion, an exasperated parent may respond, "I don't care what your friend is doing! If your friend were going to jump off a bridge, would you do it too?" The teen's response varies from understanding and compliance to the eye-rolling and groaning. Resistance could also include arguing, anger, defiance, and the slamming of bedroom doors.

I once had a conversation with a junior-high girl who began by expressing, "My bedroom door is gone, again." I had no idea what she was talking about, so I asked her to explain. "My dad told me that if I kept slamming my door, he was going to take it and put it in the basement. I broke part of the wall. So I don't have a door anymore. Again."

Adolescent newcomers will undergo the same identity formation and changes in physical and emotional maturity as other teens, and yet the newcomer will experience stress associated with a dual source of identity. They will take cues for things like clothing, behavior, and relationships from the culturally diverse peer group instead of the family.[4] This creates a clash of cultures, and according to the research conducted by Anisef and Kilbride, it is only one of the stressors for newcomer teens. Other stress points include issues related to language, school (including lack of recognition of prior learning), conflicts in norms and values between the peer group and the home, and cultural gender differences.

This tension between the peer group and the family, combined with the cultural gender differences, resulted in violence in Toronto on December 7, 2010, when Muhammed Parvez strangled his daughter to death. The father was angry that the youngest of his four daughters, sixteen-year-old Aqsa Parvez, refused to wear the hijab, dressed in clothing more closely associated with her friends, and ran away in defiance of his rules.[5]

The tragic story of tragedy due to stress highlights the importance of providing resources for all of the members in the newcomer family. If you were coaching Aqsa's soccer team and heard her talking about the tension at home, what kind of support might you offer? This is a more complicated discipleship question, because leading her to faith in Jesus might also put her in danger. What challenges might you face if you had the opportunity to help a teen like Aqsa as she settled in to your community?

Reimagining Youth Ministry

In the United States, political and social tension regarding immigration is intense, and yet the number of foreign-born people living in the United States has more than quadrupled since 1965; it is expected to reach 78 million by 2065. Where once newcomers to the States were predominantly of European origin, most immigrants now come from places like Mexico, China, India, the Philippines, El Salvador, Cuba, the Dominican Republic, and South Korea.[6] In 2016, over half a million temporary residents and over a quarter million permanent residents arrived in Canada.[7] The critical point for you in youth ministry is to recognize the ministry opportunities associated with immigration, noting the high percentage of children and teens who land in Canada and in the States with little to no support.

As you think about youth ministry and discipleship, it would be good to consider people immigrating or escaping conflict zones and how their presence in your community will continue to give shape to the cultural, religious, and sociological landscape. As the ethnic diversity of your neighborhood changes, your understanding of youth ministry and mission may also need to be reimagined. Santes Beatty writes this:

> Multiethnicity must no longer be something reserved for inner city ministries or global missions—or seen as optional, as long as it doesn't cost us too much relationally and financially. Instead, churches can embrace a multiethnic reality no matter the geographical or cultural context, grounded in the scriptural call to make disciples of all nations.[8]

As the peoples of the world come to your town, so the issues of the world become local ones. I found this out when two teens right out of a conflict zone landed in our youth ministry. Now their war became *my* war. It was no longer a war that had nothing to do with me, something I could ignore. I was affected by the violence as I listened to their stories and walked with them through the pain of losing their closest friends, the anxiety of not knowing whether other friends and relatives were dead or alive, the experience of trauma, and the sadness of missing their mom and siblings.

This situation can be a tough reminder that you are no longer able to insulate yourself from the effects of famine, genocide, and war simply by staying home. In your church, camp ministry, or drop-in you might have children and teens who have faced atrocities beyond your imagination. How will your discipleship efforts need to adjust to build relationships with people from culturally diverse backgrounds? How will you build relationships with teens when there are language barriers, family suspicions regarding your intentions, and stress due to cultural transitions? How will you heal from secondary trauma as you hear stories of atrocity and violation beyond your imagination?

As Jesus demonstrated, the most effective disciple-making efforts always flow from ability to respond to human need. Your calling in youth ministry is to notice the need and to respond as Jesus would. John, the brother of Jesus, once wrote, "This is how we know that we are in him: Whoever claims to live in him must live as Jesus did" (1 John 2:5–6). Unfortunately, when you come face to face with the complications and pain associated with war and violence, responding as Jesus would might just be the most difficult youth ministry challenge you ever encounter.

Play Fighting

"Can I tell you something?" she said, nervously shifting from one foot to the other and chewing on her bottom lip. We were standing in a gymnasium, and it was the final day of our mission trip. Teens were milling around and getting ready for bed. The last thing I wanted to do was have a conversation with Leah.

On the final day of our inner-city mission trip, the agency we were serving with took us up on a hillside overlooking the city. We had a cookout and watched as the city lights chased away the shadows of nightfall. As the team was preparing our supper, I was invited to hang out with several leaders and a group of teens who were eager to explore our surroundings. After a week of serving together cutting lawns, building fences, and serving in soup kitchens, we felt relaxed with each other. It was a perfect way to end our time together—until Leah began to shove me playfully. "Wanna fight?" she challenged.

As a youth pastor, I have had my share of playful "beatings" from teens, but this was out of the ordinary. Without warning, she jumped in front of me, took a martial arts stance, and punched me in the face. She broke the only pair of glasses I had with me and split my lip open.

The entire group stood frozen, except for Leah. "She just punched the pastor," one girl observed. Leah giggled like a little girl, said something like, "Oops, sorry!" and actually skipped off to look at something of interest in the forest.

"Can I tell you something?"

I wanted to tell her to go away. I wanted to say, "Unless you're going to tell me that you know you're completely insane, then no—go away." But I knew what was coming (and likely you would, as well). I called over one of the women serving with our team, and together we sat down to talk.

As the story slowly unfolded, Leah's face clouded over. The female leader held her hand, helping her to say what needed to be said. Leah's voice was calm. There was no expression, no emotion. She could have been reading a recipe from a cookbook. It was just a story about violence that happened to be about her.

She paused several times as she told us her story while looking off into the distance. When she was done, we saw the emotion in her eyes for the first time. She was terrified, and we could tell she was uncomfortable with what she has just told us.

"I shouldn't be telling you this," she admitted. "Do you believe me? Maybe this was my fault. Sometimes I do things that make him mad." There was panic now in her voice. The woman sitting with us happened to be a professional therapist—a good pick for a volunteer youth leader—and she knew exactly what to do. This woman, compassionate and sensitive and one of the best listeners I have ever known, engaged Leah with empathy, reflected back what she was hearing, and looked deeply into Leah's eyes, saying the one thing every abuse survivor needs to hear: "This is not your fault."

Leah finally broke down and began to sob into the volunteer's shoulder. She apologized over and over for hitting me, and together we sat in the sorrow, aware that we were only at the beginning of the difficult journey with a teen traumatized by abuse.

Teens under Pressure

The experience in the gymnasium with Leah is called an *initial disclosure*, which is a term describing the very first time a person musters the courage to tell someone about their abuse. This is a critical conversation for the survivor, and the way a youth worker responds is important.

Although definitions of abuse vary, it is generally understood as taking place when an adult intentionally harms a child or teen. As an example of a variation, note the differences in the legal description of abuse in Texas, as opposed to North Dakota.

In Texas, this is how abuse is defined:

> Inflicting or failing to reasonably prevent others from inflicting mental or emotional injury, impairing the child's growth, development, or psychological functioning; physical injury resulting in substantial harm, or which is at variance with the explanation given; sexual abuse, exploitation, use of a controlled substance resulting in mental or physical harm to the child.[9]

In North Dakota abuse is described thus:

> Suffering from serious physical harm or traumatic abuse caused other than by accidental means, including sexual abuse, assault, exploitation, corruption, or solicitation.[10]

If at any time you suspect a child or teen is experiencing abuse, your legal obligation is to contact child protective services. I will have more to say about this later in the chapter.

Your response when a teen shares a story of abuse can be a determining factor in how the abuse affects her life and how she will engage with you and Jesus as she begins to face the pain on a whole new level. Writing about the response of parents to a disclosure of sexual abuse, Lynn Heitritter and Jeanette Vought state the following:

> More than any other variable, the reaction of the parents (or others who are important to the child) can have the greatest impact. Experts agree that this is the single most important factor in preventing the abuse from becoming a life-destroying event.[11]

Adult reactions can range from positive and supportive to blaming the teenager for somehow instigating the sexual or physical violence— sometimes even making excuses for the perpetrator. "He's been under a lot of stress lately." Adults might try to protect the aggressor to save a reputation or suggest that the teenager "forgive and forget."

I have also heard adults threaten teens into silence by telling them that child protective services will remove them and their siblings from the home if a report is made about abuse. This puts pressure on the teen, forcing him to choose between enduring the ongoing abuse or facing separation from everything familiar, including his bedroom, family, friends, siblings, and school, since child protection involvement could result in relocation to a new home in a different community. The pressure can be immense. Before taking a closer look at a compassionate and wise response to initial disclosure, I want to point out a few questions that might be on the teen's mind.

Pressing Questions

As soon as Leah finished telling us her story, she had a classic case of fearing she had overshared. Perhaps you have had an experience like this, when you pour out your heart to a friend, but then on your drive home you begin to feel vulnerable or even ashamed of what you said. Teens sharing stories of abuse might have some, or all, of these six questions, on their minds. They wonder,

- Will I betray someone?
- Will someone hate me?

- Will someone blame me?
- Will I be safe?
- What will happen to my family?
- What happens if I don't tell?

When you listen for and respond to these concerns, it will help the teen gain perspective and clarity at a time when he might feel he is in a fog. Reassuring a teen that it is okay to be honest with you is critical, but you must also take great care never to assure a teen that everything will work out fine if they simply tell their story. When it comes to disclosure of physical or sexual abuse, the process can be frightening, painful, and chaotic. Unfortunately, honest disclosure can often lead to greater scrutiny of the situation by strangers, increased danger at the hands of the perpetrator, accusations of dishonesty, and remorse.

Hearing an initial disclosure can also activate strong emotions in you. You might find at the moment that you feel strong and completely focused on the teen and the problem at hand—that you are a rock. After the encounter, however, you could feel a whole host of emotions associated with secondary trauma. Remember, there is a cost to caring. If you are a survivor of sexual or physical abuse, this story could send you spinning emotionally. Even if you have done considerable work in therapy and feel you have dealt with your pain, hearing a story can activate feelings you thought were resolved.

With abuse in my distant past, I felt angry when hearing Leah's story, but not overwhelmed. I found myself feeling out of control the next time I saw her assailant. Strong emotions ran through my body, and I needed to stop to catch my breath. This, too, is an *X* day. Write it in your calendar. Take some time off. Talk to a therapist. Remove the superhero cape, and let yourself feel the strong emotions swirling around inside of you.

When you listen to an initial disclosure, here are some of the things that you as a youth worker might be concerned about:

- The teen's safety
- Your own strong emotions
- Saying the wrong thing and making things worse
- Discerning fact from fiction
- Next steps and legal requirements

There is no better place for a Christian youth worker to be than sitting beside a teen during an initial disclosure. It is not that it is enjoyable; rather, it is a good place to be because the Spirit of Jesus lives in you. Your response in this sacred space will be compassionate and gentle. As you engage in crisis care, your intention will be to help this young person experience the presence of Jesus, even as he or she cries out in agony, "My God, my God. Why have you forsaken me?" (Psalm 22:1).

Sexual Abuse

In both Canada and the US you will discover a variety to laws and definitions for sexual abuse, including provincial legal definitions, federal laws, and child advocacy definitions. In Toronto, the Central Agencies Sexual Abuse Treatment Program provides a comprehensive definition. Though it is long, it is valuable for you as a youth leader to see all that child sexual abuse involves. Here is their definition:

> Child sexual abuse occurs when a person uses his/ her power over a child or youth and involves the child in any sexual act. The power of the abuser can lie in age differences, intellectual or physical development, a relationship of authority over the child, and/or the child's dependency on him/her. "Touching" is not the only way in which a child can be sexually abused. Sexual abuse includes acts such as fondling, genital stimulation, mutual masturbation, oral sex, using fingers, penis, or objects for vaginal/anal penetration, inappropriate sexual language, sexual harassment, voyeurism, exhibitionism, as well as exposing a child to, or involving a child in pornography or prostitution. The offender may engage the child in sexual acts through threats, bribes, force, misrepresentation, and other forms of coercion. Sexual abuse is usually an ongoing pattern of progressively intrusive sexual interactions. Most of the time, the offender is someone well known to the child and trusted by the child and/or family.[12]

The final point in this definition addresses the myth that strangers are the greatest risk to children and teens; in fact, most of the time the perpetrator is someone familiar. To put the risk in perspective, a study published in the *Canadian Medical Association Journal* found that 10 percent of the population, corresponding to roughly 3.6 million Canadians, reported having experienced sexual abuse before they were sixteen years old.[13] In the States, one in four girls and one in six boys will be sexually abused before they reach the age of eighteen.[14]

These statistics are important to youth workers for two reasons. First, as teens grow into young adults, it is quite common for them to begin to express the pain and strong emotions associated with childhood sexual abuse. In youth ministry, you might find yourself discipling teens as they begin to fully comprehend the violation. Second, based on these statistics, you might also find yourself discipling teens through recent sexual abuse.

Slow Hope

It was my first phone call from a parent. I had been a youth ministry intern for a few weeks, and I was having a blast. I had a few years of Bible college under my belt and plenty of zeal, but I was short on experience.

The mother wanted to bring her daughter in to speak with me. The girl was a quiet fourteen-year-old who enjoyed the youth group and had plenty of friends. As we sat in the youth room to talk, the teen never looked up. It appeared that she had been crying. Mom reached over and held her girl's hand and gently began to talk. Recently, Brit had gone to a party. As far as they could tell, someone at the party had slipped a drug into her drink. When she'd woken up sometime in the early morning, she'd realized that she had been raped.

Brit sat on the couch across from me, holding her mom's hand, feeling humiliated, ashamed, and terrified. I knew that I was walking in sacred space. They had been to the hospital, and she had already given a statement to police, though she hadn't had much to say. We cried and prayed and felt the helplessness of violation together. I spoke of the healing hope found in Jesus, but it was as if my words fell to my feet and hit the floor. It was my first youth ministry counselling session, and I literally felt like throwing up.

The number of children and youth violated through sexual abuse and rape is staggering and the need for discipleship overwhelming. To make matters even more painful, over 90 percent of child abuse cases are never brought forward to police or child welfare.[15] Due to the secrecy often associated with sexual abuse and rape, very few of the perpetrators who find themselves standing in front of a judge will ever be fully prosecuted for their crimes. As sad and maddening as all of this might feel, there is always hope through the healing and restoring power of Jesus Christ.

It is not fast hope that we cook up in our spiritual microwave. It is the slow hope that simmers over time, compassionate and frustrating, complete in Christ, but never quite finished. And yet, even as we sit with those overwhelmed by the violation, we know that they are not destined to identify as "broken." In Jesus Christ, we are more than conquerors, through him who loves us (Romans 8:1). He is the one who restores and transforms.

I wish that I could have offered Brit the YouTube video by Elizabeth Smart. It might not have been appropriate to suggest the video at our first meeting, but it would have been nice to pass it on to her mother to show at an appropriate time. Elizabeth was abducted at age fourteen, repeatedly raped, and held captive for nine months.[16] At the end of her moving TEDx Talk, after describing her painful ordeal, Elizabeth says, "We all have a choice. We can give in and surrender, or we can fight and move forward … When you are faced with trials, don't give up. Don't surrender. Move forward, because you never know what you'll be able to do with it; you never know the lives you'll be able to touch."[17] Elizabeth experienced horrific pain but decided that her life would not be defined—that *she* would not be defined—by evil. She decided to move beyond hatred to the courageous acts of embracing happiness, purpose, and forgiveness.

Which resources might you draw from when helping teens heal after sexual trauma? Is there a workshop you might take or a book you could read? Take some time now to list a few resources that you might access as you prepare for the next difficult conversation.

Secrets Are Bad

When you find yourself sitting with a Leah in a gymnasium or a Brit in your youth room and you hear the words "Can I tell you something?"—take a deep breath and prepare to step into sacred space. As the story unfolds, do your best to be fully present. Remember, the response of the adult to the initial disclosure may be the single most important factor for lifelong healing. Take some time to research the topic and see if you can learn how to respond. Here are five affirmations I have used over the years that you might find helpful.[18] I have used them so often that I found it helpful to write them in the back of my Bible.

First, as in the case of Leah, the teen might appear hesitant. She might ask, "Can I tell you something?" but then stop, unsure of her next step. You might begin with a simple affirmation, like "It's okay to tell me what's on your mind." It is never appropriate to promise a teen that you will help them keep a secret. Over the years, I have often said to teens, "Secrets are bad." Letting a secret go is like letting the air out of a balloon.

Second, as the teen tells you her or his story, it is common for him or her to ask, "Do you believe me?" It is unlikely that a teen would be dishonest about a story of sexual abuse, so your answer must always be, "Yes, I believe you." Even if some of the details sound far-fetched, the teen's perception of the event is what matters. Your response at this point in the conversation is affirmation. "You can talk to me about this. I believe you." You might notice, as I did with Leah, that there is no sign of emotion. During the conversation, there could be tears, or silence, or rage.

The third important statement is another affirmation. "It's okay to feel angry." Christian teens might feel hesitant expressing rage. There could be sobbing, swearing, punching the floor, anger expressed at God, or other displays of unbridled emotion. This is not the time to quote verses of scripture about loving your enemies, turning the other cheek, or forgiveness. Those things might come later, but during the initial disclosure, the primary discipleship task is to be a loving and gentle presence, representing the Prince of Peace, and to do your best to help this teen tell the story that she needs to tell.

Fourth, the teen needs to hear these words: "This is not your fault." It is common for teens who have suffered sexual abuse or rape to place the blame on themselves. Jennie Steinburg writes that self-blame is one of the ways survivors attempt to make meaning out of chaos. It is a way that survivors try to feel grounded again—a form of self-protection.[19] In her article she also reinforces the discipleship approach presented above when she writes, "The best thing you can do with your feelings of shame and your thoughts of self-blame is to share them with someone you trust. The best antidote to shame is empathy, and that's not something you can get from within yourself."[20]

Your gracious and empathic presence is an act of generosity as you make space for survivors to express shame and self-blame in the safety of your kindness and love.

The final response is one that will come naturally to you, because you love teenagers. It is simple but powerful when said under these circumstances. The final response is to simply affirm, "I care about you." It is not wise to tell the teen that everything is going to be okay. Nor can you say, "I'm going to stick with you. We'll get through this, together!" These are tempting affirmations, but there is no way you can know how things are going to proceed, and you do not want a teen feeling betrayed by you for not keeping a promise.

While serving in my first full-time youth ministry role, a teen disclosed to me that her father had been violent, and she was afraid to go home. I contacted child protective services, who went to the home to do an assessment. A few days later I got a very angry and threatening call from the father. He told me that I was never to speak to his daughter again, and he very clearly articulated what he would do to me should I choose not to heed his advice. I never saw his daughter again.

You can affirm your care for teens, but it is wise to always keep in mind that disclosures can lead in directions you cannot anticipate. Here are your affirmations:

- "It's okay to tell me what's on your mind."
- "I believe you."
- "It's okay to feel angry."
- "This is not your fault."
- "I care about you."

Making the Call

There may be tears, but you can tell that there is also a sense of relief. The power of the secret has been broken. The teen sits with you, not quite knowing what to do or say next. It is quiet. You must now step into your role as an advocate and inform him that your next step is to call child protective services.

This information typically results in resistance. You might see fear, as the teen sits in the vulnerability of exposing someone responsible for a violent crime. You might experience anger, as the teen expresses feelings of betrayal. He might say, "How could you do this to me?" or "I trusted you to keep this between us." The teen might begin to shut down. "I'll never tell anyone else what happened to me."

One of the significant challenges for policing services and child protection is that a survivor often refuses to tell her story to anyone but a trusted confidant. The teen simply can't be forced to retell the story to a stranger—and often won't. You might also hear threats of self-harm. "If you tell anyone, I'll kill myself." Suicide will always be a risk with initial disclosure, and threats must always be taken seriously.

Ultimately, the purpose of the call to child protective services is protection of the child or teen. Your hope is that the justice system will be able to intervene, hold the perpetrator accountable, and make the abuse stop. The safety of the child is your highest priority. The reality, however, is that abuse typically takes place in secret, where there are no witnesses and no evidence. Making the call does not guarantee the teen's safety, and in some cases it may even place him or her in greater danger. It is, however, your *legal obligation*.

I suggest that you invite the teen to make the call. It is a way of empowering him to act in the face of perceived powerlessness. If the teen does not want to call, you will do it on his behalf. Before making the call, discuss with the teen how he would like you to tell his story. Since abuse steals power and imposes helplessness, provide opportunities in the process for the teen to regain control over his or her own life.

Abuse creates profound wounds associated with strong feelings—like powerlessness, shame, betrayal, ambivalence, self-hatred, hopelessness, and rage, just to name a few. In your discipleship role as a first responder hearing an initial disclosure, you need to listen well and to use the five affirmations, making sure the teen hears you say, "This is not your fault." As a first responder, you want to stop the bleeding per se and make sure you get the teen to professionals of the next level of critical care, at child protective services. This is beautiful discipleship, even though you may not feel as though you have done anything *spiritual*. Once the initial disclosure is done and the child and family services are involved, then what? Here are a few ideas for discipling teens after an initial disclosure.

Join the Team

You are now part of a multidisciplinary team working to help the teen keep safe, manage the internal chaos, draw close to the Lord, and ultimately heal from the pain of abuse. Following an initial disclosure, child protective services will interview the teen. Police will likely also be involved. Doctors, psychologists, psychiatrists, adolescent mental health workers, and school counsellors might come and go as they play their roles as part of the support team. You play a unique role as a youth worker, because you are one of the few adults easily accessible for support. You also know the teen well and can function as an advocate, and sometimes a translator, for other professionals. You can encourage the teen to attend sessions with counsellors or to join a support group for young abuse survivors. You might be the only follower of Jesus on the support team, but take care to speak positively about others and the importance of their roles.

Acting in a supportive role may not feel very spiritual, but do not be fooled. This kind of caring is significant. Never underestimate the transforming power of love, demonstrated through simple acts of kindness. It could be a ride to the doctor's office or a lunch after small group meeting. It could be a walk through a park to debrief after a trip to the counsellor. In Matthew 25, Jesus makes it clear that he takes acts of compassion like these very personally—just as if you were doing them for him.

Pass the Peace

Liturgical practices shape your mind and your faith. By this I mean that your consistent practices in worship are supposed to influence the way you live your life. One of my favorite liturgical practices takes place in churches around the world every Sunday. At a certain point in the service, the worship leader will stand and say, "The peace of our Lord Jesus Christ be with you," to which the congregation will respond, "And also with you." The people in the congregation will then turn to one another, extending a hand of friendship or sharing an embrace and saying the words, "The Peace of Christ be with you," and receiving the response, "And also with you."

In chapter 1 of the book of Ephesians, the Apostle Paul writes of the glorious riches of God's grace (1:7); in chapter 2 he reminds the Church that God made them alive with Christ (2:5); and in chapter 3 he tells them that, because of Jesus, they can approach God with freedom and confidence (3:12). Building on these central ideas, the apostle begins chapter four by urging the church members to live lives worthy of their calling. He then writes, "Make every effort to keep the unity of the Spirit through the bond of peace" (4:3). This comment does not stand alone, but it flows out of all that God has done for them, and us, in Christ. Passing peace and keeping the peace is central to the gospel.

In his beatitudes, Jesus will say, "Blessed are the peacemakers, for they will be called children of God" (Matthew 5:9). Beatitudes are descriptions of the good life, of the way life could be, if lived for God's glory and for the common good. The idea of peacemaking is rooted in Psalm 34:14: "Turn from evil and do good; seek peace and pursue it." I wonder how you might understand this call to be a peacemaker, in the context of abuse? Is it even moral to speak of peace, in the devastation caused by sexual or physical trauma?

My gut reaction when face to face with Leah's abuser was not to make peace but violence. I was a pastor, yet I wanted to hurt him—to make him suffer. The hardest part of pastoral care with those who have suffered violation is extending the same kind of compassionate care to those who have caused the suffering. How important it is to remember that our struggle is not against flesh and blood but against the powers of this dark world and against the spiritual forces of evil (Ephesians 6:12).

Supporting violence and vengeance with your words or actions as you engage in youth ministry is contrary to the teachings of Jesus. The peacemaker is called the child of God because of the orientation to peace.[21] Peacemaking is a characteristic that determines whether the child belongs to God, being a true reflection of God's character. In what ways can you advocate for peace as you minister to those wounded by abuse?

Remember the Triangle

Violence has a way of marking its territory in your life, and events that traumatize often separate memories into life before and life after. While I was in seminary, a professor in a leadership course gave the class an assignment. We were to create a time line, marking significant events and people who had influenced us over the years. As I worked on my assignment, I placed crosses on my line, indicating those times when Christ had revealed himself to me in unique and memorable ways. It was a profound experience for me, as I came to realize that even though Jesus was transforming me, I was still finding my identity in the life I'd lived before I came to faith—the abuse, reckless living, and addiction. But as I created my time line, it became clear to me that God was calling me to change my orientation. God was inviting me to find the core of my identity, not in my suffering and failures but in the redemptive work of the cross.

In chapter 1, I wrote about a balanced approach to youth ministry that calls for theological reflection, meaningful relationships, and purposeful action. As you think about your role as one who nurtures faith, invite teens who are wounded by violence to consider the violence Jesus endured in order to rescue humanity from themselves. The temptation with people in pain is to lean too heavily on the relational part of the triangle, when healing can be found as we wrestle with important theological questions like "How could God let this happen?" Although teens need solid theological engagement and biblical learning, it is ironic that restoration often grows not in answering questions like these but when you experience the freedom to ask hard questions in the context of a safe relationship.

Healing and restoration may also come when teens are given the opportunity to engage in purposeful action. Inviting teens to tell their stories to help others, as Elizabeth Smart has done, is one way you can help them fight the controlling power of despair. It can be as simple as writing a poem, making a testimonial video to put online, writing a blog, or speaking at a support group. It is not appropriate to tell a teen that God allowed the violence so they could have a ministry, but you can reinforce the idea that God does not "waste pain."

Every Easter I am reminded that the crucifixion is not the end of the story. In Jesus, there is always the potential for resurrection and for life where you least expect it. God calls each of us to live our lives, not out of the evil we find in our past or the depression that clouds our present but rather out of our relationship with this incredible person, Jesus, who has loved us and called us his own.

No Safe Space

Nigel Shelby, fifteen. Raniya Wight, ten. Kashala Francis, thirteen. These young people may not have known each other, but they share a common story. Each of their lives ended prematurely in the past few months because of bullying. Although schools have legislated a zero-tolerance policy on bullying and increased their attentiveness to safety for all students, behavior-management is not as easy as it sounds.

"Bullying happens when there is an imbalance of power; when someone purposely and repeatedly says or does hurtful things to someone else. Bullying can occur one on one or in a group(s) of people."[22] Bullying is a form of violence that can lead to depression, stress-related health problems, and suicidal thinking. Physical bullying might include bodily aggression like hitting, punching, kicking, spitting, or breaking someone's belongings. Verbal bullying might include things like name-calling, put-downs, threats, or teasing. Social bullying might include spreading rumours, gossiping, excluding others from a group, or making others look foolish or stupid.[23] Cyberbullying involves the use of communication technologies such as the internet, social networking sites, websites, email, text messaging, and instant messaging to repeatedly intimidate or harass others.

When I was growing up, if you could get home, you had a safe space from bullies—until you had to go to school the next day. Today, if the bully has a phone and online access to social media, there is no safe space. The bully literally has access to the victim every hour of every day. Cyberbullying is also a form of violence, and it includes things like sending mean or threatening emails or text/instant messages, posting embarrassing pictures, creating a website to humiliate someone, pretending to be someone by using his name, and tricking someone into revealing personal information and then sending it to others.[24]

In adolescent culture, bullying can happen with a raised eyebrow. It can be as subtle as a look of disgust, and it can quickly escalate into violence. Think *Lord of the Flies*. If you were not made to read this disturbing little gem of a book in high school, pick it up sometime. It provides a detailed, yet fictional, account of what happens when teen bullies are left unchecked. Youth groups must maintain a commitment to providing a safe, bully-free zone for children and teens. One way to do this is to look at the policies used in your local school and adapt them for your context. Parents and teens will be familiar with these policies and will appreciate the consistency. It is also wise to communicate how you will respond to bullying and to be consistent in your discipline.

Here is a word of wisdom from a retired youth pastor who made a few mistakes over the years: never threaten discipline that you cannot carry out. For example, one night at our junior-high meeting, a young man was acting aggressively with several of his friends. When he was asked to settle down, he flipped me the bird (middle finger). A youth leader took him aside and spoke to him, reinforcing how great it was to have him at youth group. Then the teen was asked to be respectful of others in the room. He did not respond as requested. When we threatened to call his parents, he laughed and handed us his phone, saying, "Go ahead." He knew his parents would not come, and sure enough, when I called, his father told me it was my problem, not his. What then? It is a good idea to have a plan in place, should you find yourself in a similar situation. Eventually this young man and his friends were asked not to return. With the renewed sense of safety, the group began to grow.

Finally, let's talk about online safety. We must help teens make the connection between online etiquette and following Jesus. There is always room in youth ministry discipleship for conversations about friendship and how our friendship with Jesus can influence our relationships with people (Matthew 22:37). In chapter 1, I described a disciple of Jesus this way: "A disciple is a person-in-process who is eager to learn and apply the truths that Jesus teaches, which will result in ever-deepening commitments to a Christlike lifestyle" (Christopher Adsit).

Teens will make mistakes; sometimes, they will act violently toward others, while at other times they will be the victims of aggression. As a disciple maker, you understand that whatever they have done and whatever they have experienced, they are *people-in-process*, learning to follow Jesus. Like all of us, they are desperately in need of wise and godly mentors who will patiently lead the way.

Ideas for Discussion and Reflection

1. How will you need to adjust your discipleship efforts in order to build relationships with people from culturally diverse backgrounds?
2. What resources might you draw from when helping teens heal through sexual trauma? Is there a workshop you might take or a book you could read? Take some time now to list a few resources that you might access as you prepare for the next difficult conversation.
3. How might you live out the biblical invitation to be a peacemaker while you provide spiritual care for a teen survivor of abuse? What challenges might you face as you try to live this out?
4. If you can find it online, watch the TEDx Talk by Elizabeth Smart. What do you find moving about her story? How might her story inspire hope for a teen survivor?
5. You notice a teenager in the youth group bullying someone. Describe how you would respond. Do you have expectations about safety for all participants that are clearly communicated on a regular basis?

1   Elizabeth Smart, "My Story," TEDx University of Nevada, posted January 31, 2014, https://www.youtube.com/watch?v=h0C2LPXaEW4

2   Chris McGreal, "Rwanda's Himmler: The man behind the genocide," *The Guardian*, posted December 18, 2008, https://www.theguardian.com/ world/2008/dec/18/ rwanda-genocide-theoneste-bagosora

3   Lee Mannion, "More than 350 million children living in conflict zones, says charity," *Reuters*, posted February 14, 2018, https://www.reuters.com/article/ usglobal-war-children/more-than-350-million-children-living-in-conflict-zonessays-charity-idUSKCN1FZ00M

4   Paul Anisef and Kenise Murphy Kilbride, "The Needs of Newcomer Youth and Emerging Best Practices to Meet Those Needs," *The Joint Centre of Excellence for Research on Immigration and Settlement* (CERIS), 2008, accessed January 18, 2019, http://atwork.settlement.org/downloads/Newcomer Youth Best Practices.pdf

5   Bob Mitchell, "I killed my daughter… with my hands," *The Star*, posted June 16, 2010, https://www.thestar.com/news/ crime/2010/06/16/i killed my daughter with my hands.html

6   Michael D. Nicholson, "The Facts on Immigration Today: 2017 Edition," *Center for American Progress*, April 20, 2017, https://www.americanprogress.org/issues/ immigration/reports/2017/04/20/430736/ facts-immigration-today-2017-edition/

7   "Migration Flows," *Canadian International Development Platform*, accessed April 27, 2019, https://cidpnsi.ca/migration-flows/

8   Santes Beatty, "We're not all just alike: Challenges and opportunities in multiethnic youth ministries," *Fuller Youth Institute*, posted July 11, 2016, https://fuller youthinstitute.org/blog/challenges-opportunities-multiethnicyouth-ministry

9   "Texas Child Abuse Laws." *FindLaw*, 2019, accessed April 27, 2019, https:// statelaws.findlaw.com/texaslaw/texas-child-abuse-laws.html

10 "North Dakota Child Abuse Laws," *FindLaw*, 2019, accessed April 27, 2019, https:// statelaws.findlaw. com/north-dakota-law/north-dakota-child-abuse-laws.html

11 Lynn Heitritter and Jeanette Vought, *Helping Victims of Sexual Abuse: A Sensitive Biblical Guide for Counselors, Victims, and Families* (Bloomington: Bethany House, 2006), 31.

12 Loree Beniuk and Pearl Rimer, "Understanding Child Sexual Abuse: A Guide for Parents & Caregivers," *Central Agencies Sexual Abuse Treatment Program: Child Development Institute*, 2006, accessed January 19, 2019, https://www.childdevelop. ca/ sites/default/files/files/Understanding-Child-Sexual-Abuse.pdf

13 "Child Sexual Abuse," *Canadian Centre for Child* Protection, posted June 12, 2018, https://protectchildren.ca/pdfs/C3P CSAinSchoolsReport en.pdf

14 "Get Statistics," *National Sexual Violence Resource Center*, 2018, accessed April 27, 2019, https://www. nsvrc.org/statistics

15. "Understand and Identify Child Sexual Abuse," *Canadian Centre for Child Protection*, 2018, accessed April 28, 2019, https://www.protectchildren.ca/en/resources-research/understanding-child-sexual-abuse/

16. Elizabeth Smart, "My Story," *TEDx University of Nevada*, posted January 31, 2014, video, 11:36. https://www.youtube.com/watch?v=h0C2LPXaEW4

17. Ibid.

18. You will find a version of these affirmations in *Unlocking the Secret World: A Unique Christian Ministry to Abused, Abandoned, and Neglected Children* by Wayne and Diane Tesch (Carol Stream: Tyndale House Publishing, 1995), page 136.

19. Jennie Steinburg, "Why Sexual Assault Survivors Blame Themselves," *Through the Woods Therapy Center*, October 27, 2017, http://www.throughthewoodstherapy.com/sexual-assault-survivors-blame/

20. Ibid.

21. R. T. France, "The Gospel of Matthew," *The New International Commentary of the New Testament* (Grand Rapids: Wm B. Eerdmans, 2007), 169.

22. "Bullying and Cyberbullying," *Royal Canadian Mounted* Police, posted February 20, 2019, http://www.rcmp-grc.gc.ca/cycp-cpcj/bull-inti/index-eng.htm

23. Ibid.

24. Ibid.

CHAPTER 10
When Winter Comes:
Making Space for Uncomfortable Honesty

He is called to be the wounded healer,
the one who must look after his own
wounds, but at the same time be
prepared to heal the wounds of others.
–Henri Nouwen

Ernie had rare blood anemia.[1] Passed through a recessive gene, this condition caused loss of blood cells and bone marrow function, as well as congenital disorders including dwarfism, microcephaly (small skull size), and kidney problems. Ernie had lived with the disease for several years and he had come to the National Institutes of Health for an experimental drug to boost the function of his bone marrow. The treatment did not work, and he was left with only one option to reverse the disease—a bone marrow transplant. Without some reversal, the disease would be fatal.

The hospital chaplain wrote, "As I talked with both Ernie and his parents, the kinds of questions they asked were different. For Ernie, the questions were, "When will I get out of here? Why does everything have to be so painful?" He resented the limits being in the hospital placed on his childhood, and he was angry. He was angry at the staff, who poked him with needles and made him stay in bed. He was angry with his parents, who had no solutions, and he was angry with God.[2]

Anger with God is common for those experiencing trauma. In the Bible you will find Job expressing his own strong feelings:

> I cry out to you, God, but you do not answer; I stand up,
> but you merely look at me. You turn on me ruthlessly;
> with the might of your hand you attack me. (Job 30:20–21)

The despair you will find in Job 16:9 is even more striking. "God assails me and tears me in his anger and gnashes his teeth at me; my opponent fastens on me his piercing eyes." The person who wrote Psalm 10 cries out in a similar voice: "Why, Lord, do you stand far off? Why do you hide yourself in times of trouble?" (verse 1). Jesus knew a similar kind of agony, captured in his use of Psalm 22, as he hung on the cross. In Mark 15:34, you will read his cry, translated as, "My God, my God, why have you forsaken me?"

Throughout this book I have given you the opportunity to think about discipling teens though crisis. You have thought about teen grief, unhealthy dependence, sexual behavior, intentional self-harm, disordered eating, depression, and violence. Every one of these topics will result in suffering for at least some of the teens you will disciple—if not for themselves, then certainly for some of their friends. As you come face to face with suffering teenagers, you will need to learn to make space for uncomfortable honesty.

Ernie questioned why God would allow him to suffer. Instead of defending God's honor, you might respond with, "That's a good question. What do you think?" Job, the Psalmist, Jesus, and even little Ernie in his hospital bed have expressed pain in words that we might want to chastise or correct. Sometimes the most difficult part of discipling teens in pain is choosing to sit with them, through the anger and the sadness, *in silence*.

Reimagining God

Professor Lewis B. Smedes was confident that he knew what God was like. He had his theological ideas well-ordered—until the day his baby boy died. In his article titled *What's God up to? A Father Grieves the Loss of his Child*, he writes this painfully honest reflection: "With one morning's wrenching intuition, I knew that my portrait of God would have to be repainted."[3]

Honesty with teens in pain will likely be difficult. It may lead you to the realization that your portrait of God no longer makes sense. You may find, as Dr. Smedes did, that suffering plunges you into the disorienting process of reimagining God, as you are forced to ask in your own agony, *"Who is God now?"*

Speaking at a conference of therapists on the book of Job, John Ortberg once said, "When winter (suffering) comes to people, it will force them to re-examine what they really believe about God. When winter comes, your sense of identity changes. Your sense of who you are changes."[4]

There are few things more disorienting than finding yourself lost in familiar places. Sacred space, like your church, can become irritating and intolerable when your portrait of God no longer makes sense. The worship leader is too happy. The music is too hopeful. The sermon is too neatly packaged and the people in the audience too perfect. Teens can feel completely alone, even in a public worship space, when the family is ripped apart by divorce, a family loses a child to prison, or a parent is diagnosed with a terminal illness.

No one wants to reimagine God; there is comfort in the familiar. It is hard and terrifying work, which often includes entertaining the possibility that God might not be anything like what you had imagined. As you reimagine, you come to the cliff's edge, wrestling with questions about God's goodness, or kindness, or mercy. This kind of work requires a teenager to compare these biblical characteristics of God with the cold and hard reality of his or her life.

I knew a teenager once who loved the Lord. He was a worship leader in his church, was known as a follower of Jesus in his high school, and was serious in his devotional life—until his best friend was tragically killed in a car accident. *"Who is God now?"* In his pain, the only thing that made sense to him was to conclude that God is not good. His parents grieved with him, prayed with him, loved him, and supported him, but that event had shattered his portrait of God.

It is much easier to let someone feed you the bottle of faith and to remain a spiritual infant than to choke on the meat that leads to Christian maturity and Christlikeness. In chapter 5 of Hebrews, the writer chastises readers for choosing to remain bottle-fed infants (5:12–14). You would not wish this kind of agony on any of the teens in your life, but the truth is that Christian faith cannot become mature faith unless the believer is refined through suffering. All the topics in this book have the potential of helping teens come to know Jesus in a way that they could never have known him had their stories been different. A part of me wishes that this were not true, that there was another way.

The Apostle Paul captures this idea beautifully when he writes, "I want to know Christ—yes, to know the power of his resurrection and participation in his sufferings, becoming like him in his death, and so, somehow, attaining to the resurrection from the dead" (Philippians 3:10–11).

Dark Doorways

The word *theodicy* comes from two Greek words, *Theos*, meaning "God," and *dike*, meaning "justice." Christian theodicy is an attempt to understand the righteous ways of God in a world where physical and moral evils are disastrous realities."[5]

Little Ernie in his hospital bed was engaging in theological reflection—asking questions that fall into the category of theodicy—as he questioned his own suffering. Anytime a teenager asks you, "How can God be good and loving when I'm experiencing so much pain?" you are thinking about theodicy. Other common questions might include the following: If God is good and fully in control, how can evil exist in the world? How do we justify the actions of God in causing evil, suffering, and pain? If God is all-powerful and good, and in control, how is he not the author of evil?"[6]

These questions are often addressed academically, depersonalized, and removed from emotion, but in youth ministry, face to face with questioning teens or children like Ernie, you do not have that luxury. Perkins-Buzo accurately concludes that "theodicy can't be addressed as an abstract concept but only as a pastoral concern."[7]

Your goal in discipleship is not to be God's lawyer. It is not your job to come up with a good answer for every difficult theological question or to defend God's actions. Your calling is to lead people into the mystery of God, to help them to speak of God with their own words, in their own language, and with their own thoughts and feelings—not removed from their pain but out of the depths of their suffering.[8]

Your ministry is to help teens prayerfully and biblically engage with Jesus—with all that they are and all that they have experienced—and to know personally the love that Jesus has for them. In youth ministry, it will not take you long to discover that you cannot adequately address all of life's difficult questions. Even if you could, you will find that many people do not have the patience required to do the hard work of thinking theologically. What you can do, and what is incredibly meaningful, is to help teens find adequate ways of communicating their pain, disappointment, doubt, and anger in the natural process of faith formation. These things do not have to be an indicator that teens are tossing faith to the wind. They may very well represent the dark doorway through which the teens must pass in order to discover the unshakable, immovable, unchanging love of God.

Going Deeper

Teens who feel the disconnect between God's goodness and the reality of their own discomfort might want to engage in a deeper theological conversation. It is not uncommon to hear questions like, "If God is good, why is there suffering and evil in the world, in *my* world?" In those moments, you might consider referring to these three ideas: *Satan, sin, and selfishness.*[9]

In the parable of the weeds, found in Matthew 13:24, Jesus explains how the weeds got into the farmer's good field. Jesus does not apologize for evil in his world. In the parable, a servant asks, "Sir, didn't you sow good seed in your field? Where then did the weeds come from?"

In verse 28, the owner of the field responds by saying, "An enemy did this." As you walk with teens, there will be opportunities for you to lead them into deeper theological conversations about the problem of evil. Be patient. It is challenging for teens to move from the black-and-white world of childlike faith, where the idea of the love of God made perfectly good sense, and into the ambiguity of adult belief.

As you think together, consider helping the teen by discussing these three ideas about the existence of suffering:

1. Suffering finds its source with God's enemy.
2. Jesus comes into the world to transform the despair associated with suffering and to break the power of sin. On the cross, Jesus takes your suffering upon himself, destroys the power of God's

enemy, and gives you the power, by his Holy Spirit, to look suffering in the face and still experience peace (Isaiah 53:1–6, John 16:33).

3. God is moving the world toward a new creation, where suffering will come to an end.

Christian faith isn't remarkable because it acts as an inoculation to the effects of suffering; rather, what makes Christianity truly remarkable is that followers of Jesus believe that horrendous evil, overwhelming misery, hopelessness, and suffering do not have to control our lives. The hope of the gospel is found in Luke 4:18–19, where Jesus, sitting in the synagogue, is handed a scroll from Isaiah and reads this:

> The Spirit of the Lord is on me because he has anointed me to proclaim good news to the poor. He has sent me to proclaim freedom for the prisoners and recovery of sight for the blind, to set the oppressed free, to proclaim the year of the Lord's favor.

As Elizabeth Smart and so many others like her have proven, Jesus speaks freedom to those imprisoned behind impenetrable bars by inexcusable violence and violation. He did this when the disciples were gathered after his resurrection; he slipped into the room, unimpeded by walls or doors, and was there with them, showing them the nail marks in his hands.

Jesus comes to offer freedom to those oppressed by inner and outer turmoil, and his presence, love, compassion, and strength provide Spirit-empowered courage to grow beyond the pain.

A Way of Being

This book has been about discipling teens through their experience of trauma. Sometimes the trauma is in the past, and you will help teens in the present to prayerfully walk through the darkness, releasing crippling emotions like bitterness, unforgiveness, anger, and rage. At other times the trauma will be in the present. A friend has died suddenly in a car accident, an acquaintance has taken his own life, rape is terrifying someone, or a person is being physically assaulted. The common denominator in these situations is *trauma*.

The *Trauma-Informed Practice Guide* was created on behalf of British Columbia's Provincial Mental Health and Substance Use Planning Council.[10] It is an excellent resource, and you may still be able to find it online. The guide defines *trauma* this way:

> Experiences that overwhelm an individual's capacity to cope. Trauma early in life, including child abuse, neglect, witnessing violence, and disrupted attachment; as well as later traumatic experiences such as violence, accidents, natural disaster, war, sudden unexpected loss, and other life events that are out of one's control, can be devastating.[11]

It describes five types of trauma:

1. Single-incident trauma
   - related to an unexpected and overwhelming event, like an accident, natural disaster, or sudden loss
2. Complex trauma
   - related to ongoing abuse, domestic violence, war, or ongoing betrayal; often involves being trapped emotionally and/or physically
3. Developmental trauma
   - from exposure to early ongoing or repetitive trauma involving neglect, abandonment, physical abuse or assault, sexual abuse or assault, emotional abuse, witnessing violence or death, and/or coercion or betrayal
4. Intergenerational trauma
   - psychological or emotional effects that can be experienced by people who live with trauma survivors
5. Historic trauma
   - cumulative emotional and psychological wounding over the lifespan and across generations, emanating from massive group trauma like genocide, colonialism, slavery, and war.[12]

Although the guide was written for mental-health service providers and others working in a variety of health-care contexts, I could not help but think of its value for youth ministry. Trauma-informed youth ministry is a new way of thinking about discipleship. It is like wearing an expensive pair of polarized sunglasses on a sunny day. When you have the glasses over your eyes, it affects how you see your environment. When you begin to look at teenagers through this new pair of sunglasses, it not only affects the way you hear their stories but also your response. Trauma-informed discipleship is a way of being in a relationship with teens.

Utilizing a trauma-informed approach does not necessarily require disclosure of the trauma. Rather, services are provided in ways that recognize the need for physical and emotional safety, as well as choice and control in decisions affecting treatment. Trauma-informed practice is more about the overall essence of the approach, or *way of being in the relationship* than it is a specific treatment strategy or method.

How might your new trauma-informed sunglasses change the way you see discipleship? What do you think would change?

The Ministry Space

With a trauma-informed approach, creating a safe environment takes on new importance. Although the guide refers to *services* and *service providers*, you can easily substitute the words *ministry* and *youth workers* to make the material fit your context. As you engage in ministry, you will find that preparing your program, teaching, and worship will include only three-fourths of your preparation. You will also need to consider the preparation of your context.

It is no longer enough to gather a bunch of teens together in a room, a camp, or a drop-in to have fun and learn about Jesus. Due to violation at the hands of clergy and ministry volunteers, you will need to place a high priority on the protection of vulnerable people, ensuring your volunteers have completed vulnerable-sector checks and criminal-record checks. They must be fully aware of and compliant with organizational policies regarding ministering to minors, including the following subjects:

- appropriate and inappropriate touch
- the pictures you take and post

- whether you can have minors as friends on social media
- the legalities associated with texting minors
- adults meeting with minors during the week
- adults providing counsel

It gets even more complicated for Christian camps, which require policies related to the safety of minors sleeping in cabins with older staff. The critical point here is this: you need to spend as much time thinking about the safety of people in your ministry space as you do about the program, teaching, and worship. On a scale of 1 to 10 (1 being bad and 10 amazing), how would you rate your own youth ministry context regarding your policies for safety? What steps could you take to increase your score?

Cultivate Trauma Awareness

Now that you know about trauma-informed discipleship, consider teaching the team of people you work with. Teach your team to listen for trauma-related language and to understand the impact of trauma. Describe trauma. Look closely at the five kinds of trauma, and talk about which one you see the most in your context. Talk about the creation of safe space. Spend some time teaching about appropriate vulnerability and things to consider when adults share their own trauma stories with teens. It is not enough for *you* to have a new pair of sunglasses; make sure everyone on the team is also learning to see ministry through a trauma-informed lens.

Reorient toward Restoration

A trauma-informed youth worker understands that unhealthy adolescent behavior does not always stem from the teen's own willful rebellion or sin. Instead, unhealthy—or even sinful—behavior might be a coping strategy that is helping a teen manage the pain of trauma. Reorienting the focus of conversation away from sin and confession will likely bring about better overall results for the disciple and help him or her draw closer to Jesus.

I am not suggesting that we do not invite teens to confess sin. What I am suggesting is that medicating behaviors often get labelled as sin, and the behaviors, rather than the trauma, can become the focus of the ministry intervention. A youth worker looking through trauma-informed sunglasses will at least consider the possibility that the behavior is a symptom of a much deeper pain and will reorient efforts toward healing, restoration, and collaboration.

Engage in Collaborative Disciple Making

The *Trauma-Informed Practice Guide* highlights the need for trauma-informed services to create an environment where teens will not experience further traumatization and where they can make decisions about their growth at a pace that feels safe to them.[13] In like manner, trauma-informed discipleship creates safe environments that provide for teen success, self-determination, dignity, and personal control for those engaged in the relationship. Youth workers try to communicate openly, equalize power imbalances in relationships, allow for the open expression of feelings without fear of judgment, provide choices regarding the discipleship, and work collaboratively with the teens they serve.[14]

In other words, discipleship is not something you do *to* a teen; it is a relationship in which you offer your wisdom and support, prayerfully engaging in collaborative decision making, as together you follow Jesus.

Wounded Healers

There is a cost to caring. Discipling teens in pain can leave you tired and discouraged, and at times their pain will bring you uncomfortably close to your own. In his book *The Wounded Healer*, Henri Nouwen reflects on an old story from the Talmud.

A rabbi asked Elijah, "When will the Messiah come?"

Elijah replied, "Go and ask him yourself."

"Where is he?"

212

"Sitting at the gates of the city."

"How shall I know him?"

"He is sitting among the poor covered with wounds. The others unbind all their wounds at the same time and then bind them up again. But he unbinds one at a time and binds it up again, saying to himself, "Perhaps I shall be needed; if so, I must always be ready, so as not to delay for a moment.""[15]

Nouwen explains that the Messiah is sitting among the poor, binding his wounds one at a time, waiting for the moment when he will be needed. So it is with you. Since it is Jesus's task to help others experience healing, he must bind his own wounds carefully, in anticipation of the moment when he will be needed. He is called to be the wounded healer, the one who must look after his own wounds, but at the same time be prepared to heal the wounds of others.[16]

Brené Brown once wrote that vulnerability is the emotion you experience during times of uncertainty, risk, and emotional exposure.[17] Caring for your own wounds so that you can care for the wounds of others is a healthy way to think about ministry; however, it implies that you will be prepared to slow down long enough to look closely at your own history of trauma, and do the necessary work of wrapping your own bandages.

If it means uncertainty, risk, and emotional exposure, few of us would sign up to be a wounded healer. We would rather look composed, prepared, anointed, chosen by God, maturing in faith, and ready to serve. The truth is that in the real world of honest self-evaluation we are all wounded healers, and those who choose to view ministry through a trauma-informed lens will come to recognize that God does not waste painful experience. As a matter of fact, God will often take the darkest moments of your life and use that part of your story as your greatest resource for ministry and for love.

One Life at a Time

Tony Campolo tells a funny story about a party that he and his wife, Peggy, attended with university professors. A female professor started a conversation, and at one point, she turned to Mrs. Campolo and, knowing she was a stay-at-home-mom, asked in a condescending tone, "And what is it that *you* do, my dear?"

Not wanting to be outdone by a woman in the "workforce," she replied this way:

> I am socializing two Homo sapiens into the dominant values of the Judeo-Christian tradition in order that they might be the instruments for the transformation of the social order into the kind of eschatological utopia that God willed from the beginning of creation![18]

Then, she followed this brilliant summary of motherhood with a question of her own. "And what is it that *you* do?"

The woman answered humbly, "I ... I ... teach sociology." At the close of his story, Campolo draws attention to his point. "We must recognize that raising children is a high and holy task!"[19]

I, too, have been asked to explain what I do, but never have I been this eloquent. As I bring this book to a close, I want to thank you for taking this difficult journey with me. My hope for you is that you will understand that what you do for teenagers is incredibly important, especially for teens who have no safe adults in their life. Let me give it a shot, Peggy Campolo-style: what is it *you do*?

You are changing the world, one life at a time, by communicating the biblical *Missio Dei* with an attentiveness to adolescent formation, in the context of spiritual and moral depravity, resulting in life transformation for the common good, social reconfiguration, and eternal salvation, all in the name of the Kings of Kings and Lord of Lords.

Not too shabby. Youth ministry matters, because teenagers are important to God. When teens experience trauma, they become vulnerable, and they need safe, loving, wise, consistently present adult followers of Jesus in their lives. These adults must have thick skin and be able to stay the course, even when there is profanity, anger, difficult questions, and reckless immorality. This is what God has *seized* you to do. This is what God is calling you to—to be the one who stands in the gap.

Engaging in this kind of discipleship nurtures transformation, healing, and hope for teens all over the world, every day. The next time someone asks you why you *waste* your time with *those kinds* of kids, smile and lift your chin. God has given you the opportunity to make an eternal difference.

Ideas for Discussion and Reflection

1. What would you do, or say, if you were Ernie's chaplain? Take another look at Job 16:9. Can you describe a time when you felt like Job?
2. John Ortberg speaks of suffering as a "winter." How has this winter forced you to re-examine what you believe about God? Do you think the process has destabilized your faith or made your faith stronger?
3. What do you think about the three affirmations? Do you think they would be helpful for teens eager to dig deeper? Take a moment to add your own additional points.
4. How might your new trauma-informed sunglasses change the way you see discipleship? What do you think would change?
5. On a scale of 1-10 (1 being bad and 10 amazing), how would you rate your own youth ministry context regarding your policies for safety? What steps could you take to increase your score?

1   J. Reid Perkins-Buzo, "Theodicy in the Face of Children's Suffering and Death," *The Journal of Pastoral Care*, Vol. 48, No. 2, Summer 1994: 155.

2   Ibid., 155.

3   Lewis B. Smedes, "What's God Up To? A Father Grieves the Loss of his Child," *Christian Century*, Vol. 120, Issue 9, May 2003: 38–39.

4   John Ortberg, "Take Me to the Cross," (2005 DVD), *The American Association of Christian Counselors*.

5   Ellis W. Hollon, "Pain, Suffering, and Christian Theodicy," *Perspectives in Religious Studies* 6, Spring 1979: 24.

6   Gary W. Crampton, "A Biblical Theodicy," *The Trinity Foundation*, 2019, accessed May 8, 2019. http://www.leaderu.com/theology/theodicy.html

7   J. Reid Perkins-Buzo, 158.

8   Michael J. Dodds, "Thomas Aquinas, Human Suffering, and the Unchanging God of Love," *Theological Studies*, Vol. 52, Issue 2, June 1991: 336.

9   "Theodicy," *GoodNews Tube*, posted August 14, 2015, https://www.youtube.com/watch?v=aXrPIvGWuII

10 Cristine Urquhart and Fran Jasiura, "Trauma-Informed Practice Guide," *British Columbia's Provincial Mental Health and Substance Use Planning Council*, 2013, http://bccewh.bc.ca/wp-content/uploads/2012/05/2013 TIP-Guide.pdf

11 Ibid., 6.

12 Ibid., 6.

13 Ibid., 12.

14 Ibid., 14.

15 Henri Nouwen, *The Wounded Healer: Ministry in Contemporary Society* (New York: Image Doubleday, 1972), 87.

16 Ibid., 88.

17 Brené Brown, *Dare to Lead: Brave Work, Tough Conversations, Whole Hearts* (New York: Random House, 2018),

18 Tony Campolo, *Let Me Tell You a Story: Life Lessons from Unexpected Places and Unlikely People* (Grand Rapids: Thomas Nelson Publishing, 2000), 145.

19 Ibid.

Appendix A

Discipleship Triage Model

Need	Care	Description	Youth Worker Response
The crisis could result in death	Critical Care	May include issues like: suicidal thinking, conclusion of a terminal illness, injury due to unanticipated trauma	<ul><li>Immediate reaction</li><li>Ministry of presence</li><li>Use of a suicide intervention model</li><li>Remaining present</li><li>Liaison with other helping professionals</li><li>Provision of resources for life change</li><li>Prayer ministry</li><li>Support for family members</li><li>Engaging additional resources</li></ul>
Problem is severe and may become critical if not addressed	Crisis Care	Needs immediate assistance, but not life-threatening May include issues like death of a friend or family member, sexual or physical assault, bullying, witnessing violence, major family disruption, addictions, an encounter with police services, breakup with dating partner, diagnosis of a severe or terminal illness, diagnosis of a mental illness	<ul><li>Immediate, personal visit (within 24–48 hours)</li><li>Ministry of presence</li><li>Consistent prayer ministry</li><li>Liaison with supportive services</li><li>General knowledge base</li><li>Consistent one-on-one talk with an adult leader</li><li>Ongoing small group Bible study for peer connections</li><li>Youth ministry programming</li><li>Support for family members</li><li>Resourcing</li><li>Reacting to the crisis</li></ul>

Persistent non-crisis Pain	**Compassion Care**	*The Walking Wounded* Issues are ongoing but not crisis oriented. May include issues like low self-esteem, ongoing pain in the home, fear, physical injury, damaged relationships, emotional instability, disability, mental illness, or incarceration	• Discipleship and evangelism • Ongoing small-group Bible study for peer connections • Youth ministry programming (give Companion Care people opportunity for ministry) • Consistent one-on-one talk with an adult leader • Provision of brief, solution-focused care • Connection to supportive services • Making yourself available to school administration as a support • Being a resource for parents/caregivers
Friends are experiencing pain	**Companion Care**	For ministry-minded teens, discipling friends in pain	• Ongoing one-on-one dialogue with an adult leader • Provision of ministry training and support • Training and practice in prayer ministry • Spiritual gifts inventory • Resources • Attention to compassion fatigue

About the Author

Chris Marchand (Doctor of Ministry) has been helping people grow in faith for more than thirty years. He has served in pastoral roles in both Canada and the United States, has taught youth ministry at several schools and more recently, served in camp ministry. He lives in southern Manitoba with his wife, Heather, and their two adult children, Justin and Brianna.

Reference list

Abbott-Smith, G. *A Manual Greek Lexicon of the New Testament*, 3rd edition. New York: Charles Scribner's Sons, 1922.

Adams, Kathryn Betts, Holly C. Matto and Donna Harrington. "The Traumatic Stress Institute Belief Scale as a Measure of vicarious trauma in a National Sample of Clinical Social Workers." In *Families in Society: The Journal of Contemporary Human Services* 82, no. 4 2001: 363-371.

Addiction Center. "The Twelve Steps of Alcoholics Anonymous." Last modified March 22, 2018. https://www.addictioncenter.com/treatment/12-step-programs/

Addictions Foundation of Manitoba. "Fundamentals of Addictions" (Course Manual).

Adsit, Christopher B. *Personal Disciple-Making: A Step-by-Step Guide for Leading a Christian from New Birth to Maturity.* San Bernardino: Here's Life Publishers, 1988.

Anderson, Ray. *Making the Transition: From a Theology of Ministry to a Ministry of Theology.* Grand Rapids: Wm. B. Eerdmans, 2008.

Anisef, Paul and Kenise Murphy Kilbride. "The Needs of Newcomer Youth and Emerging Best Practices to Meet Those Needs." *The Joint Centre of Excellence for Research on Immigration and Settlement (CERIS),* 2008. Accessed January 18, 2019. http://atwork.settlement.org/downloads/Newcomer_Youth_Best_Practices.pdf

Asatsa, Stephen. "Cell phone sexting and its influence on adolescence sexual behavior in Nairobi County, Kenya." *Research Gate*. Posted February 2017. https://www.researchgate.net/publication/313655458_Cell_Phone_Sexting_And_Its_In fluence_On_Adolescence_Sexual_Behavior_In_Nairobi_County_Kenya

Auld, Alison. "Nova Scotia teens treated girls' intimate photos 'like baseball cards." *The Canadian Press* July 31, 2017 at *The Globe and Mail*. https://www.theglobeandmail.com/news/national/nova-scotia-teens-treated-girls-intimate-photos-like-baseball-cards-crown/article35841245/

Axelrod, Julie. "The Five Stages of Grief and Loss." *Psych Central*. Accessed February 21, 2018. https://psychcentral.com/lib/the-5-stages-of-loss-and-grief/

Baker, Rafferty. "City on Drugs: The Dark Pull of Vancouver's Downtown Eastside." CBC Radio. August 1, 2017. http://www.cbc.ca/radio/ondrugs/city-on-drugs-the-dark-pull-of- vancouver-s-downtown-eastside-1.4229455

Balswick, Judith K. and Jack O. Balswick. *Authentic Human Sexuality: An Integrated Christian Approach*, 2nd ed. Downers Grove: InterVarsity Press, 2008.

Beale, Stephen. "Saints and Sexual Temptation." *Catholic Exchange*. Posted March 20, 2012. https://catholicexchange.com/saints-and-sexual-temptation

Beaton, R. D. and S. A. Murphy, "Working with People in Crisis: Research Implications." In *Compassion Fatigue: Coping with Secondary Traumatic Stress Disorder in Those Who Treat the Traumatized*, edited by Charles R. Figley, 58. New York: Brunner and Mazel, 1995.

Beatty, Santes. "We're not all just alike: Challenges and opportunities in multiethnic youth ministries." *Fuller Youth Institute.* Posted July 11, 2016. https://fulleryouthinstitute.org/blog/challenges-opportunities-multiethnic-youth- ministry

Beniuk, Loree and Pearl Rimer. "Understanding Child Sexual Abuse: A Guide for Parents & Caregivers." *Central Agencies Sexual Abuse Treatment Program: Child Development Institute,* 2006. Accessed January 19, 2019. https://www.childdevelop.ca/sites/default/files/files/Understanding-Child-Sexual- Abuse.pdf

Benner, Benner G. *Care of Souls: Revisioning Christian Nurture and Counsel.* Grand Rapids: Baker Books, 1998.

Beresin, Eugene and Jennifer Derenne. "Two Psychiatrists Weigh in on Netflix's 'To the Bone': A Missed Opportunity to Understand Anorexia Nervosa." *Psychology Today,* July 21, 2017. https://www.psychologytoday.com/ca/blog/inside-out-outside-in/201707/two- psychiatrists-weigh-in-netflix-s-the-bone

Blocher, Henri. *In the Beginning: The Opening Chapters of Genesis.* Downers Grove: InterVarsity Press, 1984.

Block, Daniel I. *The Book of Ezekiel Chapters 1–24.* Grand Rapids: Wm. B. Eerdmans Publishing, 1997.

Bock, Darrell L. *Baker Exegetical Commentary on the New Testament: Luke 9:51–24:53.* Grand Rapids: Baker Books, 1996.

Boscarino, Joseph A., Richard E. Adams and Charles R. Figley. "Secondary Trauma Issues for Psychiatrists." In *Psychiatric Times* 27, no. 11 (2010): 24–26. https://www.ncbi.nlm.nih.gov/pmc/articles/PMC3014548/

Bosch, David J. "The Structure of Mission: An Exposition of Matt. 28:16-20. In *Exploring Church Growth,* edited by Wilbert R. Schenk, 228. Eugene: Wipf and Stock, 2010.

Brown, Brené. *Dare to Lead: Brave Work, Tough Conversations, Whole Hearts.* New York: Random House, 2018.

Brueggemann, Walter. *Genesis: A Biblical Commentary for Teaching and Preaching.* Louisville: John Knox, 2010.

Buechner, Frederick. *Wishful Thinking: A Seeker's ABC.* New York: HarperSanFrancisco, 1993.

Campolo, Tony. *Let Me Tell You a Story: Life Lessons from Unexpected Places and Unlikely People.* Grand Rapids: Thomas Nelson Publishing, 2000.

Canadian Centre for Child Protection. "Child Sexual Abuse." Posted June 12, 2018. https://protectchildren.ca/pdfs/C3P_CSAinSchoolsReport_en.pdf

Canadian Centre for Child Protection. "Self/Peer Exploitation: It's Not OK. A Resource Guide for Families Addressing Self/Peer Exploitation." Accessed February 2, 2019. https://www.cybertip.ca/app/en/internet_safety-intimate_images

Canadian Centre for Child Protection. "Understand and Identify Child Sexual Abuse." Accessed April 28, 2019. https://www.protectchildren.ca/en/resources-research/understanding-child-sexual- abuse/

Canadian International Development Platform. "Migration Flows." Accessed April 27, 2019. https://cidpnsi.ca/migration-flows/

Canadian Mental Health Association. "Eating Disorders." Accessed February 10, 2019. https://www.cmha.ca/mental-health/understanding-mental-illness/eating-disorders

Canadian Mental Health Association. "Youth and Self-injury." Accessed January 16, 2019. https://cmha.ca/documents/youth-and-self-injury

Catholic Strength. "Oh, Blessed Night of Pure Faith: A Bird's-eye View of the Spirituality of St. John of the Cross." Accessed January 16, 2019. https://catholicstrength.com/tag/a-summary-of-the-spirituality-of-saint-john-of-the- cross/

Centers for Disease Control and Prevention. "Smoking and Cardiovascular Disease." Accessed March 5, 2019. https://www.cdc.gov/tobacco/data_statistics/sgr/50th- anniversary/pdfs/fs_smoking_CVD_508.pdf

Centre for Suicide Prevention. "A Suicide Prevention Toolkit: Self-Harm and Suicide." Accessed January 5, 2019. https://www.suicideinfo.ca/self-harm-suicide-toolkit/

Center for the Study of Social Policy. "Youth Resilience: Protective and Promotive Factors." Accessed March 10, 2019. https://www.cssp.org/reform/strengtheningfamilies/practice/body/HO-3.1e-YT_Youth-Resilience.pdf

Chriscaden, Kimberly. "More than 1.2 million adolescents die every year, nearly all preventable." News Release, *World Health Organization*. Accessed February 24, 2018. http://www.who.int/mediacentre/news/releases/2017/yearly-adolescent-deaths/en/

Christianity Today. "Origen: Biblical scholar and philosopher." Accessed January 15, 2019. https://www.christianitytoday.com/history/people/scholarsandscientists/origen.html

Christianity Today/CT Pastors. "The Apprentices." Accessed January 29, 2018. http://www.christianitytoday.com/pastors/2005/summer/2.20.html

Clark, Chap. *Hurt: Inside the World of Today's Teenagers*. Grand Rapids: Baker Academic, 2004.

Clark, Jerusha. *Inside a Cutter's Mind: Understanding and Helping Those Who Self-Injure* Colorado Springs: THINK, 2007.

Clear, James. "Vince Lombardi on the Hidden Power of Mastering the Fundamentals." Accessed April 14, 2018. https://jamesclear.com/vince-lombardi-fundamentals

Comfort Zone Camp. https://www.comfortzonecamp.org/locations

Costin, Carolyn. *The Eating Disorders Sourcebook*, 3rd ed. New York: McGraw Hill Books, 2007.

Crampton, Gary W. "A Biblical Theodicy." *The Trinity Foundation*, 2019. Accessed May 8, 2019. http://www.leaderu.com/theology/theodicy.html

Cruz, Cynthia. "Diagnosis." In *The New Yorker*, February 1, 2010. https://www.newyorker.com/magazine/2010/02/01/diagnosis-10

Daane, J. "Theology." In *The International Standard Bible Encyclopedia* Vol. 4, 827. Grand Rapids: Wm. B. Eerdmans, 1988.

DePaulo, J. Raymond Jr. and Leslie Alan Horvitz. *Understanding Depression: What We Know and What You Can Do About It*. New York: John Wiley & Sons, 2002.

DeVries, Katie. "Slow Suicide." *Eating Recovery Center*. Published November 29, 2017. https://www.eatingrecoverycenter.com/blog/november-2017/slow-suicide-katie-j- devries

Disaster Medicine. "Mass Triage." Accessed February 3, 2018. https://disastermedicine.wordpress.com/triage/

Dodds, Michael J. "Thomas Aquinas, Human Suffering, and the Unchanging God of Love." *Theological Studies*, Vol. 52, Issue 2, June 1991: 336.

Doka, Kenneth. "Did You Know: Children and Grief Statistics." Children's Grief Awareness Day. Accessed February 24, 2018. https://www.childrensgriefawarenessday.org/cgad2/pdf/griefstatistics.pdf

Dunn, Richard. *Shaping the Spiritual Lives of Students:* A *Guide for Youth Workers, Pastors, Teachers & Campus* Ministers. Grand Rapids: Zondervan Publishing, 2001.

Dutton, M. A. and F. L. Rubinstein. "Working with people with PTSD: Research Implications." In *Compassion Fatigue: Coping with Secondary Traumatic Stress Disorder in Those Who Treat the Traumatized*, edited by Charles R. Figley. New York: Brunner and Mazel, 1995.

Eating Disorder Referral and Information Center. "Magnolia Creek: How to Stop the Binge- Purge Cycle of Bulimia Nervosa." Accessed March 31, 2019. https://www.edreferral.com/blog/magnolia-creek-how-to-stop-the-binge-purge-cycle- of-bulimia-nervosa-551

Figley, Charles R. "Compassion Fatigue as Secondary Traumatic Stress Disorder: An Overview." In *Compassion Fatigue: Coping with Secondary Traumatic Stress Disorder in Those Who Treat the Traumatized*, edited by Charles R. Figley, 2. New York: Brunner-Routledge, 1995.

FindLaw. "North Dakota Child Abuse Laws." Accessed April 27, 2019. https://statelaws.findlaw.com/north-dakota-law/north-dakota-child-abuse-laws.html

FindLaw. "Texas Child Abuse Laws." Accessed April 27, 2019. https://statelaws.findlaw.com/texas-law/texas-child-abuse-laws.html

Findlay, S. M. "Dieting in Adolescence." *Canadian Pediatric Society.* Accessed January 15, 2019. http://www.cps.ca/documents/position/dieting-adolescence

France, R. T. "The Gospel of Matthew." In the *New International Commentary of the New Testament*. Grand Rapids: Wm. B. Eerdmans, 2007.

GoodNews Tube. "Theodicy." Video, 50:33. Posted August 14, 2015. https://www.youtube.com/watch?v=aXrPIvGWuII

Government of Canada. "Heart Disease – Heart Health" Modified: 2017-01-30. https://www.canada.ca/en/public-health/services/diseases/heart-disease-heart- health.html

Grant, Jon E., Marc N. Potenza, Aviv Weinstein, and David A. Gorelick. "Introduction to Behavioral Addictions." *American Journal of Drug and Alcohol Abuse* (2010) September: 36(5): 233–241. https://www.ncbi.nlm.nih.gov/pmc/articles/PMC3164585/

Hartley, J. E. "Lament; Lamentation." In the *International Standard Bible Encyclopedia* Vol. 3, edited by G. W. Bromiley. Grand Rapids: Wm. B. Eerdmans Publishing, 1986.

Haugk, Kenneth C. *A Time to Grieve: Journeying Through Grief.* St. Louis: Stephen Ministries, 2004.

Hayes, Robert E. "Healing Emergency Worker's Psychological Damage." In *USA Today*, 128, no. 2650, 1999. https://www.questia.com/magazine/1G1-55149343/healing-emergency- workers-psychological-damage

Heitritter, Lynn and Jeanette Vought. *Helping Victims of Sexual Abuse: A Sensitive Biblical Guide for Counselors, Victims, and Families.* Bloomington: Bethany House, 2006.

Hendriksen, William. *The Gospel of Luke.* Grand Rapids: Baker Book House, 1978.

Herman, Judith. *Trauma and Recovery: The Aftermath of Violence—From Domestic Abuse to Political Terror.* New York: Basic Books, 1992.

Hiebert, Dennis. *Sweet Surrender: How Cultural Mandates Shape Christian Marriage.* Eugene: Cascade Books, 2013.

Hiebert, Edmund D. "An Expository Study of Matthew 28:16–20." In *Bibliotheca Sacra* 149, no. 595, 1992: 338-354.

Hoehner, Harold W. *Ephesians: An Exegetical Commentary*. Grand Rapids: Baker Academic, 2002.

Hollander, Michael. *Helping Teens Who Cut: Using CBT skills to end self-injury*. New York: The Guilford Press, 2017.

Hollon, Ellis W. "Pain, Suffering, and Christian Theodicy." *Perspectives in Religious Studies 6*, Spring 1979: 24.

Hospice of the Chesapeake. *Grief Out Loud: Teens Talk About Loss*. Posted August 10, 2016. Video, 11:46. https://www.youtube.com/watch?v=qgrRoJyljeQ

Hu, Tina and William Watson. "Nonsuicidal self-injury in an adolescent patient." *Canadian Family Physician,* March 2018, 64 (3) 192–194. http://www.cfp.ca/content/64/3/192

Internet Safety 101. "Sexting." Accessed May 3, 2019. https://internetsafety101.org/sexting

Jacober, Amy E. *The Adolescent Journey: An Interdisciplinary Approach to Practical Youth Ministry*. Downers Grove: InterVarsity Press, 2011.

Jamison, Elise. "This is What Depression Really Feels Like." *HuffPost*. Last modified March 2, 2014. http://www.huffingtonpost.com/elise-jamison/teen- depression_b_4518746.html

Johnstone, Matthew. *I Had a Black Dog*. World Health Organization. Posted October 2, 2012. Video, 4:18. https://www.youtube.com/watch?v=XiCrniLQGYc

Journal of Youth Ministry. "Statement of Purpose." Accessed February 15, 2018. https://www.aymeducators.org/journal-youth-ministry/

Kessler, David. "The Five Stages of Grief." *Grief.com*. Accessed February 6, 2019. https://grief.com/the-five-stages-of-grief/

Kidd, Sue Monk. *When the Heart Waits: Spiritual Direction for Life's Sacred Questions.* New York: HarperSanFrancisco, 1990.

Kid's Help Phone. Impact Report. Accessed January 18, 2018. https://apps. kidshelpphone.ca/ImpactReport/en

Kohut, Heinz. *How Does Analysis Cure?* Chicago: The University of Chicago Press, 1984.

Kübler-Ross, Elizabeth. *On Death and Dying: What the Dying Have to Teach Doctors, Nurses, Clergy, and Their Own Families.* New York: Scriber, 1969.

Lacocque, Jonathan (ed). *Binge Eating.* WebMD. Accessed January 16, 2019. http://www.coatofarmspost.com/portfolio/webmd-binge-eating/

Leary, Lani. "Grief Is Like a Fingerprint." *Psychology Today.* Posted August 22, 2013. https://www.psychologytoday.com/blog/ no-one-has-be-alone/201308/grief-is- fingerprint

Lenski, R. C. H. *The interpretation of St. Luke's Gospel.* Minneapolis: Augsburg Publishing, 1946.

Lerner, Mark. *It's OK Not To Be OK ... Right Now: How to Live Through a Traumatic Experience* Melville: Mark Lerner Associates, 2006.

"Living the Spiritual Disciplines and Virtues in 12-Step Recovery: Surrender." Accessed January 20, 2019. http://practicetheseprinciplesthebook. com/surrender_311.html

London Real. *Gabor Maté: Why You Are Addicted (Part 1).* Posted July 16, 2017. Video, 47:10. https://www.youtube.com/watch?v=iKFJ3y0TdYI

Madigan, Sheri and Jeff Temple, "One in seven teens are "sexting" says new research." *The Conversation.* Posted February 26, 2018. Accessed January 3, 2019. https://theconversation.com/ one-in-seven-teens-are-sexting-says-new-research-92170

Mannion, Lee. "More than 350 million children living in conflict zones, says charity." *Reuters*. Posted February 14, 2018. https://www.reuters.com/article/us-global-war-children/more-than-350-million-children-living-in-conflict-zones-says-charity-idUSKCN1FZ00M

Marchand, Christopher. "An investigation of the influence of compassion fatigue due to secondary traumatic stress on the Canadian youth worker." Doctor of Ministry Thesis, Providence Theological Seminary, 2007.

Marchand, Christopher. "Secondary Traumatic Stress: Recognizing the Unique Risks for Youth Ministry." In the *Journal of Youth Ministry*, 4, no. 1, 2005: 9-22.

Mare, W. Harold. *1 Corinthians: The Expositor's Bible Commentary*, Vol. 10. Edited by F. E. Gaebelein. Grand Rapids: Zondervan, 1976.

Maslach, Christina. *Burnout: The Cost of Caring*. Los Altos: ISHK, 2003.

Maté, Gabor. *In the Realm of Hungry Ghosts: Close Encounters with Addiction*. Toronto: Vintage Canada, 2008.

May, Gerald G. *Addiction and Grace*. New York: Harper and Row Publishers San Francisco, 1988.

Mayo Foundation for Medical Education and Research. "Anorexia Nervosa." Accessed March 30, 2019. https://www.mayoclinic.org/diseases-conditions/anorexia-nervosa/symptoms-causes/syc-20353591

McGinn, Dave. "Canadian children consuming 5 times more sugar." *The Globe and Mail*. Posted June 5, 2017. https://www.theglobeandmail.com/life/health-and-fitness/health/canadian-children-are-consuming-five-times-more-sugar-than-they-should/article35207835/

McGreal, Chris. "Rwanda's Himmler: The man behind the genocide." *The Guardian*. Posted December 18, 2008. https://www.theguardian.com/world/2008/dec/18/rwanda- genocide-theoneste-bagosora

McKee, Katie Q. "The Monster Called Depression." *Family Friend Poems*. Accessed April 10, 2019. https://www.familyfriendpoems.com/poem/the-monster-14

Merikangas, Kathleen Ries. "Lifetime Prevalence of Mental Disorders in US Adolescents." In the *Journal of the American Academy of Child and Adolescent Psychiatry*. October 2010, Vol. 49, Issue 10, pgs. 980–989. https://www.ncbi.nlm.nih.gov/pmc/articles/PMC2946114/

Miller, William R., Robert J. Meyers, and Susanne Hiller-Sturmhöfel. "The Community- Reinforcement Approach." *Alcohol Research & Health*, Vol. 23, No. 2, 1999: 116.

Minino, Arialdi M. "Mortality among teenagers Aged 12–19 Years: United States, 1999–2006." Centers for Disease Control and Prevention. NCHS Data Brief No. 37, May 2010. Accessed February 24, 2018. https://www.cdc.gov/nchs/products/databriefs/db37.htm

Mitchell, Bob. "I killed my daughter… with my hands." *The Star*. Posted June 16, 2010. Accessed April 27, 2019. https://www.thestar.com/news/crime/2010/06/16/i_killed_my_daughter__with_my_h ands.html

Morrison, Stephen D. "Karl Barth's Revolutionary Doctrine of Sin." Accessed January 22, 2019. http://www.sdmorrison.org/karl-barth-s-revolutionary-doctrine-of-sin/

Mounce, Robert H. *New International Biblical Commentary*: Matthew. Peabody: Hendrickson Publishers, 1991.

Muller, Wayne. *Sabbath: Finding Rest, Renewal, and Delight in Our Busy Lives*. New York: Bantam Books, 1999.

National Eating Disorders Association. "Parent Toolkit." Accessed March 31, 2019. https://www.nationaleatingdisorders.org/parent-toolkit

National Eating Disorder Information Center. "Clinical Definitions." Accessed March 31, 2019. http://nedic.ca/node/806#Bulimia Nervosa

National Institute of Mental Health. "Depression." Last modified February 2018. https://www.nimh.nih.gov/health/topics/depression/index.shtml

National Institute of Mental Health. "Major Depression." Last modified February 2018. https://www.nimh.nih.gov/health/statistics/major-depression.shtml

National Sexual Violence Resource Center. "Get Statistics." Accessed April 27, 2019. https://www.nsvrc.org/statistics

New Advent. "St. Benedict of Nursia." 2017. Accessed January 15, 2019. http://www.newadvent.org/cathen/02467b.htm

New World Encyclopedia. "Benedictine." Last modified June 1, 2016. http://www.newworldencyclopedia.org/entry/Benedictine

Nicholson, Michael D. "The Facts on Immigration Today: 2017 Edition." *Center for American Progress.* April 20, 2017. https://www.americanprogress.org/issues/immigration/reports/2017/04/20/430736/fa cts-immigration-today-2017-edition/

Nouwen, Henri. *The Wounded Healer: Ministry in Contemporary Society.* New York: Image Doubleday, 1972.

O'Brian, Charles P., N. Volkow, T.K. Li. "What's in a Word? Addiction vs. Dependence in DSM-V." *The American Journal of Psychiatry*, May 2006, 163, No. 5: 764–765. https://ajp.psychiatryonline.org/doi/full/10.1176/ajp.2006.163.5.764

Online Etymology Dictionary. "bereave (v)." Accessed February 15, 2019. https://www.etymonline.com/word/bereave

Orenstein, Hannah. "We Just Want to Start a Conversation." *Seventeen* (July 14, 2017). https://www.seventeen.com/celebrity/movies-tv/a10307840/lily- collins-responds-to- critics-who-say-to-the-bone-glamorizes-eating-disorders/

Orloff, Judith. "10 Traits Empathic People Share." In *Psychology Today* (February 2016). https://www.psychologytoday.com/blog/emotional-freedom/201602/10-traits- empathic-people-share

Ortberg, John. *Take Me to the Cross*. Published by the American Association of Christian Counselors (DVD), 2005.

Owens, Eric W., Richard J. Behun, Jill C. Manning, and Rory C. Reid. "The Impact of internet pornography on adolescents: a review of the literature." In *Sexual Addiction and Compulsivity*. Taylor & Francis, 2012. http://psych.utoronto.ca/users/tafarodi/psy427/articles/Owens%20et%20al.%20(2012). pdf

Parrott, Les. *Helping the Struggling Adolescent: A Guide to Thirty-Six Common Problems for Counselors, Pastors, and Youth Workers*. Grand Rapids: Zondervan, 2014.

Pearlman, L. A. *Self-care for trauma therapists: Ameliorating vicarious traumatization* Lutherville: Sidran Press, 1999.

Pearlman, L. A. and Karen W. Saakvitne. *Transforming the Pain: A Workbook on vicarious traumatization*. New York: W. W. Norton, 1996.

Pearlman, L. A. and Karen Saakvitne. *Trauma and the Therapist: Countertransference and vicarious traumatization in Psychotherapy with Incest Survivors*. New York: W. W. Norton and Company, 1995.

Perkins-Buzo, J. Reid. "Theodicy in the Face of Children's Suffering and Death." *The Journal of Pastoral Care*, Vol. 48, No. 2, Summer 1994: 155-161.

Peterson, John, Stacey Freedenthal, Christopher Sheldon, and Randy Andersen. "Nonsuicidal Self injury in Adolescents." *Psychiatry* (Edgmont), Nov; 5(11): 20. Posted November 2008. https://www. ncbi.nlm.nih.gov/pmc/articles/PMC2695720/

Powell, Kara E., Brad M. Griffin and Cheryl A. Crawford. *Sticky Faith: Practical ideas to Nurturing Faith in Teenagers*. Grand Rapids: Zondervan, 2011.

Power, Elizabeth. "Seven Key Traits of a Trauma-informed Congregation." *Institute for Congregational Trauma and Growth* (blog). Posted March 1, 2018. http://www.ictg.org/

Providentia. "Saint Rose." Posted January 23, 2011. https://drvitelli. typepad.com/providentia/2011/01/saint-rose.html

Robbins, Duffy. *This Way to Youth Ministry: An Introduction to the Adventure*. Grand Rapids: Zondervan Publishing, 2004.

Rogers, Carl R. *A Way of Being*. Boston: Houghton Mifflin Publishing, 1980.

Root, Andrew. *Taking Theology to Youth Ministry*. Grand Rapids: Zondervan Publishing, 2012.

Ross, Shana and Nancy Heath. "A Study of the Frequency of Self-Mutilation in a Community Sample of Adolescents." *Journal of Youth and Adolescence*, Vol. 31, No. 1, February 2002: 67-77. http://citeseerx.ist.psu. edu/viewdoc/download?doi=10.1.1.414.4759&rep=rep1&type= pdf

Rowatt, Wade. *Adolescents in Crisis: A Guide for Parents, Teachers, Ministers, and Counselors* Louisville: John Knox Press, 2001.

Royal Canadian Mounted Police. "Bullying and Cyberbullying." Accessed May 5, 2019. http://www.rcmp-grc.gc.ca/cycp-cpcj/bull-inti/index-eng.htm

Sarris, Jerome. "Nutritional medicine as mainstream in psychiatry." *Lancet Psychiatry* (2015), 2:271–74. Posted January 26, 2015. http://dx.doi.org/10.1016/S2215-0366(14)00051-0

Schneider, Mike. "Sinkholes: Why So Frequent in Florida?" *Associated Press*. Posted August 13, 2013. https://weather.com/science/news/sinkholes-why-so-frequent-florida-20130813

Senter III, Mark H. "A Historical Framework for Doing Youth Ministry." In *Reaching a Generation for Christ: A Comprehensive Guide to Youth Ministry*, edited by Richard R. Dunn and Mark H. Senter III. Chicago: Moody Publishers, 1997.

Slattery, Juli. "The Importance of Sexual Discipleship." *Authentic Intimacy*. Posted February 3, 2016. https://www.authenticintimacy.com/resources/2641/the-importance-of-sexual- discipleship

Smart, Elizabeth. "My Story." TEDx University of Nevada. Posted January 31, 2014. Video, 11:36. https://www.youtube.com/watch?v=h0C2LPXaEW4

Smedes, Lewis B. "What's God Up To? A Father Grieves the Loss of his Child." *Christian Century*, Vol. 120, Issue 9, May 2003: 38–39.

Smith, Christian and Melinda Lundquist Denton. *Soul Searching: The Religious and Spiritual Lives of American Teenagers*. Oxford: Oxford University Press, 2009.

Smith, Gordon T. *The Voice of Jesus: Discernment, Prayer and the Witness of the Spirit* InterVarsity Press: Downers Grove, IL, 2003.

Smith, Melinda, Lawrence Robinson, and Jeanne Segal. "Coping with Grief and Loss: Understanding the Grieving Process and Learning to Heal." *HELPGUIDE.ORG*. Last modified October 2017. https://www.helpguide.org/articles/grief/coping-with-grief- and-loss.htm

Smithson, Sinead, Sharon Pearce, and Laurie Potter. "Understanding Self-harm in Children and Young People." Primary Mental Health Team: Community CAMHS, Nottinghamshire. Accessed March 2, 2019. https://slideplayer.com/slide/12486357/

Soifer, Kelly. "Limping Through the Valley of the Shadow of Death: Lessons from One Who Is Acquainted with Grief." Youth Worker 2018. https://www.youthworker.com/articles/limping-through-the-valley-of-the-shadow-of-death-lessons-from-one-who-is-acquainted-with-grief/

StatsCan. "Perceived Need for Mental Health Care in Canada: Results from the 2012 Canada Community Health Survey/Mental Health," Last modified November 27, 2015. https://www150.statcan.gc.ca/n1/pub/82-003-x/2013009/article/11863-eng.htm

Statistics Canada. "Table 5.5 Leading causes of death of children and youth, by age group, 2006 to 2008." Accessed February 24, 2018. http://www.statcan.gc.ca/pub/11-402-x/2012000/chap/c-e/tbl/tbl05-eng.htm

Steeves, Valerie. *Young Canadians in a Wired World, Phase III: Sexuality and Romantic Relationships in a Digital Age*. Ottawa: MediaSmarts, 2014.

Steinburg, Jennie. "Why Sexual Assault Survivors Blame Themselves." *Through the Woods Therapy Center*. October 27, 2017. http://www.throughthewoodstherapy.com/sexual- assault-survivors-blame/

Strong, Marilee. *Bright Red Scream: Self-Mutilation and the Language of Pain*. New York: Penguin Books, 1998.

Tantam, Digby and Nick Huband. *Understanding Repeated Self-injury: A multidisciplinary approach*. New York: Palgrave Macmillan, 2009.

Tesch, Wayne and Diane. *Unlocking the Secret World: A Unique Christian Ministry to Abused, Abandoned, and Neglected Children*. Carol Stream: Tyndale House Publishing, 1995.

The Disciples Study Bible. New International Version. Nashville: Holman Bible Publishers, 1988.

The Search Institute. "The Developmental Assets Framework." Accessed February 5, 2019. https://www.search-institute.org/our-research/development-assets/developmental- assets-framework/

"The TV Parental Guidelines." Accessed December 15, 2018. http://www.tvguidelines.org/history.htm

Thiessen, Henry C. *Lectures in Systematic Theology*. Grand Rapids: Wm. B. Eerdmans Publishing, 1983.

Thom, Michael. "Bible camp asks for prayer after tragedy." CHVN Radio, July 2017. https://www.chvnradio.com/news/bible-camp-asks-for-prayer-after-tragedy

Thompson, Francis. "The Hound of Heaven." *Amazing Discoveries*, Winter 2016. Posted April 4, 2016. https://amazingdiscoveries.org/the-hound-of-heaven

Ungar, Michael. *Nurturing Resilience: Nine Things Children Need*. Heart-Mind 2016. Posted March 13, 2017. Video, 35:04. https://www.youtube.com/watch?v=gXALq7SZU7U

Urquhart, Cristine and Fran Jasiura. "Trauma-Informed Practice Guide." *British Columbia's Provincial Mental Health and Substance Use Planning Council*, 2013. http://bccewh.bc.ca/wp-content/uploads/2012/05/2013_TIP-Guide.pdf

Van Dernoot Lipsky, Laura. *Trauma Stewardship: An Everyday Guide to Caring for Self While Caring for Others*. San Francisco: Berrett-Koehler, 2009. Accessed January 20, 2019. https://www.bkconnection.com/static/Trauma_Stewardship_EXCERPT.pdf

Wainwright, Geoffrey. "Sanctification." In the *Westminster Dictionary of Christian Theology*, edited by Alan Richardson and John Bowden. Philadelphia: The Westminster Press, 1983.

Webber, Robert E. *Worship Old and New*. Grand Rapids: Zondervan, 1994.

White, R.E.O. "Sanctification." In the *Evangelical Dictionary of Theology*, edited by Walter A. Elwell, 1051-1054. Grand Rapids: Baker Book House, 1984.

Willard, Dallas. *The Great Omission: Reclaiming Jesus's Essential Teachings on Discipleship*. New York: HarperCollins Publishing, 2006.

Willard, Dallas. *Renovation of the Heart: Putting on the Character of Christ*. Colorado Springs: NavPress, 2002.

Willimon, William. *Pastor: The Theology and Practice of Ordained Ministry*. Nashville: Abingdon Press, 2002.

World Health Organization. "Depression: Key Facts." Last modified March 22, 2018. https://www.who.int/en/news-room/fact-sheets/detail/depression

CPSIA information can be obtained
at www.ICGtesting.com
Printed in the USA
LVHW021528311220
675538LV00013B/1655